Serving Food and Drink in the Restaurant

Student Guide

The complete material for Serving
Food and Drink consists of three books:
Serving Food and Drink in the Bar: *Student Guide*
Serving Food and Drink in the Restaurant: *Student Guide*
Tutor Resource Pack

Catering and Hospitality

NVQ/SVQ 2

Serving Food and Drink in the Restaurant

Student Guide

Sarah Brazil, Ann Bulleid, David Rimmer, Caroline Ritchie,
Tim Roberts, Nick Wilson

First published in 1994 by:
Stanley Thornes (Publishers) Ltd
Ellenborough House
Wellington Street
CHELTENHAM GL50 1YD
England

A catalogue record for this book is available from the British Library.

ISBN 0 7487 1518 5

Reprinted 1994

Typeset by Tech-Set, Gateshead, Tyne & Wear.
Printed and bound in Great Britain.

Contents

Acknowledgements

The authors and publishers gratefully acknowledge the help and advice of all those without whom the preparation of this book would not have been possible: Barry Eustice and Trish Smith for their very considerable contribution to Units 2C1, 2C3 and 2C6; also Jeffrey T Clarke, Ron Evans, Bill Moorcroft and Gerry Shurman. They would also like to thank Gee's Restaurant, Oxford, for their help in providing photographs and artwork; and Bass Taverns for their permission to use the cover photograph.

UNIT G1

Maintaining a safe and secure working environment

ELEMENTS 1–5: Carrying out procedures in the event of fire, accident or discovery of suspicious packages. Maintaining a safe and secure environment

What do you have to do?

- Identify all company procedures for dealing with emergency situations.
- Comply with all relevant health and safety legislation.
- Take account of customers', staff and visitors' reactions when involved with emergencies and deal with them accordingly.
- Identify hazards or potential hazards and take appropriate action to deal with the situation.
- Ensure that safety and security procedures and practices are followed at all times in a calm, orderly manner.

What do you need to know?

- What action to take when dealing with an emergency situation such as fire, accident or the discovery of a suspicious item or package.
- Why suspicious items or packages should never be approached or tampered with.
- Why suspicious items or packages must always be reported immediately.
- Why keys, property and storage areas should be secured from unauthorised access at all times.
- How to identify and deal with safety hazards or potential safety hazards for customers, staff and visitors.
- Why preventative action must always be taken quickly when a potential hazard is spotted.
- What action to take when challenging suspicious individuals.
- Whom to contact in the event of an emergency and the information they will need.
- The procedures for ensuring the security of the establishment and property within it.
- Why and what preventative actions are needed to maintain a safe environment.
- What action to take when establishment, customers' or staff property is reported missing.

ELEMENT 1: Carrying out procedures in the event of a fire

Introduction

Fires occur regularly on premises where staff are working and customers or visitors are present. Many, fortunately, are quite small and can be dealt with quickly. Others lead to tragic loss of life, personal injury and destruction of property.

Some of these fires could have been prevented with a little forethought, care and organisation. The commonest causes are misuse of electrical or heating equipment, and carelessly discarded cigarette-ends. People are often the link needed to start a fire: by acting negligently, perhaps by leaving rubbish in a dark corner; or by being lazy and taking shortcuts in work methods.

Fire hazards

Fire hazards can exist wherever there is a combination of flammable materials, heat and oxygen. As part of your responsibility in ensuring the safety of yourself, colleagues and customers you need to be aware of some of the most common causes of fire. These are:

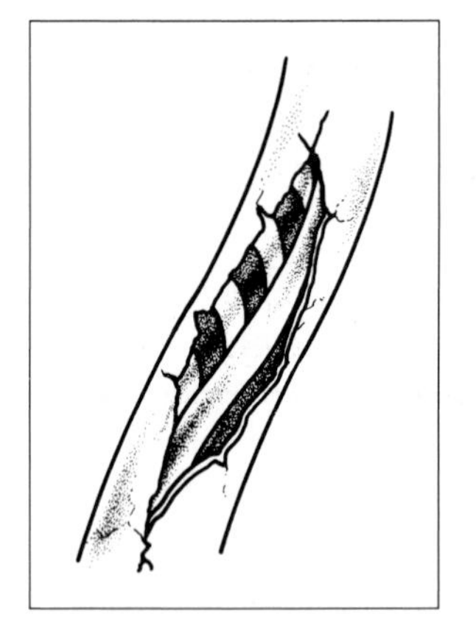

Damaged wiring

- *rubbish.* Fires love rubbish. Accumulations of cartons, packing materials and other combustible waste products are all potential flashpoints
- *electricity.* Although you cannot see it, the current running through your electric wiring is a source of heat and, if a fault develops in the wiring, that heat can easily become excessive and start a fire. Neglect and misuse of wiring and electrical appliances are the leading causes of fires in business premises
- *smoking.* The discarded cigarette-end is still one of the most frequent fire starters. Disposing of waste correctly will help reduce fires from this source, but even so, remember that wherever cigarettes and matches are used there is a chance of a fire starting
- *flammable goods.* If items such as paint, adhesives, oil or chemicals are stored or used on your premises they should be kept in a separate store room and well away from any source of heat. Aerosols, gas cartridges and cylinders, if exposed to heat, can explode and start fires
- *heaters.* Portable heaters, such as the sort used in restaurants and offices to supplement the general heating, can be the cause of a fire if goods come into close contact with them or if they are accidentally knocked over. Never place books, papers or clothes over convector or storage heaters, as this can cause them to overheat and can result in a fire.

Fire legislation

The Fire Precautions Act 1971 requires companies to comply with certain legal conditions, such as those listed:

- providing a suitable means of escape, which is unlocked, unobstructed, working and available whenever people are in the building
- ensuring suitable fire fighting equipment is properly maintained and readily available
- meeting the necessary requirements for a fire certificate. On larger premises, where more than twenty people are employed, the owners are required to have a fire certificate which regulates the means of escape and markings of fire exits. These premises must also have properly maintained fire alarms and employees and visitors must be made aware of the means of escape and the routine to follow in the event of a fire
- posting relevant emergency signs around the area giving people guidance on what to do in the event of a fire and where to go.

Preventing fires

Being alert to the potential hazard of fire can help prevent emergencies. Potential fire hazards exist in every area of the workplace, so regular preventative checks are essential as part of your everyday working practice.

- As far as possible, switch off and unplug all electrical equipment when it is not being used. Some equipment may be designed to be permanently connected to the mains (e.g. video recorders with digital clocks); always check the manufacturer's instructions.
- If new equipment has been installed, ensure that you are trained in its use and follow the manufacturer's instructions. If you are involved in carrying out maintenance on the equipment follow the schedule properly.
- Electrical equipment is covered by British Safety Standards, so look for plugs that conform to BS1363 and fuses that conform to BS1362.
- Ensure there are sufficient ashtrays available for smokers to use.
- Inspect all public rooms, kitchens, staff rooms and store rooms to ensure all discarded smoking equipment is collected in lidded metal bins and not mixed with other waste.
- As often as possible, look behind cushions and down the side of seats to check a cigarette-end has not been dropped by mistake. You could check for this whenever you are tidying cushions, or after guests have left an area.
- Ensure rooms and corridors are free of waste and rubbish, especially in areas where litter tends to collect, such as in corners and underneath stairwells.
- Place all accumulated waste in appropriate receptacles, away from the main building.
- Check that all external stairways and means of escape are kept clear.
- Make sure that fire doors and smoke stop doors on escape routes are regularly maintained. These doors are designed to withstand heat and to reduce the risks from smoke. They must not be wedged open or prevented from working properly in the event of a fire.

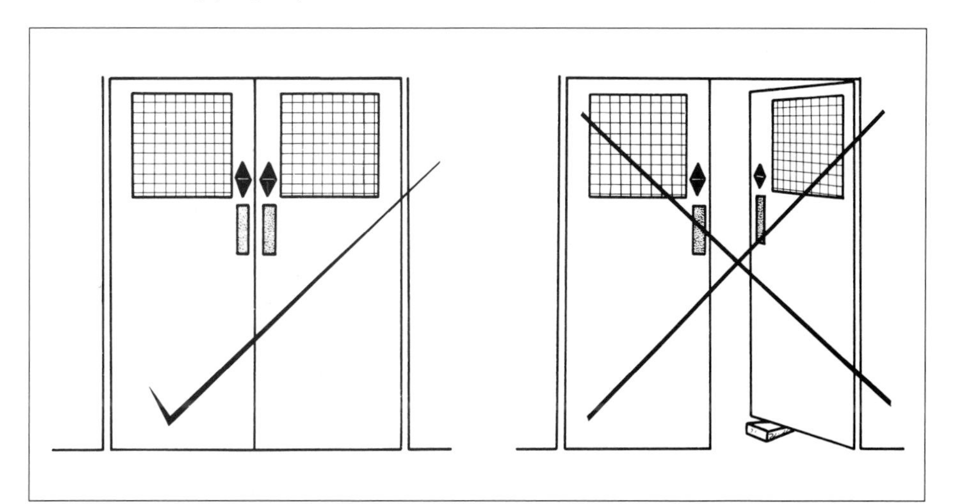

Fire doors used correctly (left) and incorrectly (right)

In the restaurant

Fire hazards

In a restaurant there are additional hazards that you should be aware of. Note the following points.

- Any cooking operations in the restaurant or service area should be kept under constant supervision.

- Electrical equipment (e.g. toasters) with faulty controls or thermostats can cause food (e.g. toast) to overheat, ignite and cause a fire. All equipment must be maintained and kept free from build-up of grease or dirt.
- Cloths, aprons and loose clothing should be kept away from any open flames (such as lamps, candles, etc.). It is very easy for fabric to catch alight and cause a fire to spread.
- Gas cylinders and methylated spirit or jelly containers used in the restaurant should be in good condition and undamaged. Staff using the cylinders must be thoroughly trained in their use and aware of dangers from inadequate storage and damage to the cylinders.
- Flare lamps used for cooking, reheating or flaming dishes in the restaurant must be regularly cleaned and maintained by trained personnel.
- Candle holders used on guests' tables must be checked before service, recharged where appropriate and maintained by trained personnel. Care must be taken to ensure candles are positioned on tables away from flamable material.
- In food service areas with open grills and barbeques, care must be taken to protect customers and staff from flames, smoke and heat generated by the equipment. Ensure you are trained how to light and replenish barbeques and open grills where appropriate.

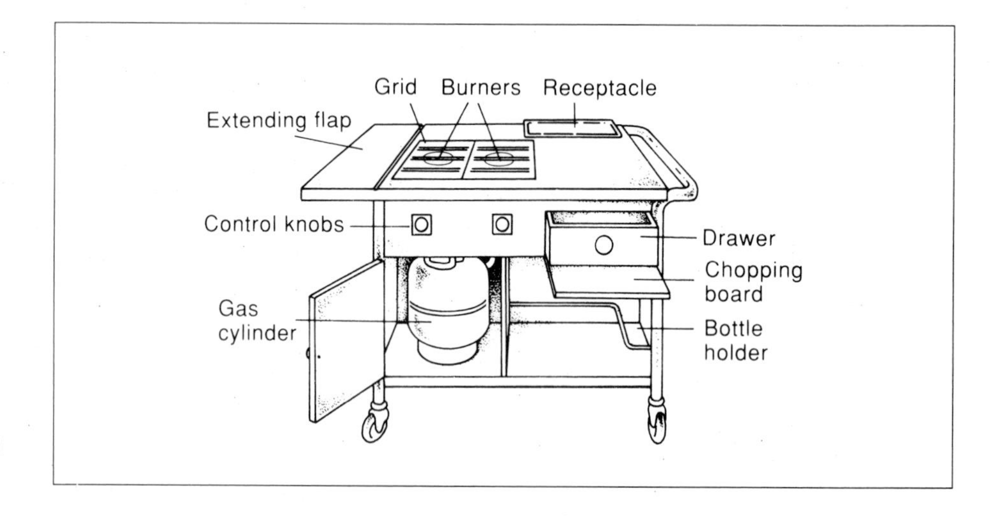

Gueridon trolley showing gas cylinder in place

- Any CO_2 cylinders in cellars must be properly secured and free from damage.
- If there is an open fire in the restaurant, customers, visitors and staff must be protected from the flames by a fire guard.

Fire safety conditions

The following conditions must always be met within a working area.

- Fire doors should not be hooked or wedged open (see illustration on the previous page). Check that they close automatically when released. Fire stop doors held by magnets need to be closed from 11 p.m.–7 a.m.
- Fire extinguishers should be available, full and not damaged.
- Fire exit doors should be easy to use and secure.
- Emergency lighting should be maintained and visible at all times. Make sure that the lights are not obscured by screens, drapes, clothing, etc.
- Signs and fire notices giving details of exit routes must be available in all areas and kept in good condition.

- Alarm points should be readily accessible and free from obstruction.
- Fire sprinklers and smoke detectors must be kept clear of obstruction for at least 24 inches in all directions.
- Fire exit doors and routes must be kept clear at all times and in a good state of repair.

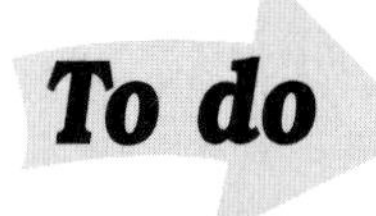

- Carry out a full survey of your own work area and identify any potential fire hazards. List the hazards under the following categories: combustible material, flammable liquids, flammable gases, electrical hazards.
- Discuss the potential dangers with your colleagues and agree ways of minimising the risk.
- Revise your own working methods to minimise fire risks.

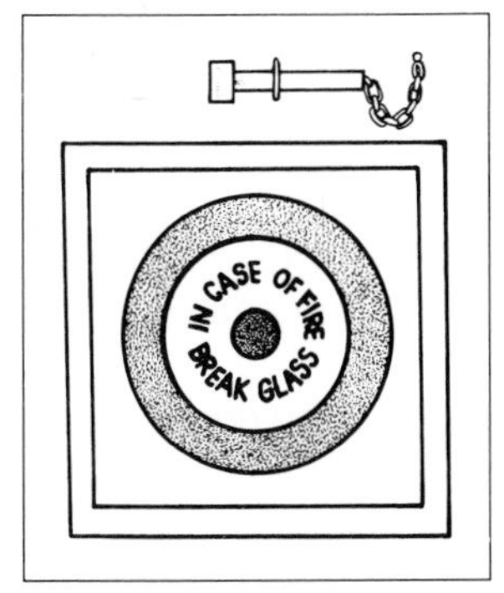

A break glass alarm

Discovering a fire

If you discover a fire, follow the sequence of events given below:

1 sound the alarm immediately
2 call the fire brigade
3 evacuate the area
4 assemble in the designated safe area for roll call.

Sounding the alarm

The function of the alarm is to warn every person in the building that an emergency has arisen and that fire evacuation procedures may need to be put into action. Most alarms are known as *break glass* alarms, and, as the name suggests, you have to break the glass to make the alarm sound.

Calling the fire brigade

The responsibility for calling the fire brigade falls to different people in different establishments. Often it is a receptionist or telephonist who will be expected to deal with the call. Make sure that you know who is responsible for this in your establishment.

When calling the fire brigade, be ready with the following information:

- your establishment's address
- your establishment's telephone number
- the precise location of the fire.

You may like to write down the necessary information about the establishment and keep it near the telephone in case of an emergency. If you do have to make an emergency phone call, make sure that you listen for the address to be repeated back to you before replacing the telephone receiver.

Evacuating the area and assembling outside

It is essential for everyone to be able to escape from danger. If you do not have specific duties to carry out in the evacuation procedures you should leave the premises immediately on hearing the alarm.

When evacuating the premises:

- ensure guests are informed immediately of the escape procedure and assisted in their escape in a calm but firm manner
- switch off equipment and machinery
- close windows and doors behind you
- follow marked escape routes

- remain calm, do not run
- assist others in their escape
- go immediately to an allocated assembly point
- do not return for belongings, no matter how valuable.

You and all of your colleagues should be instructed on what to do if fire breaks out. Customers and visitors should also be made aware of what to do in the event of a fire and should be made familiar with the means of escape provided. Although this is usually done by means of notices in all public areas (often in several languages), it is not always possible in a restaurant. Be prepared to inform guests of escape procedures as soon as you hear the alarm sound.

Fighting fires

Fighting fires can be a dangerous activity, and is generally to be discouraged. Personal safety and safe evacuation must always be your primary concern. If a fire does break out, it should only be tackled in its very early stages and before it has started to spread.

Before you tackle a fire:
- evacuate everyone and follow the emergency procedure to alert the fire brigade. Tell someone that you are attempting to tackle the fire
- always put your own and other people's safety first; never risk injury to fight fires. Always make sure you can escape if you need to and remember that smoke can kill. Remember the rule: *if in doubt, get out*
- never let a fire get between you and the way out. If you have any doubt about whether the extinguisher is suitable for the fire do not use it; leave immediately
- remember that fire extinguishers are only for 'first aid' fire fighting. Never attempt to tackle the fire if it is beginning to spread or if the room is filling with smoke
- if you cannot put out the fire, or your extinguisher runs out, leave immediately, closing doors and windows as you go.

Fire fighting equipment

Types

On-premise fire fighting equipment is designed to be used for small fires only and is very specific to the type of fire. Hand extinguishers are designed to be easy to use, but can require practice and training in how to use them.

All fire fighting equipment is designed to remove one of the three factors needed for a fire: heat, oxygen or flammable material. Fire extinguishers are filled with one of the following:
- *water.* This type of extinguisher provides a powerful and efficient means of putting out fires involving wood, paper and fabric
- *dry powder.* These extinguishers can be used to put out wood, paper, fabric and flammable liquid fires, but are more generally used for fires involving electrical equipment
- *foam.* The pre-mix foam extinguishers use a combination of water and aqueous film, and are effective for extinguishing paper, wood, fabric and flammable liquid fires
- *carbon dioxide.* These extinguishers are not commonly in use, but can be used in situations where there is electronic equipment.

Fire blankets are also used to extinguish fires. These are made from a variety of materials: some are made of woven fibreglass while others have a fibreglass base and are coated with silicone rubber on both sides. Fire blankets are generally housed in a wall-mounted plastic pack with a quick-pull front opening.

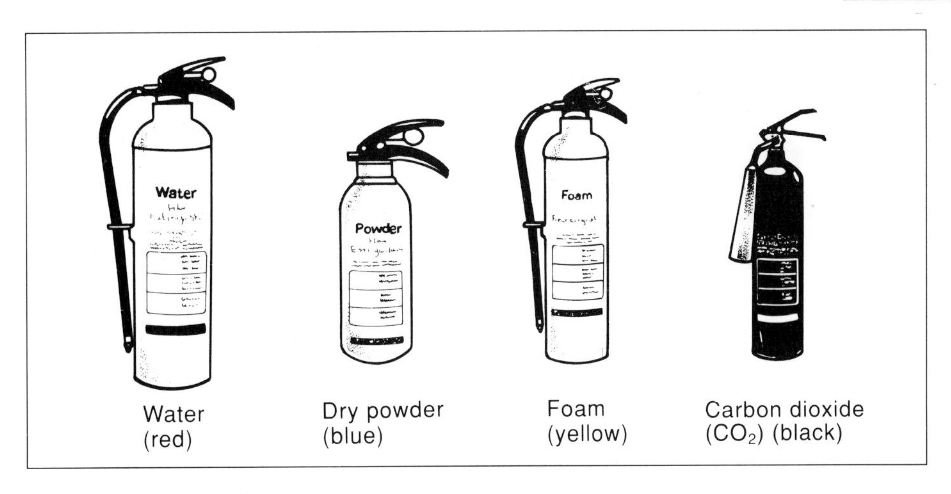

Fire extinguishers

Maintaining equipment

Fire fighting equipment is needed in areas where there is a potential risk from fires. It is essential that equipment is:

- *maintained regularly and kept in good condition.* The fire brigade or your supplier will carry out annual checks and note on the extinguisher when the check was carried out
- *kept clear from obstruction at all times.* The equipment must be visible and readily available. Obstructions can prevent easy access and may result in unnecessary damage to the equipment
- *available in all areas of work.* Different types of extinguishers are needed for different fires, so the most suitable extinguisher should be available in the area. Guidance can be sought from the fire brigade or equipment suppliers
- *used by trained operators.* Fire extinguishers can be quite noisy and powerful and can startle you if you have not used one before. It is important that you know the best way of utilising the extinguisher to tackle a fire in the most effective way.

How to use a fire blanket

To do

- Find out where your nearest fire exits are located and the route you need to follow to reach your nominated assembly point.
- Identify the fire extinguishers available in your area and learn how to use them.
- Look out for potential fire hazards in your area and remove or report them immediately.
- Take part in practice fire drills in your establishment and learn to recognise the type of sound made by the alarm in your building.

What have you learned?

1 What are the four most common types of fire extinguisher?

2 What should you do first on discovering a fire?

3 What type of extinguisher would you use for putting out:

- an electrical fire?
- a fire on a gueridon trolley?
- a fire in a store room where chemicals are stored?

4 List four points you need to remember when evacuating your work area if the fire alarm sounds.

5 How can you ensure that fire fighting equipment is ready to use whenever you need it?

6 How does a fire blanket work in preventing a fire from spreading?

____

____

____

____

7 Why should fire escapes and exits be kept free from rubbish and doors unlocked when people are on the premises?

____

____

____

____

ELEMENT 2: Carrying out procedures on discovery of a suspicious item or package

Introduction

In any area of work there may be times when an unattended item, package or bag raises suspicion. This could lead to an emergency, and, if not handled correctly, may result in danger or injury to people in the area.

A full carrier bag left next to an empty rubbish bin might be enough to arouse suspicion

In recent years there has been an increase in the number of bombs and incendiary devices used by terrorists in pursuit of their particular cause. Evacuations, or closure of shops, transport systems and public areas are no longer an unusual occurrence, especially in large cities. Often these evacuations occur as a result of a hoax, and, although no explosion or fire takes place, businesses often suffer significant damage through the loss of income or delays caused by the need for an evacuation.

Because of the 'chance' or transient nature of custom, restaurants are a prime target for terrorists. It is important to treat any suspicious item seriously. Be aware of the danger it potentially contains and be prepared to inform people of your suspicions quickly and calmly.

A suspicious package which is not dealt with immediately may result in serious injury to people in the area or serious damage to the building. It is an essential part of your daily work to keep alert to dangers from suspect packages and follow laid down procedures when dealing with the problem.

Recognising a suspicious item or package

It is difficult to give precise guidance about where you may discover a suspicious package, or what size or shape it might be. Either of the types of package listed below might raise your suspicions.

- Something that has been left unattended for some time, such as a briefcase next to a chair, or a suitcase left in a reception area.
- Something that looks out of place, like a man's holdall in the ladies' cloakroom, or a full carrier bag near a rubbish bin.

In fact, anything that sticks out in your mind as somewhat unusual. Always check on and under tables and chairs when guests leave; if you find anything left behind, politely remind the relevant guests.

On discovering a suspicious item

- Do not attempt to move or touch the item. The action of moving or disturbing the item may be enough to start off a reaction leading to an explosion or fire.
- Remain calm and composed. Try not to cause panic by shouting an alarm or running from the item. People and property can be injured through a disorderly or panicked evacuation.
- Report the matter to your supervisor or the police immediately. Check your establishment's procedures to find out whom you should inform.
- If possible, cordon off the area and move people away. It may be difficult to do this without causing people in the area to panic, but it is essential that no one attempts to move or touch the item, so you will need to warn people to keep clear.
- At some point it may be necessary to evacuate the building, or the part of the building nearest to the suspect package. This may be a decision taken by your supervisor, or the police if they are involved. If it is thought necessary to clear the area, follow your company procedures for the evacuation of the building.

Essential knowledge

- Suspicious items or packages must never be approached or tampered with in case they contain explosive materials which may be set off.
- Suspicious items or packages must always be reported immediately, to prevent serious accidents occurring involving bombs and explosives.

Reporting a suspicious item

If you are reporting a suspicious item make sure you are able to tell your contact:

1 what the suspicious package looks like:

2 the exact location of the suspect device:

3 the precautions you have taken so far:

4 the existence of any known hazards in the surrounding area, e.g. gas points:

5 the reason for your suspicion:

6 any witnesses to the placing of the package or item:

To do

- Carry out a survey of your work area to identify places where suspicious items or packages could be left.
- Find out what procedures your establishment follows for dealing with suspect packages.
- Carry out regular checks in your area.

What have you learned?

1 Why is it important to report any suspicious packages or items you may spot?

2 Why is it important you do not attempt to move the package yourself?

3 What might happen if you fail to report suspicions you might have?

4 What might make you become suspicious about a package or bag?

5 What do you need to do if you find a suspicious package or item?

____

____

____

____

____

____

____

ELEMENT 3: Carrying out procedures in the event of an accident

Introduction

Within the normal course of your work you may be required to deal with an accident or an emergency resulting in someone sustaining an injury. Often these injuries are not life-threatening, but occasionally they may be serious enough to warrant the person involved being taken to hospital, or being unable to carry on their work for that day.

Most organisations have several people trained in dealing with emergencies and administering first aid. These *first aiders* are often spread around the different departments to ensure that someone is available at all times. Organisations are legally required to have trained first aiders on the premises and to display a list detailing their place of work and contact telephone number on notice boards.

First aiders are usually the people who deal with an emergency before a doctor or an ambulance arrives (if necessary). They have a responsibility to respond to emergencies as they arise, and are trained to diagnose the course of action needed to deal with the injured person. You would immediately call a first aider when an accident occurs.

Who is a *first aider*?

The term *first aider* describes any person who has received a certificate from an authorised training body indicating that they are qualified to render First Aid.

The term was first used in 1894 by the voluntary First Aid organisations and certificates are now offered by St John's Ambulance, St Andrew's Ambulance Association and the British Red Cross. The certificate is only valid for three years, to ensure that first aiders are highly trained, regularly examined and kept up to date in their knowledge and skills.

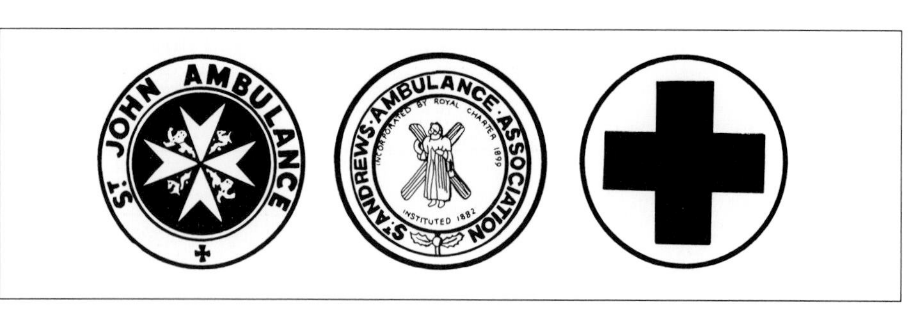

First Aid organisations (left to right): St John's Ambulance, St Andrew's Ambulance, British Red Cross

When a first aider is dealing with the casualty their main aims are to:

- preserve life
- prevent the condition worsening
- promote recovery.

Their responsibility is to:

- assess the situation
- carry out diagnosis of the casualty
- give immediate, appropriate and adequate treatment
- arrange, without delay, for the casualty to be taken to a hospital or to see a doctor if appropriate.

Giving information to the first aider

Once the first aider arrives at the accident they will need certain information from you before they begin their treatment.

Be prepared to tell them as much as you know about:

- *the history of the accident.* How the accident happened, whether the person has been moved, what caused the injury
- *the symptoms.* Where the casualty is feeling pain, what other signs you have observed, whether the symptoms have changed
- *the treatment given.* What has already been done to the casualty and whether the casualty has any other illness or is receiving treatment or medication to the best of your knowledge.

Initial response to an accident

Whether you are a first aider or not, in the event of an accident it is the initial response to the situation and the way laid down procedures are followed that can make the difference to the treatment received by the injured person.

You need to know what immediate response you should give if a person near you sustains an injury. Many of the points are common sense, and will depend upon the extent of the accident and the speed with which you can contact the relevant people.

When dealing with accidents the following points are important.

- *Remain calm when approaching the injured person.* The injured person will probably be frightened by the situation they are in, or may be in pain, and they will benefit from someone taking control of the situation. This may help reduce the feeling of panic, helplessness or embarrassment they may be experiencing.
- *Offer reassurance and comfort.* Keep the casualty (if conscious) informed of the actions you are taking by talking in a quiet, confident manner. Do not move the person but keep them warm, covering them with a blanket, or a coat if necessary. By keeping them warm you are minimising the risk of shock which can often cause the condition of the injured person to deteriorate. By preventing them from moving you are allowing time for them to recover and reducing the possibility of further injury.

Initial response to an accident

- *Do not give them anything to drink.* If the casualty is given something to drink they may not be able to have an anaesthetic if necessary. A drink may also make them feel worse and may cause nausea.
- *Contact or instruct someone else to contact a first aider.*
- *Stay by the casualty* if you can, to reassure them and ensure they do not cause further injury to themselves.
- *Minimise the risk of danger* to yourself, the injured person and any other people in the area.

In the case of:

1. *gas or poisonous fumes:* if possible, cut off the source.
2. *injury from electrocution:* switch off at the source – do not attempt to touch the injured person until they are clear of the current.
3. *fire, or collapsing buildings:* move the casualty to a safe area after temporarily immobilising the injured part of the person.

To do

- Find out the name and work location of your nearest first aider (a list should be displayed in your work area).
- Find out how you can become a first aider.

Contacting the emergency services

If either you or your supervisor decide that assistance is required from the emergency services, or you have been asked to call them by the first aider you will need to pass on certain information:

1. *your telephone number*, so that if for any reason you are cut off, the officer will then be able to contact you
2. *the exact location of the incident.* This will help the ambulance or doctor to get to the scene of the accident more quickly
3. *an indication of the type and seriousness of the accident.* This will allow the team to bring the most appropriate equipment and call for back-up if necessary

4 *the number, sex and approximate age of the casualties involved.* If possible, you should also explain the nature of their injuries
5 *any special help you feel is needed.* For example, in cases where you suspect a heart attack.

It might be a good idea to write down the information you need to pass on before calling the emergency services.

If you do call 999, you will be asked to state the service required: in the case of accidents you would normally state 'ambulance'. The officer responding to your call will be able to pass on messages to any other emergency services necessary, such as gas or fire.

Establishment procedures

Procedures vary from company to company as to who has authority to call the emergency services so it is important that you find out how you are expected to deal with the situation in your own place of work.

Recording an accident

All accidents need to be reported as soon after the event as practicable. Any accident is required by law to be reported and recorded in an accident book located on the premises. Any accident resulting in serious injury must be reported to the Health and Safety Executive within three working days. Your establishment should have procedures for dealing with this.

In the case of an accident to a member of staff, ideally the person who received the injury would complete the accident book. However, it may be necessary for an appointed person to report the accident on their behalf.

The following information is mandatory:
1 the date and time of the accident
2 the particulars of the person affected:
- full name
- occupation
- nature of injury or condition

3 where the accident happened
4 a brief description of the circumstances.

If an accident happens to a customer or visitor there will probably be different records available. Check the type of records kept by your own establishment.

Accident record keeping is important, not only to comply with the legal requirements under health and safety legislation, but also to ensure details are available for possible insurance claims. Accident reporting can also be a great help when analysing trends and identifying where there may be a need for preventative training.

To do

- Establish where the Accident Recording Book is located.
- Find out whether there are different procedures and records for accidents involving customers and visitors to those involving staff for your establishment.
- Find out the procedure for reporting accidents to the emergency services.

What have you learned?

1 Why is it important that you deal with an accident quickly?

2 State three things you should remember when dealing with an accident.

3 Why is it important that you remain calm when approaching an injured person?

4 Why should you not attempt to move a person if they have sustained an injury?

5 What information do you need to pass on to a first aider or the emergency services to help them?

ELEMENT 4: Maintaining a safe environment for customers, staff and visitors

Introduction

The safety of everyone who works or visits the premises should be foremost in your mind if accidents are to be prevented and the wellbeing of the business assured.

Under the *Health and Safety at Work Act 1974* (HASAWA) there are certain responsibilities both employers and employees must comply with. Those given on the next page are ones you should be particularly aware of.

Employers' responsibilities

Employers must, as far as reasonably practicable:

- provide and maintain plants and systems of work that are safe and without risks to health
- make arrangements to ensure safety and the absence of risks to health in connection with the use, handling, storage and transport of articles and substances
- provide such information, instruction, training and supervision as will ensure the health and safety of employees
- maintain any place of work under their control in a safe condition without risks to health and provide at least statutory welfare facilities and arrangements.

These duties also extend to include customers and others visiting the premises.

Employees' responsibilities

As an employee you also have responsibilities and must:

- take reasonable care of your own health and safety
- take reasonable care for the health and safety of other people who may be affected by what you do or neglect to do at work
- cooperate with the establishment in the steps it takes to meet its legal duties
- report any physical conditions or systems which you consider unsafe or potentially unsafe to a supervisor.

These responsibilities have been drawn up for the benefit of everyone in the workplace, to ensure that the risk of accident or injury to anyone is minimised through promotion of a thoughtful and considerate approach to work practices. Customers place themselves under your protection as far as safety is concerned when visiting your work area.

Many working days can be lost through accidents, which more often than not are caused through carelessness and thoughtlessness. As a result the business suffers reduced productivity and, in serious cases, considerable trading time if forced to close while the premises are made safe.

Under the HASAWA, Health and Safety inspectors (often under the umbrella of the Environmental Health Office) have the authority to place prohibition notices on premises if they persistently fail to meet the standards set by law. This might occur if there were a physical problem in the building or in equipment, or an outbreak of food poisoning caused by poor hygiene practice.

Whatever the cause, it is important that you and your colleagues have a positive and active approach to maintaining the safety of the environment in which you operate.

The Health and Safety Executive has the responsibility of advising on safety matters and of enforcing the HASAW Act if the obligations of this Act are not met. This is one reason why serious accidents must always be reported to the Executive.

In the case of hotel and catering establishments, local authorities appoint their own inspectors: Environmental Health Officers who work with companies and colleges on matters associated with health and safety.

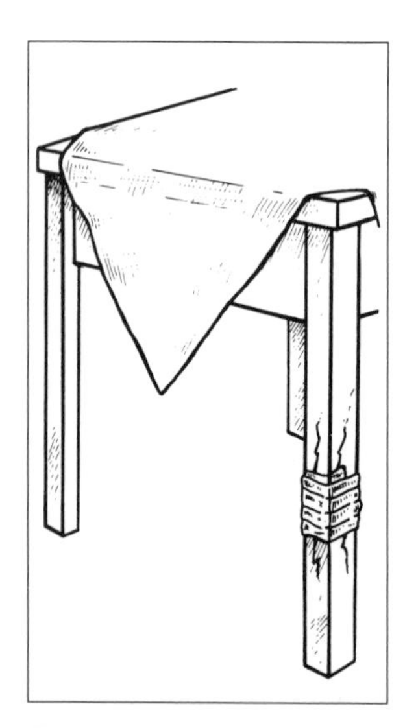

Faulty table legs can cause accidents

Hazard spotting

Much of the health and safety legislation is aimed at preventing accidents from happening and ensuring the environment is safe for everyone within it. Some of the most common causes of accidents in the workplace are caused through basic mistakes, such as someone not cleaning up a spillage, or a cable left trailing across a walkway.

By being aware of the potential danger of hazards you will be able to contribute effectively to the safety of the area in which you work. The guidelines given on the next page show areas in which you can start contributing towards maintaining a safe environment.

Safety points to remember

- Be constantly aware of obstacles on the floor or in corridors and remove them, returning them to their rightful place.
- Watch out for damaged floor coverings or torn carpets: it is very easy to catch your heel and trip over a carpet edge.
- Make sure electrical cables or wires never run across walkways. Always keep them behind you when you are working to reduce the risk of damage to them.
- Clean up spillages as soon as they occur. If grease is spilt use salt or sand to absorb the spillage before cleaning the area.
- If cleaning up spillages on non-porous floors use wet floor signs to warn people of the danger.
- Never handle electrical plugs with wet hands. Water conducts electricity: this can cause death.
- Never use equipment that appears faulty or damaged. You are increasing the risk to yourself by doing so. Report the problem immediately and ensure the equipment is repaired.
- Use a step ladder to reach to the top of shelves. Never stand on piles of cases or boxes.
- If lifting a load, make sure it is not too heavy or awkward for you to move on your own. If you need help, ask. Back injuries are another of the most common reasons for people having to take time off from work.
  The picture below illustrates the correct way of lifting a heavy object.

The correct way to lift a heavy object

Restaurant hazards

In the restaurant area there are some special hazards to be aware of. The following points show how these can be kept to a minimum.

- When using knives, always use the correct knife for the job you are doing. Use of incorrect knives can lead to accidents. Always leave a knife with its blade flat: if you leave the blade uppermost it would be very easy for you or a colleague to put a hand down on top of the blade and cut the plam of the hand. Never leave a knife immersed in water.

- If walking while carrying knives, always point the blade towards the floor, away from your body; or place it on a service plate or salver. If you were to trip when carrying the knife incorrectly you might accidentally stab someone or injure yourself.
- Always use a dry cloth when handling hot containers: wet cloths can transmit heat and burn you, causing you to drop boiling liquid or hot items on yourself or a colleague.
- Think about your customers, and ensure that they are protected from potential hazards as you are preparing the food service area. Check that table legs are level, table corners do not jut out awkwardly, space between tables is adequate and that walkways to kitchen and sideboard areas are clear. Restaurants are sometimes dimly lit and some clients may be unsighted, partially sighted or disabled; remember that an obstacle you may walk around easily can constitute a hazard to these guests.
- Ensure that you are trained in how to use hot water boilers, still sets, coffee machines, etc. before use. Both boiling water and steam can cause severe burns.
- Stack unused chairs and tables in a safe area and in a manner that does not cause a potential safety hazard or block access to those needing the equipment at a later date.

Much of the health and safety legislation focuses on people having a thoughtful and commonsense approach to their work and the safety of others. Many of the accidents which happen on premises, whether they be to staff, customers or visitors, occur as a direct result of someone not doing the right thing at the right time.

Preventative action

1. When you spot a hazard, remove it immediately (if you can) and report the situation to your supervisor. Most organisations have a standard Health and Safety Report Form stating action to be taken and follow-up procedures. If you are unable to remove the hazard, as in the case of a doorway blocked by a delivery of goods, monitor the situation and if it appears the goods will not be moved quickly, report the problem to your supervisor. By taking immediate action over a potential hazard you will be contributing to your own wellbeing and that of your colleagues. Some hazards, however, may be due to poor working practices or faulty building design and they will need a different approach and more time to solve.
2. Take note of all signs warning of dangers or potential hazards, especially those associated with:
   - use of machinery
   - hazardous chemicals
   - cleaning fluids.

Essential knowledge

Preventative action should always be taken quickly when a hazard is spotted, in order to:

- prevent injury to staff and customers
- prevent damage to buildings and equipment
- comply with the law.

Reporting hazards

Under the HASAWA, every company must have a procedure in place for employees to report potential hazards they have identified. In some companies there may be *Safety Representatives* whose role is to bring the hazard to the supervisor's attention. The Safety Representative may be part of a *Health and Safety Committee* who will meet regularly to deal with matters of safety and to ensure appropriate action is taken.

Your department may have a standard Hazard Report Form which you would complete to help you and your supervisor deal with the hazard through a formalised procedure. You may also be involved in carrying out regular safety audits in your department aimed at ensuring that planned preventative work is implemented.

Under *The Health and Safety at Work Act* it is your responsibility to be aware of potential hazards and to take the necessary action to prevent them from becoming actual hazards.

To do

- Carry out a hazard spotting tour of your area noting any actions needed and highlighting potential dangers.
- Find out how you are required to report health and safety hazards in your place of work.
- Examine the equipment you use in your department. Is the wiring in good condition? When was the equipment last serviced? Discuss any problems found with your supervisor.

What have you learned?

1 Why is it important for you to be aware of the HASAW Act?

____

____

____

2 What are the main responsibilities for employees under the HASAW Act?

____

____

____

____

3 What is required of an employer under the HASAW Act?

____

____

____

4 Why is it important to carry out hazard spotting exercises?

____

____

____

____

5 Give three examples of potential hazards in your workplace.

____

____

____

6 What should you do if you identify something as a hazard?

____

____

____

____

7 Whose responsibility is it to report hazards?

____

____

ELEMENT 5: Maintaining a secure environment for customers, staff and visitors

Introduction

Maintaining effective security should be the concern of everyone working within an establishment and is an essential part of good business practice. There may be staff within your own organisation employed as Security Officers whose role will include all aspects of protecting people on the premises, looking after the security of the building and the property contained within it.

Effective security practices can help protect the profit of the business by reducing the likelihood of losses through, for example:

- *theft,* whether through break-ins causing damage to the building or through walk-outs where customers leave without paying for their service
- *fraud,* by customers or staff
- *missing stock.*

Profitability can be affected both by the immediate loss of property or damage to the building and by bad publicity, which can damage the business through loss of custom.

Your role

Whether or not there are security staff employed within your organisation, you will find there are many situations within your working day where you need to be security conscious. It is easy to become complacent or lazy in your working habits, which can lead to an opportunity being seen and seized by a thief. A common example of this is a member of staff leaving a cash drawer open after transactions for speed or ease of use, allowing a customer to remove cash from the till when the cashier turns away.

Daily work patterns may also present an opportunity to be exploited by a thief. When we work in an area we become familiar with our surroundings, used to seeing things in a certain place and following procedures in a certain way. It is often these patterns that are observed by potential thieves and which can lead to break-ins or thefts.

Being aware of potential breaches of security and knowing how to report them or the action to take is an essential starting point. Think about the way you work and how security conscious you are. Make sure that you always follow the basic security practices listed below.

- Handle all cash transactions away from the customer and preferably out of their sight.
- Keep display materials beyond the reach of any customers and as far away from main entrances as possible, making it difficult for people to remove the items without being spotted.
- Keep security issues and procedures confidential: you can never be sure who might overhear you discussing a sensitive issue.
- Keep your own belongings, such as handbags or wallets, secure and out of sight in a locked compartment or drawer.
- Keep alert to anyone or anything that looks suspicious, for example: an occupied car parked outside the building for a long period of time, boxes or ladders placed near to windows, fire exits left open.
- Keep keys, especially master keys, under close supervision. You will probably find that your establishment has a log book for recording the issue of keys.

It is important for you to follow any particular security procedures that are in place in your establishment. These procedures are there both for your benefit and to minimise any loss to the business.

To do

- Think about your working day. List the things you do where attention to security is essential.
- Now write down your ideas for improving security within your job. Discuss your ideas with your supervisor.
- Find out what security procedures you are required to follow within your work area.

Dealing with suspicious individuals

Since you are working in the business of hospitality, there will inevitably and frequently be strangers within the building.

As part of your job you should keep yourself alert to the presence of strangers in areas reserved for staff, i.e. in the staff restaurant, offices and corridors.

Non-staff may have a legitimate reason for being there: they may be visiting or delivering some material. On the other hand, they may have found their way in and be looking for opportunities to steal.

An individual may seem suspicious to you for a number of reasons. The following list will give you some pointers to potential problems, but remember that behaviour and situations may or may not indicate that an offence is taking place. An individual fitting any of these descriptions might be said to be acting suspiciously:

- someone wearing an incorrect uniform, or a uniform that is ill-fitting or worn incorrectly
- someone asking for directions to certain areas where you would not expect them to work; for example, someone wearing kitchen whites and asking directions to a bedroom
- someone carrying company property in an area not open to them
- someone who appears lost or disorientated (remember however that the person *may* be an innocent new employee)
- someone who just *looks* suspicious: perhaps they are wearing heavy clothing in summer, or carrying a large bag into the restaurant. Large bags or coats can be used to remove items from your premises
- someone who seems nervous, startled or worried, or is perspiring heavily
- someone booking into accommodation without luggage
- a guest asking for details of someone else staying in the establishment. (In this case, it is better to pass on the enquiry rather than give out information to a stranger.)

Responding to a suspicious individual
If you see someone on the premises you do not recognise, or who looks out of place it is important that you:

1. challenge them politely: ask if you can help them, or direct them to the way out
2. report the presence of a stranger to your supervisor immediately.

Procedures for dealing with strangers will vary depending upon the establishment in which you work.

In all cases, *do not put yourself at risk.* Do not approach the person if you feel uncomfortable or potentially threatened by them. Merely reporting any suspicions you have, whether about customers, staff or visitors, can often be of great help to the security and long-term health of the business.

To do

- Find out what procedures are laid down by your organisation for dealing with people acting in a suspicious manner.
- Discuss with your supervisor how you think you might challenge someone should you need to.

Securing storage areas

Throughout the building there will be areas designated as storage, whether for customers or staff. These areas can often be used by a variety of people in the course of a day, so security of the area and the contents is essential.

Storage areas, particularly those allocated for use by customers such as coat racks or cloakrooms, are especially sensitive and can lead to a great deal of damage to the business if items from such areas are lost or go missing. Store rooms, refrigerators, freezers and cellars often contain a great deal of stock which constitutes some of the assets of the business and must be protected from potential loss.

Some items can be easily removed from the premises and are therefore of particular concern.

- *Small items* such as glasses, ashtrays, cutlery, etc. can be easily concealed in a handbag or carrier bag and removed without too much difficulty.
- *Larger items* such as candlesticks or table lamps can also be removed, but will generally need more thought and planning beforehand.
- *Valuables* such as money and credit cards can be easily removed from coat pockets if left unattended in a cloakroom, or at a table when a client goes to the cloakroom during their meal.

It is sometimes extremely difficult to make an area completely secure, especially as the premises are often host to a large variety of people. It is therefore important to minimise the risk as much as possible by following some fundamental guidelines.

Before we explore those guidelines, complete the exercise below. This will help you to identify areas which are not as secure as they could be. This may be due to a lost key, poor working practice or laziness on the part of the staff concerned.

To do

- Draw up a list of all of the designated storage areas within your work area and indicate whether they are secured storage areas (i.e. lockable) or unsecured storage areas. Make sure you include every area in your list, including those made available for customers, staff and the storage of company property.
- Once you have drawn up the list, tick those areas which are kept secure at all times. Identify the gaps, then discuss with your colleagues ways of improving the security of these areas.

Securing access

By carrying out regular checks like those given in the example above, you could highlight the need for improvement and increase the security of your area.

The following points show how you might prevent unauthorised access to certain areas.

- Where access to storage areas is restricted to certain people ensure you comply with the rule. If you see anyone you think could be unauthorised report it to your supervisor, or ask the person to leave the area.
- If you have been issued with a duplicate or master key keep it safe at all times. Ensure you follow any recording procedures there might be when you take and return the key.
- Never leave keys lying around or in locks: this is an open invitation to an opportunist thief.
- Never lend keys to other staff, contractors or visitors; especially master keys. If you have been issued with a master key, you have responsibility for the access to that particular storage area.
- Follow any organisational procedures regarding the reporting of lost keys. It may be necessary to trace the lost key or have a new lock fitted to ensure the security of the area.
- If you are working in a secure area, e.g. a liquor store room, always lock the room when you are leaving, even if only for a few moments.
- When closing the restaurant, check all windows, shutters and doors are secure and the area including toilets has been cleared of customers.

These guidelines are by no means exhaustive, but should help you maintain security within your area of work and raise your awareness about the potential risks.

To do

- Add your own ideas to the guidelines listed above, taking into account the list of storage areas you drew up earlier.
- Keep the list in a prominent position, such as your notice board or locker to remind you about the 'do's and don'ts' of effective security practice.

Dealing with lost or missing property

From time to time company, customer or staff property may go missing. This can be due to a variety of reasons, such as:

- customer property may have been left behind in a guest room or public area
- company property may have been moved without people knowing and may, in fact, be misplaced rather than lost
- a member of staff may have been careless about returning property, such as dirty linen to the linen room, or crockery to the crockery store
- items may have been stolen from the premises. You may hear this type of loss called *shrinkage* or *pilfering*, especially when referring to food or liquor missing from refrigerators or cellars.

In most establishments there will be procedures for dealing with any missing property. If you discover that property has gone missing it is important you follow the correct procedure. The type of information you should report will probably include:

- a description of the missing item/s
- the date and time you discovered the item/s were missing
- the location where item/s are normally stored
- details of any searches or actions taken to locate the item/s.

In some cases your organisation may decide to report the loss to the police. This is common where the item missing is of value or where a substantial amount of goods has gone missing. In some organisations all losses are reported to the police whether theft is thought probable or not. If the police are involved, you may be required to give them information, so it is essential for you to be clear on the circumstances of the losses.

Essential knowledge

Keys, property and areas should be secured from unauthorised access at all times in order to:

- prevent theft
- prevent damage to property
- prevent damage to the business from loss of customer confidence.

Recording lost property

In most establishments there are procedures for recording lost property. This usually covers personal property lost by customers, visitors or staff rather than property which may have been deliberately removed from the premises.

If someone reports they have lost an item it is usual for this to be recorded in a Lost Property Book. An example page from a book is shown on the following page.

- The information required should be recorded clearly and accurately. This information can then be used as a reference point for any property found on the premises.
- When recording lost property it is particularly important to take an address or telephone number so that the person can be contacted should the item/s be found.

- If you find property it is your responsibility to report the find so that it can be returned to the appropriate person.
- In some organisations, found property is retained for a period of, for example, three months and then either returned to the person who reported it or sent to a charity shop.

LOST PROPERTY RECORD					
Date/time loss reported	Description of item lost	Where item lost	Lost by (name, address, tel. no.)	Item found (where, when, by whom)	Action taken

A page from a Lost Property Book

What have you learned?

1 Why is it essential to maintain secure storage areas within your establishment?

2 List any potential security risks within your own area.

3 How can you prevent keys from being misused?

____

____

4 What should you ensure you do when leaving a secure area?

____

____

____

____

5 What should you do if you see someone acting in a suspicious manner?

____

____

____

____

6 How can you reduce the risk of items being taken from your own work area?

____

____

____

Extend your knowledge

1. Find out about the *recovery position* in first aid. When would you need to use this? Why is it effective?
2. Find out what immediate response you could give in the case of burns and scalds, fainting, strokes and heart attacks.
3. Talk to your security officers. Find out what kind of events they commonly deal with in your establishment.
4. Invite a fire prevention officer to your establishment to talk about fire prevention and fire fighting in more detail.

UNIT G2

Maintaining a professional and hygienic appearance

ELEMENT 1: Maintaining a professional and hygienic appearance

What do you have to do?

- Maintain personal cleanliness and hygiene to meet required standards.
- Keep all appropriate clothing and footwear clean and in good repair.
- Comply with all procedures about the use of perfume, cosmetics and the wearing of jewellery.
- Report illnesses and infections in accordance with laid down procedures.

What do you need to know?

- Why it is important to wear appropriate clothing and footwear.
- The ground rules for good personal hygiene.
- How to deal with wounds and cuts when you are at work.
- Why it is essential to report illness and infection and the procedure you need to follow.

Introduction

When dealing with customers the image you project can say a lot about the way the company operates. People are more likely to use a restaurant or food outlet if they have confidence in the way the staff take care of their appearance and follow good hygiene practice when dealing with food and drink.

Besides looking good, everyone involved in the service of food and drink has a duty under the Food Hygiene Regulations to protect the food from risk of infection through careful storage and handling.

As someone involved in the service of food and drink there are a number of points you need to be aware of about the way you dress, your habits and your cleanliness that can greatly reduce any risk of food poisoning to yourself, your colleagues and your customers. Attention to these will also increase customers' confidence in their visit to your restaurant.

In food areas in particular there are legal requirements laid down which influence all aspects of the way you work.

Take care of your appearance

The number of reported cases of food poisoning has been increasing in recent years and many of the outbreaks can be traced to people as the main cause of the spread of infection.

Chemical contamination can occur accidentally

Sources of food poisoning

If you are involved in the service of food and drink in the restaurant it is important to be aware of the most common sources of infection so that you can take practical measures to prevent poisoning outbreaks.

There are three main sources of food poisoning:

1 through *naturally occurring poisons* in, for example, poisonous plants such as toadstools, deadly nightshade

2 through *chemical or metal contamination*, such as pesticides, cleaning fluids, mercury, lead or copper. Food poisoning from this source can be caused through the chemical being inadvertently spilt into the food or drink

3 through *bacteria and germs*, such as Salmonella, Staphylococcus, Clostridium perfringens. These are naturally present all around us and can easily contaminate food unless we follow good personal hygiene practices. Bacteria are microscopic and invisible to the naked eye, so it is difficult to know when you may be carrying bacteria which may cause food poisoning. Bacterial food poisoning is by far the most common source of illness in humans.

Food Hygiene Regulations

The Food Hygiene (General) Regulations 1970, particularly those related to people involved in the preparation and service of food, identify and lay down the legal requirements for the main risk areas.

In these regulations the food handler's responsibilities are clearly detailed and have formed the basis for the guidelines you will follow if you are involved in the preparation or the service of food and drink.

In the regulations it is stated that food handlers must:

1 protect food from risk of infection

2 wear suitable protective clothing

3 wash hands after visiting the toilet
4 not smoke, spit or take snuff in food rooms
5 cover cuts or wounds with clean washable dressing
6 report illness or contact with illness.

These regulations are enforceable by law and can result in fines if they are not complied with. The Environmental Health Officer (EHO) is charged with overseeing the implementation of these regulations, as well as with giving help and advice to businesses involved in preparing and selling food. You may hear of an EHO visiting your workplace, or be involved in one of the visits yourself.

Much of the guidance for those involved in the service of food and drink in the restaurant is aimed at reducing the risk of bacterial food poisoning. By protecting the food from people through the wearing of a uniform or protective clothing and by ensuring that staff follow some basic guidelines for good personal hygiene the risks are greatly reduced.

Bacteria such as Staphylococcus is found naturally on the human body, particularly in the ears, nose, throat and on the hands.

Other bacteria can be carried in the intestines and can contaminate food through poor personal hygiene, for example, using the toilet and not washing your hands afterwards.

Some bacteria, such as Salmonella, can be transferred from one source to another through clothes, dirty hands and equipment.

Personal hygiene

By following the basic principles of good personal hygiene when serving food in a restaurant you can reduce contamination risks. This will benefit you, your customers, colleagues and employer.

Most of these principles are common sense and have a place in our daily life, but they need to be emphasised to ensure that you comply with your responsibilities under the Food Hygiene Regulations.

The points are in no particular order of importance as each one is essential to you in demonstrating good hygiene practice at work.

Clean hands

Bacteria (germs) on your hands can be one of the main methods of spreading infection. Germs are easily transmitted by touching, for example, some dirty cutlery, then picking up food by hand to put on a plate for a customer. This moves the bacteria from one place to the other and could result in cross-contamination.

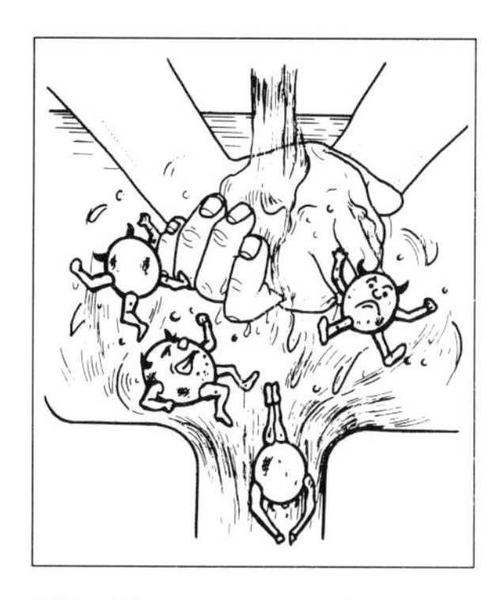

Washing your hands regularly prevents germs from contaminating food

Or it may be that you have visited the toilet, returned to work without washing and now have bacteria on your hands. If you then return to the still room to, for example, make sandwiches, bacteria present on your hands can be easily transmitted to the food while you are preparing it. By washing your hands in hot soapy water after visiting the toilet you will be greatly reducing the risk of infection.

When involved in serving food and drink in the restaurant, it is important you bear the following points in mind.

Keep your hands clean

Wash your hands as often as necessary, but particularly:

- before starting work
- before handling food
- when moving between jobs
- after visiting the toilet
- after touching your nose, hair or ears
- after coughing and sneezing
- after smoking.

You will probably be aware that you are not allowed to smoke behind the food preparation areas, in storage areas or when on duty serving food. Some companies have gone as far as to ban smoking in their restaurants altogether. This rule about smoking is to improve the atmosphere of the eating area for the customers, and to reduce the risk of contamination. When smoking you can easily transmit germs from your mouth to your hands and then to any items of food or equipment you handle. Smoking can also lead to ash being dropped into food and drink, contaminating it and making it unpleasant for the customer.

Use disposable tissues in food areas

Germs are present in our ears, noses and throats. It is very easy to transfer bacteria to your hands by sneezing without using a tissue, coughing, spitting or picking your ears or nose, and you should *never* do this. If you need to use a tissue, use a disposable one and wash your hands immediately afterwards. Always use a tissue away from service areas to avoid your customers' attention.

Keep fingernails short, free from polish and use a nail brush to clean them

Bacteria can gather under nails and spread when your hands touch food. This is why it is a legal requirement that all hand wash-basins in food and bar areas are equipped with nailbrushes as well as soap and disposable paper towels or hot air dryers.

Avoid wearing nail polish, even clear polish, as it can hide the presence of bacteria under nails. Nail polish can also chip, fall into or onto food thereby contaminating it.

Wear only plain rings or jewellery

This will, of course, depend upon the particular operational standards where you work. Some establishments limit their staff to wearing plain rings and very little jewellery, whereas others are more flexible and allow a more ornate style.

The amount of jewellery allowed can be influenced by the style of the operation and the type of customers who frequent the restaurant.

If you are involved in preparing or serving food it is important to remember that ornate jewellery can harbour bacteria and cause infection. Food particles can also damage the stones, or cause them to become loose and fall out. Rings can also be a safety hazard as they can become hot and burn you or you may trap them in machinery.

To do

- Find out the standards for wearing jewellery within your own establishment.
- Find out which areas are designated 'no smoking' areas in your workplace.

Keep hair away from food

Food can become very unappetising and offputting to the customer if a stray hair has been allowed to fall into it. Apart from being unsightly, hairs also carry germs and can infect food.

If you are involved in serving food, and you often need to be in areas where the food is prepared or maintained, you may be required to wear head covering to reduce the risk of loose hair falling into food.

Always:
- wear a head covering if required
- keep hair clean by washing it regularly.

This will reduce the risk of bacteria accumulating on hair and will improve your general appearance.

Do not comb or brush hair anywhere near food
Make sure that you always look smart and professional while on duty. Do not brush or comb hair behind a food service area, or in front of customers, as this can appear unprofessional and be offputting to them. It can also result in stray hairs finding their way into food or drink. Always ensure you groom yourself in an appropriate area and away from customers.

Keep hair, moustaches and beards neat and tidy
This will reduce risks from bacteria carried on hair.

Different establishments vary the standards they set for the personal appearance of the staff employed. These standards will depend on the theme of the restaurant, the house style, the uniform worn (if any) and the type of customers attracted.

Trim and tidy hair gives your customers the right impression, and reflects your own professionalism and pride in your work.

If you are involved in serving food you will be required to comply with the Food Hygiene Regulations. Long hair must be tied back or up, and kept away from your eyes. This will help discourage you from touching or playing with your hair when serving customers.

Essential knowledge

Correct clothing, footwear and headgear should be worn to:
- maintain a clean and professional appearance
- avoid the risk of contamination of food from hair and bacteria
- ensure personal freshness and eliminate the risk of body odour
- prevent accidents from clothes/jewellery coming into contact with machinery
- ensure your comfort.

General health

People involved in the service of food and drink should be in general good health. Healthy looking staff can do a great deal to increase customers' confidence in the food and drink they consume. Healthy staff will also minimise the risk of infection, which, if serious, can lead to ill customers, lost trade and damaged reputation.

When employed in a job that involves you handling food and drink you have a responsibility to be aware of some of the potential dangers.

1 Do not work if you have any symptoms linked to food poisoning, or have been in contact with someone suffering from, for example: vomiting, diarrhoea, stomach pains or infections. Report your symptoms to your supervisor.
2 Wash and shower daily to reduce body odour and risks from bacteria. Working in a busy restaurant can often be a very hot activity. Customers will soon notice if you sweat too much and develop a strong body odour. This can make both them and you very uncomfortable, especially if you are in close proximity, for example, when clearing tables, and may mean they choose not to return to the restaurant.

Staff Sickness Notice

If you develop any illness involving vomiting or diarrhoea, or have come into contact with anyone with these symptoms, you must report it to your Department Manager before commencing work.

Other illnesses you must report to your Manager include: abdominal pain, skin rashes, fever, septic skin, lesions or discharges from your ear, nose or throat.

The Food Hygiene legislation requires you to report any sickness

3 Cover cuts or bruises with clean waterproof dressings. Open sores or cuts can harbour germs and can look, to a customer or colleague, very unpleasant. If you are required to help with food preparation in the lead up to the restaurant opening you will find that waterproof plasters in the first aid kit for a food preparation area are blue, so that they can be seen if they fall into the food.
4 Avoid working with food if you have any wounds that are infected, unsightly and likely to cause danger to customers.
5 Avoid bad habits such as:
   - licking fingers when preparing food
   - picking, scratching or touching your nose
   - scratching your head or any spots
   - tasting food, or picking at food returned to the preparation area
   - coughing or sneezing over food
   - smoking
   - using hand wash-basins for washing food or utensils
   - tasting food with an unwashed spoon.

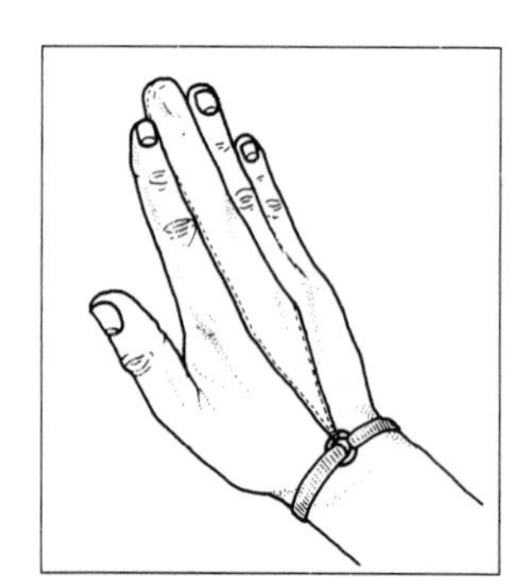

A dressed, covered finger

All of these habits can cause bacteria to spread and must be avoided at all times. They are also unpleasant for your customers and colleagues to see.

Essential knowledge

Illness and infections should be reported:
- to avoid disease spreading among staff members
- to avoid contamination of food and drink
- so that appropriate action may be taken to alert staff.

Protective clothing

Many restaurants today require their staff to wear a uniform, or some form of protective clothing, such as an apron or a tabard. This is often a good idea as it can help project a particular image or style which complements the operation. Uniforms also help project a much more professional image and increase customers' confidence in the operation.

Uniforms, or any other form of protective clothing, can also be of benefit to you, reducing the wear and tear on your own clothes and perhaps minimising costs of buying new clothes for the job.

If you are provided with a uniform to wear you may find it will be your responsibility to ensure you wear it, keep it clean and in good repair.

There are a few guidelines to follow.

- *Wear protective clothing when in a food preparation area.* This can prevent the risk of transmitting bacteria from everyday or outdoor clothing. Everyday clothing can easily be contaminated by contact with pets, dirt and other people.
- *Keep your uniform in good condition*, with no tears nor missing buttons. Damaged protective clothing can look unsightly and be a danger to you if you catch it on equipment or edges of tables.
- Keep your uniform clean and change it daily. Uniform is often light-coloured and washable to show up food stains and dirt which can harbour bacteria. Avoid using aprons and glass cloths for drying your hands as this can lead to cross-contamination.
- *Do not wear protective clothing outside food areas*, for example, to travel to and from work as this can eliminate its effectiveness in protecting food from contamination.
- It is a good idea to *wear different shoes for indoors and outdoors* to reduce risks of infection. Alternating the shoes you wear ensures foot odour is kept to a minimum, helps reduce the strain on your feet and protects them.
- *Do not wear worn or open shoes* in case of spillages or falling items (such as trays or crockery) being dropped onto your feet. Open shoes offer little support if you slip on a wet floor, or trip. Low heeled, closed shoes give you the most protection and help you move quickly and efficiently about your place of work. Ensure your shoes are always clean and comfortable.
- Depending upon the style of the uniform, always ensure the socks, stockings or tights you wear are clean and complement the uniform to project a professional and hygienic appearance.

General appearance

When serving food and drink in the restaurant you will be the focus of attention for your customers. They will be looking to you to provide the level of service and professionalism projected by the company image. It will be this that will have attracted them into the restaurant in the first place. You represent your company to your customers, so it is essential that you reflect this in the way you deal with your customers and in the image you present. Your appearance will say a lot about you and the service the customer should expect.

Whether or not you have a uniform to wear ensure your overall appearance is professional and hygienic, by:

- making sure any make-up is not overdone and distracting to the customers
- not wearing heavy perfumes or aftershave as it may be unpleasant to the customers. Strong perfume or aftershave can be transferred to glasses and crockery, tainting the food or drink

- wearing deodorant to protect against perspiration and odours
- not carrying excess items in your pockets, such as pens, tissues, or money as this can look untidy and unprofessional.

Remember to:

1. check your appearance in a mirror before starting duty and take pride in your appearance and that of your uniform
2. follow good personal hygiene practice at all times whether in front of customers or not by:
   - keeping yourself clean, washing your hair and body regularly
   - wearing a clean uniform, protective clothing at all times and keeping it in good repair
   - washing your hands regularly especially after visiting the toilet, touching your hair or face, smoking or preparing food
   - using only disposable tissues when sneezing or blowing your nose – and disposing of them
   - keeping all cuts and wounds covered with clean waterproof dressing.

Follow these basic practices, and you will enhance the service you provide as well as minimise any risks from food poisoning there may be to your customers, yourself and your colleagues.

To do

- Find out what the correct uniform standard is for your job.
- Examine the uniform or protective clothing you have and check it is clean and in good repair.
- Check yourself against the points we have listed to see if you comply with personal hygiene requirements.
- Check 'wash hands' notices are prominently displayed near hand wash-basins and in toilet areas.

What have you learned?

1 What could cause a food poisoning risk to your customers?

____

____

____

____

2 Which parts of the body can harbour harmful bacteria?

____

____

3 When should you wash your hands?

____

____

4 Why is it necessary to wear protective clothing if you are involved in preparing and serving food?

5 Give five examples of good personal hygiene practice.

UNIT G3

Dealing with customers

ELEMENTS 1–3: Maintaining customer care. Dealing with customer complaints and incidents

What do you have to do?

- Deal with all customers in a polite and professional manner at all times.
- Identify all individual customer needs accurately and anticipate them, where possible.
- Identify all company procedures for dealing with customer enquiries, complaints and incidents.
- Give accurate information to customers concerning the restaurant and other areas if applicable.
- Identify which members of senior management are available and at what times, should any difficult enquiries or serious incidents arise.
- Deal with all customer incidents, or refer them appropriately with as little delay as possible.
- Comply with all health and safety regulations.
- Become familiar with all the facilities that your establishment offers and promote them where appropriate.
- Become familiar with all the common local facilities, e.g. where the bus stops are.
- Assess the seriousness of a complaint and take action to remedy it, either yourself, or by passing it to the appropriate person as soon as possible.
- Identify an incident and assess its seriousness.
- Prioritise your response to the incident.
- Remain calm under stress.
- Correctly identify a complaint.
- Reassure a customer that they are being taken seriously.
- Be able to identify quickly any incident you are unable you deal with and refer it to the appropriate person as soon as possible.

What do you need to know?

- Why it is important to greet and welcome customers.
- Why it is important to bid customers farewell.
- Why it is important to deal with all customer enquiries and complaints in a polite and professional manner.
- Why customers' comments should be passed on, where appropriate, as swiftly as possible.
- Why you should deal with incidents involving customers appropriately and without unnecessary delay.
- The importance of providing accurate information to customers.
- Why an angry customer must be dealt with straightaway.
- Why tact and diplomacy are very important.
- Why the complaint should be resolved as soon as possible, either by you or the appropriate person.
- Why it is important to find out exactly what the incident is, and how serious it is.

- Why the actual complaint must be accurately identified.
- Why a complaint or incident must be accurately recorded, according to company procedures.
- Why it is important to deal with all incidents quickly and seriously.
- When an incident is beyond your ability to respond to it, how and to whom to refer it.

Introduction

When serving food and drink in the restaurant one of the most important tasks is dealing with customers. For some customers you will be the first and last person they deal with, and for a few the only one. This means that how you behave is crucial to how the customer perceives the rest of the establishment, and whether or not they enjoy their meal. You will have to develop great skills of tact and diplomacy in order to be able to cope with all the situations which will arise, and learn to remain calm under all circumstances. Without customers you will have no work.

All customers are individuals and need to be treated as such. Most of the work involved in dealing with customers will be routine, and you will easily be able to help them if you have a good enough knowledge of the food and drink which you are serving, how your establishment works and the facilities available within the local environment.

ELEMENT 1: Maintaining customer care

Greeting and talking to customers

Verbal and non-verbal communication

Communication can be verbal as well as non-verbal. *Verbal communication* is using speech. *Non-verbal communication* is the information which you convey

Make customers feel welcome

by your body language. For instance if a customer comes up to you and you continue with what you are doing, without acknowledging them in any way, they will feel ignored and angry. You may be busy, perhaps answering a telephone enquiry from another customer; however, you can still smile at the new customer. They will then know that you have seen them, and will be with them as soon as you can. They will feel noticed and welcome.

Verbal communication is also an important skill for you to develop, and you should try to become aware of the following points.

- Customers must be able to understand what is being said to them.
- You should, therefore, be very careful about the words you use and their pronunciation.
- If you use slang words, the customer may never have heard of them or never have heard them used in that context, and so will not understand you.
- If you do not enunciate your words clearly, or slur them, or mumble them instead, even the most intelligent and patient customer will not be able to understand you and will become dissatisfied.

Key points

- You will probably be the first representative of the establishment that the customer meets, so the impression that you make on them will colour their views about the rest of the establishment.
- You may also be the only person that the customer talks to and your behaviour will be the lasting impression that they take away about the establishment.
- If you do not understand a customer you will not be able to help them satisfactorily.
- If you smile most people will smile back and feel relaxed.
- Non-verbal communication is as important as verbal communication.

Welcoming and addressing your customers

Everyone likes to be made to feel welcome when they arrive somewhere, especially if they have had a long or difficult journey. Saying 'good morning' or 'good afternoon' with a smile on your face as soon as the customer appears is a very good start. If you know the customer, who may be a regular visitor, or have been staying in your establishment for a while, use their name to personalise the conversation, for example, 'Good afternoon Mr Johnson, it's nice to see you again', or 'Good morning Mrs Smith, how can I help you?'

Useful pointers

It will be useful for you to learn the following points so that you become more skilled in talking to customers.

- If you do not know the name of the customer you should use the more impersonal forms, such as 'Good afternoon sir/madam, how can I help you?'
- When you do find out the customer's surname then you can start to use it, but you should never use their first name, as this would be considered over-familiar.
- If the customer is a small child you should use their first name. This is because most children would be very puzzled to be addressed by their surname and to do so would not put them at their ease.
- It requires great tact and experience to know when a child is old enough to be addressed as an adult. Addressing a young person as a child when they consider that they are an adult may be seen by them as patronising and insulting.

- If the customer you are talking to is hard of hearing, or their English is not very good, speak slowly and clearly while looking directly at the customer. Check to see if any other member of staff speaks the appropriate language.
- If a customer does not understand what you say, repeat yourself using other words and appropriate gestures. For instance, if the customer does not understand when you ask them to take a seat, walk over to the seat and make a motion of sitting down.
- Listen very carefully when the customer says something to you, and do not be afraid to ask them to repeat themselves if you did not understand the first time. Accuracy in helping people is more important than short conversations.

Be helpful and attentive to customers

If a second customer requires your attention while you are still dealing with the first, greet the second customer immediately and explain that you will attend to them as soon as you have finished with the first one. As long as the second customer knows that they have been seen and if they can see that you are already helping someone, most people are happy to wait a few minutes. They will not be happy if you ignore them.

To do

- Try to put yourself in the position of a customer. Next time you are in a shop observe and remember how quickly they served you and whether you felt happy with the service or not.
- Find out if your establishment has a particular way in which they would like you to address the customers.
- Practise becoming aware of people entering the restaurant, and smiling a greeting to them as soon as they appear.
- Get one of your friends to put on a pair of ear muffs and try to explain something to them.
- Make a list of all the people who work in your area who speak a foreign language and list what languages they speak.

Dealing with customer enquiries

Enquiries fall into two categories: those that require confidential information and which you may not answer and those which require non-confidential information which you may answer. Deal with them as follows.

Non-confidential enquiries

Many customers believe that every member of staff will be able to answer any query that is put to them, and nine times out of ten you should be able to do so. This is because although you will be asked many questions most of them will be about the same subjects. As long as you know about these areas you will be able to help. Most questions fall into the four categories listed below.

1 *One type of question concerns the establishment and its facilities.* This means that you are as likely to be asked if you can heat a baby's bottle, as the opening times of the restaurant and what type of food it serves. You must therefore make sure that you know what facilities your establishment has, when customers can use them, and if there are any supplementary charges, perhaps for specialised food requests, such as a kosher meal. You must also be able to direct the customers accurately to any part of the establishment that they wish to get to.
2 *Another common query will be about local facilities*; e.g. how to get to the local station, what time mainline trains run, numbers of local taxi companies and so on. If you have a good working knowledge of the facilities or have easy access to guides and other sources of information, you will be able to help. If your establishment is a hotel then it will have a reception desk. It may also have a concierge or porter's desk, and it may be company policy that staff here deal with certain enquiries and bookings. In this case you should explain to the customer and direct them to the correct place.
3 *Some queries may need to be answered by another member of staff*; perhaps a customer has special dietary needs, or wants to make a special party booking. In this case you should locate the required member of staff and enable the customer and staff member to talk to each other. In order to deal with this type of enquiry you will have to know the names and responsibilities of all the supervisory staff in the establishment and how to contact them.
4 *Sometimes customers may ask you questions to which you do not know the answer.* In this case you should tell them that you don't know, but that you will find out or pass them on to someone who can help them. If you give out the wrong information, because you *think* that it may be right, you may actually cause the customer a lot of inconvenience and embarrassment. For instance, if you say that the establishment does have a vegan dish on the menu and the customer orders it, only to find when it is served that it is a *vegetarian* dish, the customer will be unable to eat it and will be angry and upset. An even worse incident would occur if you said that the establishment has easy access for wheelchair users, but when the customer arrives they find out that it has not because they are unable to enter the establishment without help.

It is not possible for you to be able to anticipate everything that customers might ask you, but if you say that you do not know the answer it will give you a breathing space to find out or to find out whom to pass the enquiry on to. When customers ask very unusual questions they do not normally expect you to be able to answer them immediately, but they do expect that whatever answer they get will be accurate.

Key points

- A comprehensive accurate knowledge of the menu, dish composition and beverages available, as well as those of the local area will enable you to answer 90 per cent of enquiries.
- Inaccurate information will result in angry and embarrassed customers.

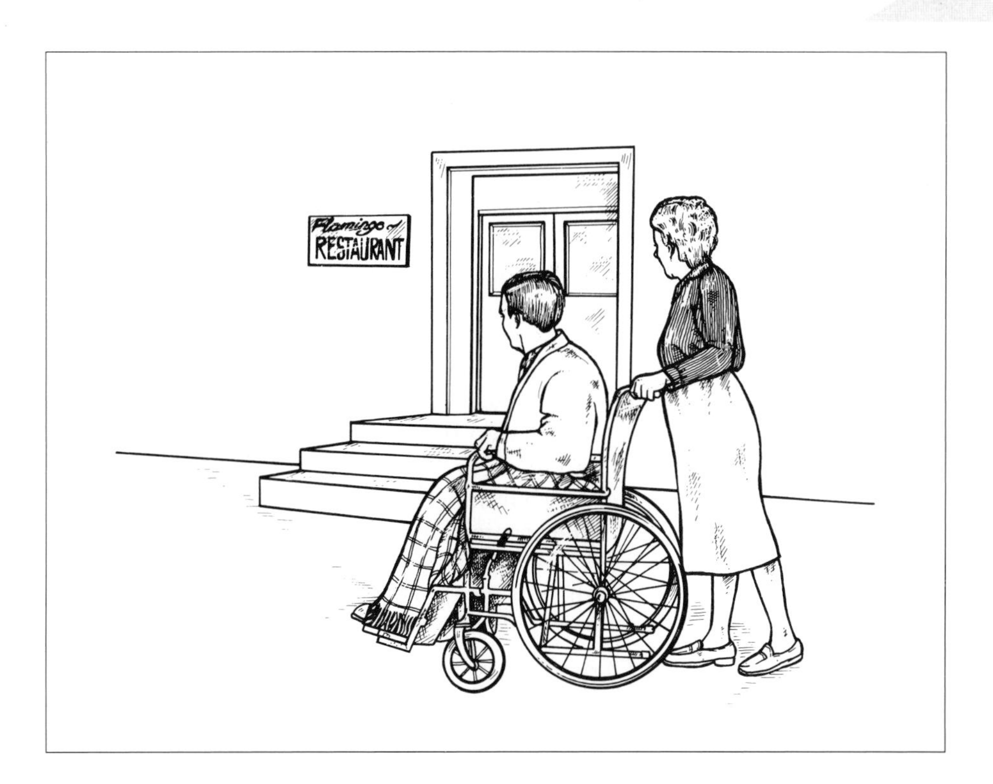

Do not give misleading information to customers

- When you are unable to deal with an enquiry, someone else *will* be able to, and the enquiry must be passed to them as soon as possible so that the customer's needs can be attended to swiftly.
- Some information is confidential: it must never be given out. To do so may break the law and/or cause the customers (or staff) great embarrassment.

Essential knowledge

It is important that information given to customers is accurate and disclosable in order to:

- maintain quality and professionalism of services
- maintain customer satisfaction
- promote sales
- maintain confidentiality and security where appropriate.

Confidential enquiries

From time to time you may be asked for information which it would be indiscreet for you to give out, or for confirmations of details that you are not authorised to give. In this situation you must exercise great tact and diplomacy. For instance, in a hotel restaurant, if someone came to you and asked the room number of another customer, you would have no way of knowing whether or not that guest wanted anyone to know they were staying in your hotel, let alone their room number. Your establishment will probably have a policy on what to do in this type of situation.

Always remember to remain calm, professional and discreet in these circumstances as it is nothing to do with you why one person may or may not want to talk to another, nor why one person might enquire after another.

To do

- Make a list of all of the special features of your restaurant, menus and bar lists which your customers may use, and, if applicable, when they are available.
- Make a list of all the reference books that it would be useful to have in the restaurant; ask your supervisor why these are not available.
- If your establishment has a concierge or porter's desk, find out what types of enquiries they deal with.
- Make a list of all of the supervisors in your establishment, what they are responsible for and how you would contact them, e.g. via a paging system, a telephone extension or some other method.
- Write down your establishment's policy on the handling of written messages if there is no one available to deal with a specialist enquiry immediately.
- Ask your supervisor what your company's policy is about giving out any type of information about the guests in your establishment.
- Write down what you should do when someone asks you for information which it would be indiscreet and against company policy to give out.

Dealing with customer comments

It is always important to treat all comments seriously. If a customer has been sufficiently motivated to bring some point to the notice of a member of staff, you should have the courtesy to listen politely, so that the customer feels that they are being taken seriously, and are important.

Customer comments differ from customer enquiries in that they are not asking you something, they are telling you something. This may be good or bad and may or may not require you to take some form of action.

A comment might range from someone saying that they like the floral arrangement on the table, to someone saying that the soup appears to be rather salty. In the first case no action other than an acknowledgement of the guest's comment is required. In the second case a message should be passed on to the supervisor and/or chef immediately, so that they are able to take remedial action.

From the establishment's point of view, dealing with a comment quickly and efficiently may prevent a major problem occurring. If a guest says that their soup is rather salty, and it is, swift action will prevent other customers from eating something which is actually unpleasant and would prevent them from enjoying their meal.

If the comment is favourable, for instance, the customer said that the service in the restaurant had been extremely good, this should also be passed on as it encourages the staff concerned to keep up their standards of service.

Essential knowledge

Customer comments should be passed on to the appropriate person or department in order to ensure:

- an efficient service is maintained
- complaints are rectified
- customer satisfaction.

To do

- Write down how you feel when you are praised for doing something well.
- Discuss with your supervisor, and then make a list, of those types of comments which should be passed on and those which should just be acknowledged.
- Find out your establishment's method of passing on comments and make yourself familiar with it.

Promoting the establishment's facilities

Key points

- You must have an accurate knowledge of the menu, dish composition and wine list as well as the other facilities of your establishment in order to be able to describe them accurately and professionally to a customer.
- You can have a direct bearing upon the success of the business if you encourage customers to use facilities which they might not otherwise use.
- If you over-promote, or 'hard sell', you may put the customers off, and prevent them from using one of the establishment's facilities.

You will often be asked many questions about the establishment. To be efficient and professional, as we have established, you will need to know about all the facilities of your establishment. Having this knowledge means that there may be times when you can encourage a customer to use more of your establishment's facilities or services than they had originally intended.

Most of the services and facilities of any restaurant are promoted using the menu and wine lists. These are usually given to the customer upon their arrival in the restaurant and in a hotel are included as part of the guest packages in the bedrooms. However, simply because something is handed out to a customer does not mean that it will be read fully. This is especially true if the guests are foreigners, as they may not be able to read English, or if the customer has poor eyesight.

Your customers may not order certain dishes because they do not know that they are available in your restaurant or because they are not aware that your restaurant can cater for their specialist needs. When a customer asks where they may be able to eat ethnic food for example, if your menu has a suitable dish you can draw their attention to it, or suggest that they might like to talk to the chef about their dietary requirements.

Not all of the establishment's services remain the same all the time. It may be company policy to offer special packages or promotions at certain times of the year, such as at Christmas. You need to become aware of these activities so that you can promote them to your customers.

The more that the facilities of your establishment are used the more likely it is that it will remain in business.

To do

- From your wine list, highlight beverages that could be offered as an alternative to any customer asking about non-alcoholic drinks.
- Make a list of all of the special activities coming up in your establishment so that you can recommend them at the appropriate time.

Bidding customers farewell

Bidding customers farewell is as important as greeting them correctly, because this is often the last impression of the establishment which they will take away with them. It is also a good opportunity to try to encourage the customer to return in the future.

A simple farewell such as 'Good-bye Mr/s Johnson, I hope you enjoyed your evening with us and that we will see you again in the future', or to a regular guest, 'Good-bye Miss Easton, it was nice to see you again and I look forward to seeing you again next month', is sufficient. (Notice the use of the guest's name to make them feel like an *individual*, and not just part of the daily business.) This should encourage the guests to pass any comments that they might have been wondering whether or not to make and it may also stimulate the customer to make their next booking there and then if they already know the date.

To do

- Find out what your establishment feels is a suitable phrase for bidding a customer farewell.
- Make a list of the names of all the people who have reservations for tomorrow, together with their table numbers; upon their departure you will be suitably prepared to say good-bye to them all.

What have you learned?

1 Why is it important to give customers accurate and disclosable information?

2 Why do your customers like to be remembered and recognised?

3 Why should you address children by their first names?

4 Why must you find out exactly what your customers want?

5 How should you communicate with people who have difficulty in understanding you?

6 What knowledge should you seek in order to be able to answer without difficulty 90 per cent of the questions you will be asked ?

7 Which is the most unprofessional?
- to be unable to answer a query immediately
- to give inaccurate information.

8 Why is some information confidential?

9 What should you do if you are unable to answer a question?

10 Why should customer comments be passed on to the appropriate person or department?

11 Why should good as well as bad comments be passed on?

12 In what ways can you directly influence the success of the establishment?

13 Even when promotional material is available why should you draw customers' attention to the special facilities of the menu or beverages list?

14 Why are you a sales person as well as a provider of food and drink?

15 Why is bidding farewell to a customer so important?

ELEMENT 2: Dealing with customer complaints

When dealing with customers who have a complaint, *always remember that they will be angry.* Perhaps not yet angry enough to shout and threaten, but certainly unhappy enough to get extremely short-tempered with you if you do not act in a very efficient and diplomatic way. This would be true even when you personally are not responsible for the problem, because you as a representative of the establishment bear a collective responsibility for everything that happens within it. You must remember, therefore, to remain calm and polite no matter how upset the customer may get with you. Do not take the anger personally.

In order to defuse the situation as swiftly as possible you should follow the course of action recommended below, always remembering to act within your establishment's policy.

- *The first thing to do is to immediately acknowledge the guest and apologise to them.* If they are not attended to swiftly, all it will do is make them more angry.
- *Listen very carefully, without comment,* unless the customer asks you to say something. Remember that when someone is angry they often tell you about lots of minor things before they get to what is really wrong. If you jump in too soon you may prevent the customer from explaining the real reason for their annoyance. Sometimes just by describing what has made them so angry will enable the customer to become more rational and calm.
- *Start to deal with the complaint immediately,* with the customer able to see that you are taking them seriously and actually doing something; e.g. returning the well-done steak to the kitchen to be exchanged for a rare one, as ordered. Tell the customer what action you are taking.

The situation and the customer should now become calmer.

When listening to the customer's complaint you should have a calm, but interested expression on your face. This is one time when a smile could be taken as a sign of a lack of interest or seriousness, and could make the situation worse.

When listening to a customer's complaint, have a calm but interested expression on your face

Key points

- A person who is angry does not always act in a rational fashion.
- A customer who is angry will be very impatient.
- If you do not start to deal with a customer with a complaint immediately, they will simply become more angry and more irrational.
- As a representative of the establishment you are responsible for any problems which your customers come across.
- All complaints are serious, because they have caused upset to your customers who are no longer satisfied with your establishment.

Types of complaint

Some complaints are very easy to deal with. Examples of these are as follows.

- If the taxi a customer has ordered has not arrived, you can phone and find out why there is a delay.
- If the customer wanted to order a drink in the lounge area and the bar person has gone missing, you can take the order and pass it on directly to the bar.

However, there are other complaints which you cannot do anything about at the time. Examples of these could be as follows.

- A customer may say when leaving that they had asked for no mushrooms with their meal as they are allergic to them, but they had found one in the sauce.
- A customer says, as they are leaving, that the mineral water which they had ordered did not arrive.

In this type of case you should write down all the details of the incident, the date, the name of the customer and what the problem is, and then you should pass on this information to your supervisor, or other appropriate person as soon as possible (according to your establishment's policy), and tell the customer that this is what you are going to do. If it is appropriate you may thank the customer for drawing the establishment's attention to the problem, for example, a customer who is making personal remarks about other people in the restaurant in a loud voice, annoying your other customers.

If you are unsure about what to do, or if the customer is being very difficult to deal with, rather than allow the situation to deteriorate, you should ask your supervisor to deal with them. If you allow the customer to get angry with you, then this will be another thing for them to complain about.

If the customer is allowed to leave the restaurant still feeling that their problem has not been dealt with then that dissatisfaction is what they will remember about your establishment and is what they will describe to their friends as typical of it. This will seriously damage the reputation of the establishment.

Essential knowledge

Complaining customers should be dealt with immediately in order to:

- defuse the situation and restore customer satisfaction
- maintain the establishment's professional image.

To do

- Find out your establishment's policy on dealing with a complaint.
- Find out if your establishment has a book in which complaints are recorded, and if it has, how to fill it in.
- Find out who has the authority to deal with very serious complaints.
- With a friend, pretend that one of you is serving food and one of you is a customer with a complaint; see if the 'waiter/ess' can deal with the incident to the 'customer's' satisfaction.
- Make a list of the things that make you angry at work, and another list of how you think that these problems could be sorted out. Discuss this with your supervisor.

What have you learned?

1 In what sort of mood will a customer with a complaint be?

2 Why must complaining customers be dealt with immediately?

3 Why might you find yourself doing things which are not strictly speaking within your job description?

4 Why should all complaints be taken seriously?

5 Will your management always be unhappy to receive complaints?

6 What is the procedure within your establishment for dealing with complaints that you cannot solve immediately?

ELEMENT 3: Dealing with customer incidents

There are many things which can happen to customers while they are in your establishment. In most cases, no matter what the incident is, they will report it to you. This is especially true if the customers are strangers to the area or from overseas, and therefore unfamiliar with the locality or the regulations of the country. As a consequence, unlike when dealing with enquiries, you will often not be able to help immediately, and will have to report the incident or redirect the customer.

As with a customer with a complaint, a customer who has been involved in some incident (they may have lost their wallet perhaps) will be in an agitated frame of mind and will need to be reassured in a very tactful manner that they are being taken seriously.

The first thing to do is to listen very carefully to what the customer says has happened. Then you will be able to decide what action to take. It may be helpful to jot down some notes.

When property is found in an establishment, it should be recorded in a Lost Property Book and stored for safekeeping (see Unit G1). If the customer remembered paying for something in the bar, and is now unable to find their wallet, you could check with the bar, and with the Lost Property Book to see if it can be located. If the action is not successful you will have to record and report the incident according to your establishment's procedures.

However, some incidents may be much more serious (for example, a customer might have been mugged or a child lost outside the establishment). In this type of incident where outside bodies such as the police have to be involved, senior management may also be involved and you must become familiar with company procedures for reporting such incidents to the appropriate person as soon as possible.

Key points

- When some incidents occur, as in the case of lost property or an accident to a customer, the establishment may have a legal responsibility.
- You must never admit responsibility for an incident, because you may have committed the establishment to some legal liabilities in the future.
- All incidents are serious, because they have caused upset to your customers.
- No matter how serious the incident is, or how agitated the customer is, you must remain calm. If you do not, then you will not be able to find out what has happened and take the appropriate action.

Essential knowledge

Customer incidents should be dealt with immediately in order to:
- maintain professionalism and efficiency of service
- maintain customer satisfaction
- comply with the law.

To do

- Find out your establishment's policy in the event of the more common incidents, such as lost property, or things getting broken or otherwise damaged.
- Find out where the Lost Property Book is kept.
- Find out the establishment procedures for dealing with a serious incident once it has been reported to the reception desk.
- Ask your supervisor about the most serious incident that they were involved in and how they dealt with it.

What have you learned?

1 Where can incidents involving your customers take place?

2 Why should all incidents be treated seriously, no matter how trivial?

3 What might be the consequences of unnecessary delay in dealing with an incident?

4 Why must customer incidents be dealt with immediately?

Extend your knowledge

1 Start to learn a new language, so that you can communicate with more people.
2 Find out how people with titles (e.g. doctors and clergymen) should be addressed.
3 Find out which are the most common mobility disabilities and what special facilities they require.
4 Find out which complaints most commonly occur in your establishment. Why is this?
5 When there is a serious complaint, which you have to pass on to your supervisor, find out how your supervisor dealt with it.
6 Make a list of all the types of incident that occur which require you to contact people outside your establishment, like the police. List those people that you would contact for each type of incident, and why.
7 Find out the most common legal problems that occur if you do not handle an incident correctly.

UNIT G4

Operating a payment point and processing payments

ELEMENTS 1–2: Opening and closing payments. Handling and recording payments

What do you have to do?

- Follow your establishment's procedures with regard to the handling of cash, tokens and vouchers and recording payments.
- Work efficiently and calmly under pressure and within the required time.
- Follow your establishment's procedures regarding the security requirements for handling cash, tokens and vouchers.
- Replenish audit rolls and receipt rolls and customer bills as appropriate.
- Complete opening, closing and handover procedures correctly.
- Ensure sufficient change is always available for use.
- Be aware of all the security aspects involved in the handling of cash.
- Report or deal with any unusual or unexplained behaviour or situations in accordance with laid down procedures.
- Deal with customers in a polite and helpful manner at all times.
- Comply with all health and safety regulations at all times.
- Register or record the correct price or code and inform the customer of the amount due.
- Create a customer bill.
- Receive cash, token and voucher payments, and give change when required.
- Issue receipts.
- Store payments securely, and in the required manner.
- Work swiftly and efficiently within the required time.
- Ensure that the payment point is secured from unauthorised access.

What do you need to know?

- Why you must be correctly prepared at the beginning of your shift with all the opening and handover procedures completed, and why you must complete all handover or closing down procedures at the end of the shift.
- Why you must follow company procedures at all times especially when handling cash, handing over change or handing over cash to authorised persons.
- Why you should never hand over cash to unauthorised persons and

should always maintain customer bills accurately and securely.
- How to look after and change as appropriate receipt and audit rolls.
- Why you should always have a sufficient amount of change and how to anticipate and deal with any shortages of change before they arise.
- Why security of both the cash and access to the payment point is so important.
- How to deal with vouchers and tokens.
- How to deal with customers in a polite and helpful manner at all times, and work swiftly and efficiently.
- All restaurant prices and the codes for them on the cashiering machines, if applicable.
- How to issue a bill, calculate change, issue change (if applicable) and how to issue a receipt.
- How to store all forms of payment securely.

Introduction

Cash handling is an important part of a food server's job. It is also one of the most vulnerable areas and one that is open to fraudulent behaviour. For these reasons security is of vital importance when handling cash: security not only of the cash but also of customer accounts and the back-up paperwork. Anyone who handles large amounts of cash is a target for thieves and fraudsters. The cash handling procedures within your establishment will have been designed to reduce the risk of theft and fraud, and your own vulnerability. You must therefore familiarise yourself thoroughly with these procedures and follow them carefully. If you do not understand why something is done in a particular way, ask your supervisor, but never deviate from the procedure without authorisation because the system may have been designed specifically to protect you and other members of staff.

ELEMENT 1: Opening, operating and closing payment points

Opening, closing and handover procedures at a payment point

In most food service operations customers are able to pay a bill at any time during opening hours. In residential catering establishments, however, such as hotels and hostels, the facility to pay bills may be available to customers 24 hours a day, seven days a week. However, there are always fairly regular high and low activity periods in establishments, although the actual routine will vary from establishment to establishment. There are therefore fairly standard shifts for most staff. Examples are as follows.

- An early shift will start sometime between 10.00 a.m and 11.00 a.m. and go on until mid-afternoon, around 3.00 p.m. A late shift will start around 3.00 p.m. and continue until around 11.00 p.m.
- Some restaurants are open until 1–2.00 a.m. In this case they are often closed during the afternoon. If not, e.g. in a tourist area, the changeover between the early and late shift usually takes place around 5–6.00 p.m.
- In other places, such as industrial canteens, those handling cash may work straight shifts with no handover necessary.

This means that the payment point is open for all of the time that the restaurant is open, and food service personnel who handle cash upon starting or finishing a shift will have to go through various different procedures depending upon what time of day or night they start or finish.

Conventional till with receipt roll and audit roll

There are two main ways of compiling and recording this information, and complying with legal requirements, either by using a conventional electronic till or via a computerised payment point.

On a conventional mechanised, electronic till there are two rolls of paper. One is a *till roll*, or receipt roll, and one is the *audit roll*. When a payment takes place the details of the payment are automatically printed on both rolls. The receipt roll is pushed out of the machine so that it can be given to the customer as proof of purchase, while the audit roll remains within the machine, printed with an exact replica of the information on the receipt roll.

At the end of the day, when the payment point is closed down, and perhaps during the day during handover periods, an authorised person will instruct the machine to print a total of the business to date onto the audit roll (it may also appear automatically upon the receipt roll as well). They will then take away the relevant part of the audit roll and compare it with the actual takings to date, to make sure that there are no discrepancies. You, the billing machine operator, will not be able to access the audit roll, but will be able to see it. You will have access to the receipt roll. At the beginning of each shift you should check to ensure that there is enough of each roll to last throughout the shift. If customers are held up while the till rolls are being replenished it will make them impatient, and make the restaurant look inefficient.

In a computerised payment point it is more likely that there will not be an audit roll. Instead there will be a program to which only authorised persons have access, and this program will automatically record each use of the payment point.

In both types of machine the receipt roll may be replaced by the customer bill. This would be quite legal as long as the items on the bill are printed out by the machine and not recorded by hand. The customer's bill then acts as their receipt.

Obviously therefore, you must make sure that there is a plentiful supply of bills available for use during the shift, whether they are individual bills or an automatic feed supply to the payment point.

The exact procedure will vary from establishment to establishment, and from machine type to machine type.

To do

- Find out what kind of audit rolls, receipt rolls, and customer bills are used in your restaurant. Are they the same for each payment point?
- Find out where the replacements are kept and if access to them is restricted.
- Make a list of who is authorised to read the audit rolls or programs. Make a note of their job titles as well.
- During a quiet period ask your supervisor to show you how to change the receipt roll of any machine that you are likely to have to use.
- If all the customer bills are numbered, ask your supervisor what to do if you have made a mess of a bill and it cannot be used. (Don't worry if you damage one or two bills at the beginning, your restaurant will have a procedure for dealing with this event.)

Security of the payment point

Given that cash is such a temptation for thieves, it is obvious that when you handle cash you have to be very careful about security. You also have a duty to ensure that the customer is only asked to pay for those meals and beverages which they have consumed, and that they are charged for every item of food and drink consumed.

You should remember the following points.

- Any amount of cash is always a temptation to a thief.
- Members of staff are just as likely to steal from an establishment as a stranger.
- It is almost impossible to prove who is the real owner of a specific piece of currency. If £50.00 goes missing from the cash drawer and some people in the vicinity of the till have over £50.00 in their pockets how do you prove who is the thief, or that none of them are?

The payment point should be near the entrance of the restaurant, allowing customers to be greeted while service is not interrupted

- While you are the operator of a payment point you are responsible for all the cash moving through that area. You are therefore responsible for any discrepancies between what money should be there and what actually is.
- In unauthorised persons gain access to customers bills, they may alter the totals for their own illegal reasons. The customer will not, therefore, be charged correctly, with serious consequences for the business.

In some establishments payment points may be physically separate from other parts of the restaurant, and even be within a secure cubicle. In other establishments the payment point is incorporated within the food service personnel's service point or sideboard.

If you are authorised to deal with payments during a shift you are automatically responsible for the security and safety of all the money in your cash drawer and for the safety and confidentiality of the customers' bills.

There are several golden rules which you should observe at all times:

- never leave an unsecured cash point unattended for any period of time
- whenever you have to leave a payment point unattended, for example, when serving a customer, make sure that the payment point is securely locked
- never hand over cash, tokens or vouchers to or receive cash from anyone, even an authorised person, without the correct explanatory paperwork
- never allow anyone except the customer or a properly authorised person to look at the customer's bills
- never allow anyone without proper authorisation into the area of the payment point
- if you have to make an adjustment to a customer's bill, get the proper authorisation and signature before you do so
- whenever you have the smallest doubt about the honesty of anyone's actions, immediately contact your supervisor.

Beyond this, each establishment has a security procedure which has been set up to deal with each payment point's security needs. You must always follow this procedure.

Essential knowledge

It is essential that payment points are secured from unauthorised access:

- to prevent strangers or members of staff stealing from the payment point
- to make sure unauthorised persons do not see customers' accounts
- to prevent anyone tampering with the payment point, for example, by making false charges or adjustments to customers' accounts
- to prevent damage to the payment points.

To do

- From time to time when you are in charge of a payment point you may need to leave it, to go to the toilet, for instance. Find out the procedure within your establishment for this type of situation.
- Make a list of all those people who are authorised to have access to customer bills, and why they have that authorisation.
- Discuss with your supervisor and then make a list of when you should hand over monies, to whom, why, and what the required authorisation is.
- Carry out the same activity but with monies received.

Dealing with customers and unexpected situations

The society in which we live teaches us to have certain expectations about what should happen in various situations. For instance, customers eating in a restaurant believe that their bill will be ready for them immediately they call for it. This should be true. Sometimes it may not be, if, for example, you have a problem with the till. Another problem which may occur is when a customer finds out at the end of a meal that they have not bought any means of payment with them, because they changed before they came out and left their money in the pockets of their other clothes. If you are unable to assist a customer straightaway, or the problem is beyond the scope of your authority, remember to remain polite and calm at all times, and contact someone who can help you deal with the situation.

Anticipating customer needs will enable you to prevent most problems. If most people finish their meal between 2.00 and 2.30 p.m. make sure that all the bills are up to date by 2.00 p.m. This is an example of being aware of a potential problem and defusing it before it occurs. The ability to do this comes through observation and experience.

You cannot, however, anticipate all potential problems. If a customer walks towards a payment point wearing a heavy coat on a summer's day, it may be that they have a gun or other weapon under the coat, as they intend to try to rob the establishment. It may also be a customer who has just come to this country from a much hotter one, and is finding the English summer a little cold. If someone comes into the restaurant and has a cup of coffee which they drink very, very slowly and watch what is going on, it may be a person with dishonest intentions, or it may be a person who is early for an appointment and is merely killing time.

When you are responsible for a vulnerable area, like a payment point, you must learn to become aware of all unexpected behaviour, because of the potential trouble it could indicate. However you must not overreact, and possibly embarrass a genuine customer who happens to be behaving in an unusual way.

Bearing in mind that you must *never* leave an open payment point unattended, the following points are useful guidelines to what you can do and what you should not do.

- If you have any reason to believe that there is something unusual going on you must immediately do something and not let it pass hoping that nothing will happen.
- Always follow the restaurant's policy in dealing with the situation. This normally means contacting your supervisor, or the security department (if your establishment has one) to report your suspicions.
- Approaching a potentially suspect person by yourself may not be a wise thing to do, nor possible if you are alone at the payment point. It could be dangerous.
- Being aware of suspect behaviour also means keeping an eye out for packages, etc. left lying unattended. These may have simply been forgotten, or they may be much more dangerous.

To do

- Find out your establishment's policy for reporting unusual or suspicious behaviour.
- Ask your supervisor, or another member of staff about problem areas which frequently arise. Find out how they deal with them.
- Make a note of when you have a problem at a payment point. After a week or so look at your notes and see if some problems are occurring regularly. If they are, discuss with your supervisor how you could anticipate them, and so prevent them from happening.

What have you learned?

1 Why must you strictly follow your establishment's procedures with regard to the operating of a payment point?

2 What problems may you cause yourself if you do not open, close and hand over a payment point correctly?

3 What is a *float*?

4 Why should you always have a sufficient amount of change available in the cash drawer?

5 What is the difference between an *audit roll* and a *receipt roll*?

6 Why shouldn't the restaurant staff on duty have access to the audit roll or program?

7 Why must the customer have a receipt of some description?

8 Why must the receipt be printed out by the cash machine?

____

____

9 Why must payment points be secured from unauthorised access?

____

____

10 Why should you never hand over any monies without the proper authorisation documents?

____

____

11 What should you do if you think that someone is behaving in an unusual fashion?

____

____

12 Why shouldn't you approach them directly?

____

____

ELEMENT 2: Handling and recording payments

Compiling a customer's bill correctly

In places like supermarkets the customer's bill is often created by swiping the bar code on an item over a computer reader. This reader then tells the cash register how much to charge for the item, and when all the items have been 'read' it totals up the amount automatically. The cashier does not need to know the price of any item individually, and so has quite an easy task when compiling a bill. This procedure cannot easily be followed in the service industries, since you cannot put a bar code, for instance, on a portion of freshly cooked spaghetti or a glass of wine.

Even in a restaurant where the menu is short and rarely changes and the billing machine can be pre-programmed with the price of each item, you still need to know the code or symbol for each item in order to press the correct key.

This means that you must be very skilful and accurate when compiling a bill, and know exactly what price to charge, or code to use for each item of food or drink that the customer has purchased. Obviously you will not be able to remember all the prices of everything that the customer can buy, especially in a very large restaurant, or if there is a very long menu or wine list. Therefore the restaurant will have a set of procedures for keeping you up to date.

The basic components of a bill in a restaurant are food and drink. The menu may either be an à la carte one where each item is charged separately, or a table d'hôte one, where there is a set price for a certain number of dishes. There may also be special dishes of the day, at special prices, or promotions where a small amount of wine is included with the meal. There are also the beverage charges to be added to the bill.

The basic principles behind compiling a bill do not vary however, whatever is on the bill. They are as follows.

- You must know what types of charges should be on the bill, whether a customer ate from the à la carte or table d'hôte menu, etc.
- If when you come to compile the bills you notice that one type of charge appears to be missing, check that this is correct. This can be done by contacting the appropriate department, e.g. the dispense bar and asking if the customer had anything to drink with their meal. They may have only had tap water so no beverage charge would occur, but this is unusual.

Mr Eaton			
V.A.T. reg no. 423 1654 39	Date 14-2-94		
Couverts	5 Dinners @ £8.50	42	50
Cafe	4 Coffees @ £1.25	5	00
Wine	2 × 23 @ £11.50	23	00
Spirits	—		
Liqueurs	1 Drambuie	2	50
	1 Tia Maria	2	50
Beers	—		
Minerals	1 Mineral Water	1	50
Cigars and tobacco			
Table no. 4	Total £	77	00
No. covers 5			
04214			

An example bill

- Once you are sure that you have collected all the charges you must ensure that you enter the correct figure on the bill. If the customer is a single person they must be charged for only one portion of everything, ensuring that all discounts, etc. are taken into account.
- When all the charges are entered onto the appropriate cash register, they can be totalled, ready for presentation to the customer, or sub-totalled, if the customer is not yet leaving and may use some other services (for example they may decide to have liqueurs after their meal). Common sense should tell you the most suitable action to take.

When compiling a bill, the most difficult part may be ensuring that the customer is charged the correct amount for any food or drink that they have consumed. This can be a problem:

a) because you are not expected to remember all the possible prices within the restaurant, and
b) because the restaurant may offer special discounts, or promotions to certain people at certain times, so that the normal prices do not apply anyway.

In order to prevent this problem occurring there should be appropriate price lists at the payment point and if any of the customers are receiving special rates you should be given details of this before the customer arrives at the restaurant or begins the meal.

Entering checks onto a cash register

In some establishments which are highly computerised, it may not be part of the duties of the person operating the payment point to compile the bill because the charges are entered at source. In this case you may merely be required to total and print bills as and when required.

For instance, food service personnel may take food orders on a computerised hand-held pad. This will automatically inform the kitchen of the dish ordered as well as inform the payment point to start compiling this new bill.

Whatever system is used in any part of your establishment, there will be a set of guidelines for you to follow so that you will know, once you have collected all the necessary charges, how to record them and create a bill. Whatever system is used you must take great care to make sure that the correct figure or code is entered accurately onto the right bill and that it is ready for presentation at the appropriate time.

You should also remember the following points.

- It is illegal to charge a price other than the one advertised for any food or beverage.
- All basic prices must be displayed for the customer to see easily, whether for food, drink, accommodation or other services.
- It is very bad for the reputation of any establishment to accidentally over- or under-charge the customers.
- A messy bill, with lots of corrections, would indicate that the establishment, and its staff, are very inefficient.

To do

- Find out if your restaurant uses a manual, computerised or semi-computerised system for compiling bills.
- Practise compiling bills according to your establishment's procedures for any payment point at which you are likely to work.
- Make a list of those bills which are compiled for immediate presentation and those for which you will receive payment at a later date.
- If your restaurant uses codes to compile bills, make a list of all the standard codes and what charges, and how much, they represent.
- Make a list of all the different price lists within your establishment. Check to see that they are available at the appropriate payment point.

The presentation of a customer's bill

There is always an appropriate time to present a bill to a customer; normally upon request. The bill may be presented either by the person working at the payment point, if the customer collects it themselves, or by a member of staff who takes the bill to the customer. This depends upon both the department within which the bill is required, and upon establishment procedure.

Bills should be presented discreetly

When a customer asks for their bill it should be presented in a written format. Normally it is printed by a cashiering machine, but in some establishments it is handwritten. In this case great care should be taken to ensure that the writing is clear and legible. The customer should be given the bill in a written format so that they can see what charges are on the bill and therefore how the total amount was arrived at. The customer should be allowed time to study the bill, if they choose to do so, before the actual payment is given.

When the bill is presented it should be done so discreetly. That is to say, so that only the customer receiving the bill can see what charges are on it. There are several reasons for this.

- The customer may be entertaining someone else, perhaps for business or as a treat, and they would prefer the other person not to know how much was spent.
- The customer may simply not want anyone else to know how much they did or did not spend, or what discounts they received, etc.

To do

- Find out how your establishment presents bills to different types of customers and in different departments, if applicable.
- Make a list of why some bills are presented in one way and some in another.
- Ask your supervisor what you should do if someone other than the customer, another guest perhaps, says that they have come to collect the bill on the customer's behalf.

The correct handling of payments, receipts and change

You may not always be able to give change to a customer; it depends upon what method they choose to pay by, but you are always able to, and by law must, give a printed receipt for each transaction that takes place.

Once a customer is satisfied that their bill is accurate they will pay. In this unit payment by cash, token or voucher is considered, and in Unit G5 (pp. 73–95), other methods of payment are considered, e.g. credit cards.

Cash payment means payment using the coinage and/or banknotes of the country which you are in. If a customer pays by this method they are entitled to the appropriate amount of change, again in the coinage or banknotes of that country.

When voucher or token payments are made, no cash changes hands. This is a method of payment where the actual exchange of cash took place before the customer visited your establishment. For instance, an employer may buy Luncheon Vouchers for their employees and include them as part of their remuneration. Each voucher represents a certain cash value, as written on it, and can be exchanged for food in those establishments which accept this type of voucher or token. When the customer has consumed their meal they will pay for it using these vouchers instead of money. If the meal comes to £5.60 and the customer gives £6.00 worth of vouchers or tokens they would not normally be entitled to any change.

Some tokens or vouchers may be a form of part payment. Sometimes organisations promote themselves by having special offers. They may say, for instance, that at the weekend a child can eat for free, if their parents or two adults have a full meal. When this type of token or voucher is presented at the payment point, a certain portion of the bill is not charged to the customers, i.e. the child's food, but the rest is, i.e. the adults' beverage and food charges.

Bill showing an allowance against a person for a meal

Although a customer is not entitled to change if they do not use up all the facilities available on a voucher or token, unused facilities are sometimes deferred. For instance, if someone in the party did not have their free bottle of wine because they were taking antibiotics at the time, the management might say that they could use up the unused facilities on their voucher at another time. However this is a decision to be made by the manager rather than a junior member of staff.

Whatever method of token or voucher payment is used, you must make sure that it is one which is accepted by your restaurant. There should be a list of those which are acceptable at the payment point. Normally, if a customer is going to settle their account using a voucher or token they will tell you when they arrive, or check in advance, perhaps by telephone, before they use the voucher or token. However there may be customers who present the voucher when they pay for their meal. If the voucher or token is one which is accepted by the restaurant it would simply be accepted and the appropriate information recorded on the bill. If, however, it is a token or voucher which is not acceptable to your restaurant, then you would have to say that you cannot accept it and ask for some other form of payment. If there are any problems here, perhaps with the customer insisting that the voucher should be accepted, then you should be courteous and polite, explaining that you are not able to help them, and ask your supervisor to deal with the problem. Problems often arise if people do not read the expiry dates, or exact terms on free/special offers.

When a voucher or token is accepted in lieu of a cash payment it must be cancelled immediately so that it cannot be used again. There are various methods of doing this. There may be a section on the token or voucher which should be filled in by you; it may be company policy to write *cancelled* across the voucher or token; or the restaurant may have special date stamps which can be used to show when the voucher was accepted and by what department.

A well organised till drawer

Assuming that everything is in order, the payment in cash, token or voucher form should be accepted, cancelled where appropriate, and stored in the correct compartment of the cash drawer.

As soon as the payment has been placed in the cash drawer it must be closed, for security reasons, to make it less vulnerable to theft, etc. See *Essential Knowledge* on page 61. On some machines it is not possible to start a second transaction until the cash drawer has been fully closed after the first one.

If cash, tokens or vouchers are not placed neatly in the cash drawer then it will be much harder, and much slower, finding change when it is necessary, and if the notes are muddled up into different denominations it is quite easy to give out the wrong change.

A disorganised till drawer

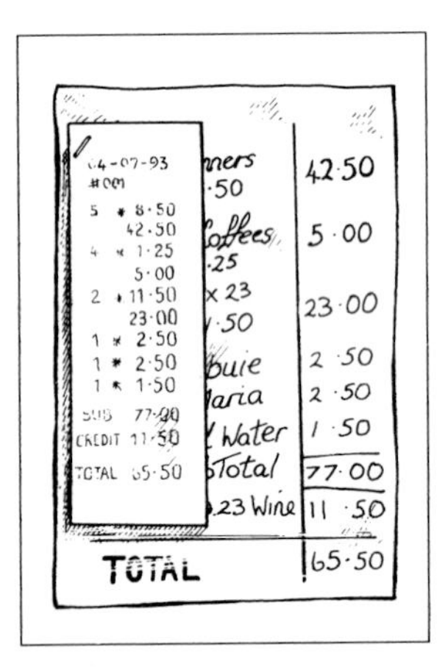

A bill with a receipt attached

Once payment in any form has been accepted the customer is entitled to a printed receipt. The receipt does not necessarily have to show the exact breakdown of the bill, but should show where and when the transaction took place, how much it was for and what type of service it covered, i.e. accommodation, food, the use of leisure facilities, etc. If the customer's bill was printed by the billing machine, this can act as the customer's receipt. This saves the customer from having to have an extra piece of paper to carry around with them, saves you time in having to produce the receipt, and is common practice in restaurants. If the customer's bill is also their receipt, it is customary for the bill to be duplicate or triplicate; i.e. it will have one or two self-duplicating copies.

The top copy of the bill is given to the customer, with their change if any, and acts as their receipt. The bottom copy/ies are kept by the restaurant and used by the accounts department to make sure that all transactions have been correctly charged for, and all monies taken correctly recorded.

If the customer's bill was handwritten they would have to be given a printed receipt from the till roll.

Exactly what you will have to do will depend upon the type of billing machines that your establishment uses, the vouchers and tokens they accept and the establishment's procedures for accepting payment. You must find out all this information as quickly as possible.

To do

- Make a list of all of the vouchers and tokens that your restaurant accepts.
- Make a note of how to cancel them once they have been accepted.
- Find out the restaurant's policy if a customer wants to pay with a voucher or token which the restaurant does not normally accept.
- Find out if the billing machines tell you how much change you should give a customer when they pay by cash, or if you have to work it out.
- Find out what type of receipts your establishment issues. Are they the same for all payment points?

What have you learned?

1 If a customer gives you a form of payment which is more than the total of the bill, under what circumstances should you not give them change?

2 Why must vouchers and tokens be cancelled immediately?

3 Why must cash drawers be kept closed when not in actual use?

4 Why must the customer be charged the correct price for food and beverages?

5 Why should the customer be able to look at the bill before they pay it?

6 Why must price lists be displayed?

7 Why must printed receipts be given?

8 Why must you never leave a payment point unattended?

____

____

9 Why must you report all unusual situations?

____

____

10 Why must you follow company procedure at all times?

____

____

Extend your knowledge

1. Find out what *fidelity bonding* means.
2. Learn how all the payment points in your establishment work, not just the ones in your area.
3. Find out how all the charges on a customer's bill are arrived at, and how they get to the various payment points in the establishment.
4. Find out what a *ledger payment* is, and how the account is settled with your establishment.
5. Find out why your establishment only accepts certain vouchers and tokens.
6. Find out why some vouchers and tokens can only be used at certain times.
7. The government says that customers must have a printed receipt for each transaction, which will protect them. From whom will it protect them and how?
8. Your establishment should have a list of procedures that you must follow when operating a payment point. Some of those procedures are to protect the establishment, some are to protect the restaurant staff, some cover both areas. Identify which procedures protect the establishment, which the restaurant staff, and which both. How do they do this?

UNIT G5

Handling and recording non-cash payments and refunds

ELEMENTS 1–2: Handling and recording payments. Handling and recording refunds

What do you have to do?

- Follow all your establishment's procedures with regard to non-cash payments and refunds.
- Enter the correct price or code and inform the customer of the amount due.
- Follow all the procedures required by the companies guaranteeing the non-cash payments.
- Acknowledge the receipt of non-cash payments.
- Produce the accompanying documentation efficiently, accurately and neatly.
- Store the payment and accompanying documentation securely.
- Give receipts and vouchers where appropriate.
- Work efficiently and calmly under pressure.
- Ensure that the payment point is secured from unauthorised access.
- Comply with all health and safety regulations at all times.
- Learn who is authorised to issue the different types of refunds.
- Report and deal with all discrepancies in accordance with laid down procedures.

What do you need to know?

- How to work in an accurate and efficient manner at all times.
- What the establishment's procedures are for processing non-cash payments.
- How to authenticate all forms of non-cash payment.
- How to prepare the appropriate documentation to accompany non-cash payments.
- How to deal with any problems or discrepancies that occur.
- Why security of the payment point and non-cash payments must be borne in mind at all times.
- How to deal with customers in a polite and helpful manner at all times.

Introduction

Non-cash payments are not as vulnerable to simple theft as cash payments, but they are more vulnerable to fraud. Another potential problem is that the credit card company or bank may refuse to honour the payment. It has the right to do this if the credit payment is not accepted correctly. You must never lose sight of the fact that any form of payment is always potentially fraudulent, as are any refund claims. This means that you must familiarise yourself thoroughly with all your bar's procedures in this area and follow them carefully. If you do not understand why something is done in a specific way ask your supervisor, but never deviate from the procedure without authorisation because the system has been designed specifically to protect you and other members of staff as well as the establishment.

ELEMENT 1: Handling and recording cheque and credit/debit card payments

Presenting and acknowledging customers' bills

The customer's bill should be created according to the procedures of the restaurant. For more information about this see Unit G4 (pp. 53–72). The bill should then be totalled and made ready for presentation to the customer when the customer requires it. Sometimes you may be able to anticipate when the customer is most likely to call for their bill. In these cases you can have the bill already prepared in advance, so as to prevent possible delays if many bills are likely to be required at once. Likely busy periods where bills can be prepared in advance are immediately after lunch and dinner.

Untidy, disorganised payment points will alienate customers

When creating or totalling a bill it is essential that the correct prices or codes are used, otherwise the bill will not be accurate and unnecessary delays and embarrassment will be caused while the errors are corrected. It is also essential to use the correct price and code when accepting payment in any form. The correct price must be entered so that:

- you can give the correct change, if applicable
- the reading on the receipt roll and audit roll match that of the amount of payment received
- you charge the customer the correct amount of money.

The correct code or ledger information (if a bill is not being paid immediately, it may be sent to a company for payment, and is called a *ledger payment*) must be entered when you receive payment so that the accounts department will know how much money to expect in cash and how much in other forms of payment. This information will either be indicated on the keys of the billing machine, or, if your establishment uses a computer, there will be a list of codes available at the payment point. You must make yourself familiar with the establishment procedures and codes.

Once payment has been made, even if it is for a non-cash payment, the customer must receive a machine-printed receipt showing the amount that they have paid. If the bill was created by machine rather than by hand it can be used for this purpose. However, if the bill was handwritten the customer must be given a receipt from the billing machine's receipt roll as proof of the transaction.

The exact procedure will vary from establishment to establishment and from machine to machine.

To do

- Find out if your restaurant creates its customers' bills manually or by machine. If more than one system is used find out why.
- Compile the bills according to your establishment's procedures for any payment point which you are likely to have to operate. For example, you may have to work in two different food service points at some time during your training.
- Make a list of all the codes that are used when operating a payment point within your restaurant, and what they mean.
- Find out what types of receipts are issued at each payment point that you are likely to work at, and learn to create them yourself.
- Ask your supervisor if there are specific times of the day when certain customer bills are most likely to be required. If there are, ask why these busy times occur and what action you can take to anticipate them so that you will be able to react swiftly and efficiently to them. (What work should you have done in advance, what should you have checked?)

Acceptance and validation of non-cash payments

There are various types of non-cash payment. Each must be treated slightly differently, but no matter what establishment you work in the basic acceptance and validation procedures for each type of payment remain the same. The main types of payment are as follows:

cheques	e.g. bank, giro or building society cheques sterling travellers cheques Eurocheques
credit cards	e.g. Access/Mastercard, Visa/Barclaycard
charge cards	e.g. American Express, Diners Club
direct debit cards	Switch cards.

Cheques

Cheques are issued by banks, the Post Office (giro cheques) and building societies. If you are presented with one of these cheques it means that the customer has an account with the issuing establishment and deposits money with them so that their cheques will be paid. This type of cheque can only be used in the country and currency in which it was issued. This means that a cheque from a branch of, for example, Barclays bank anywhere in the UK can be accepted anywhere within the UK and the amount written on it will be given in pounds sterling.

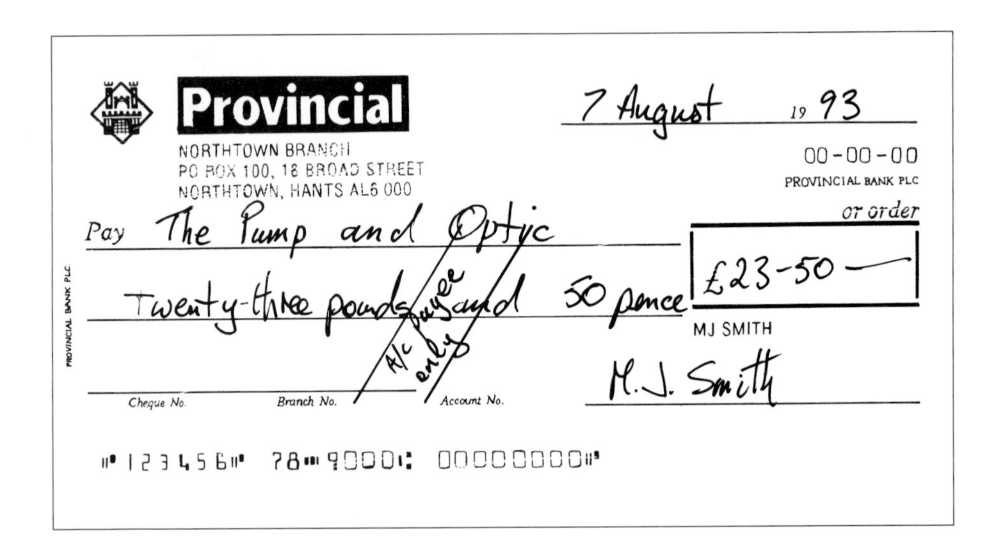

A cheque that has been filled in

A Eurocheque is similar to the type of cheque above but it can be accepted anywhere within the European Community and written in any currency. This means that a customer from France can bring a Eurocheque issued by a bank in France to the UK and pay for goods and services in sterling.

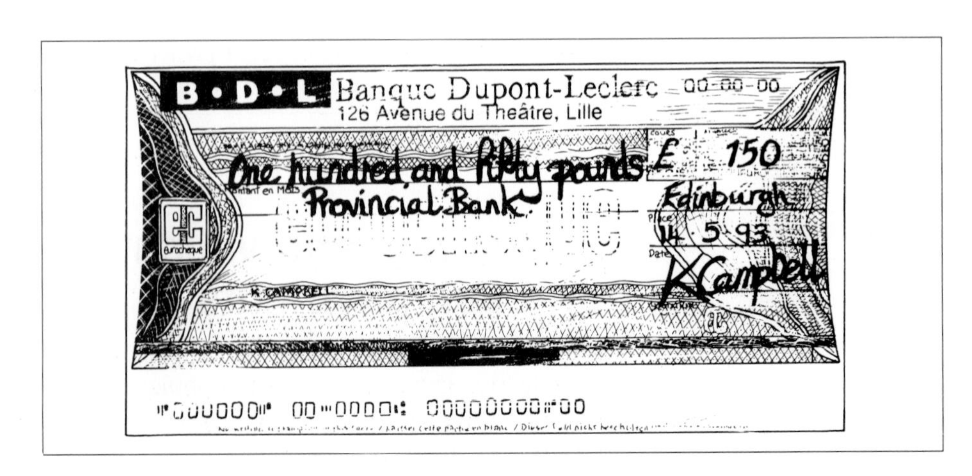

A Eurocheque that has been filled in

A sterling travellers cheque is slightly different. In this case the customer will usually have bought the travellers cheques from a financial institution, for instance, Thomas Cook or American Express, because carrying travellers cheques is safer than carrying large amounts of cash. When your establishment accepts the travellers cheque they will eventually get their money from the issuing company, which already has the customer's money.

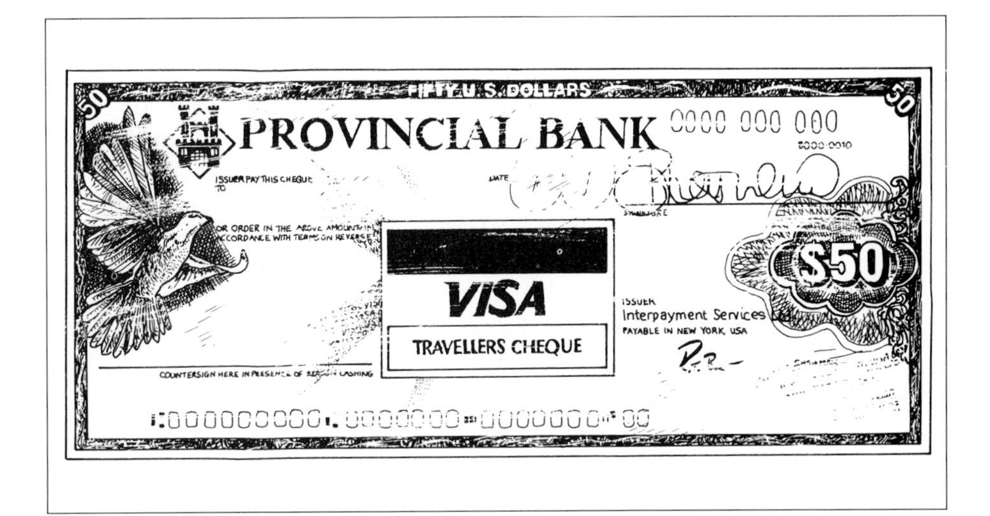

A travellers cheque that has not yet been countersigned

People tend to carry cheques with them rather than cash if they are not sure how much their bill will come to and because it is a more secure form of payment than cash. If cheques are stolen the customer can report this to the issuing company and they can cancel them, and no money is lost. This is not possible with cash. It means however, that when accepting a cheque payment you must always consult the establishment's cancelled/invalid lists. These lists will also record the number of any bank cards which are no longer valid and which should also not be accepted in payment.

ACCESS INVALID CREDIT CARD LIST 25.2.94

Card Number	Expiry date
5534 9948 7535 9630	10/94
7984 5555 2341 9804	9/95

An invalid/cancelled cheques, credit card list

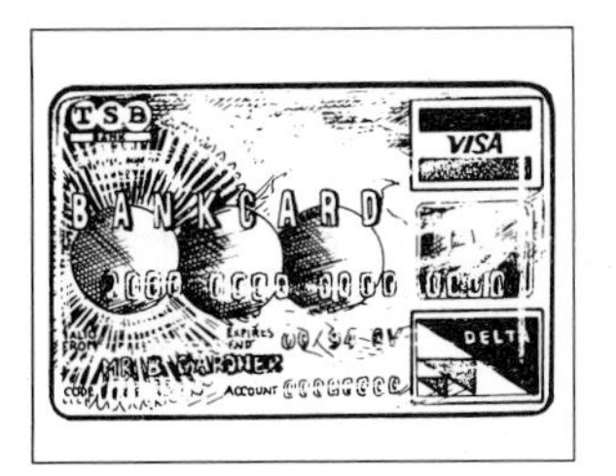

A bank guarantee card

A bank card is a small plastic card issued by a bank, the Post Office or a building society which contains information to enable restaurant staff to verify the ownership of a cheque.

Bank, giro, building society cheques and Eurocheques should all be supported by the relevant bank card. The bank card has a cash figure on it, usually a multiple of £50, and the signature of the customer. This is to enable you to check that the bill total is not for more than the issuing establishment will accept (the cash amount on the bank card). By checking the signature on the card against the signature on the cheque you can make sure that the cheque has been written by the correct person. Travellers cheques are usually supported by a passport or official ID card. Here you will be able to look at the photograph and signature and establish the identity of the customer. If there is no supporting card or passport you should not accept the cheque.

Basic procedure for accepting cheques

Bank, giro, building society cheques and Eurocheques

1 Show the customer the bill, so that they can write out the amount owing on the cheque.
2 Take the filled out cheque from the customer and check the following points:
   - the date is written in correctly
   - the amount, both in writing and figures, is written correctly
   - the signature on the cheque is the same as that on the bank card
   - the signature on the bank card is written on the original paper strip (if a new one has been pasted to the bank card, when you run your thumb over the back of the card it would catch on the different surface)
   - if your establishment has a validation machine, hold the card under the ultraviolet light to check that the hologram is a true one and not a two-dimensional fraud
   - the bank card is valid, not out of date, etc.
   - it is the correct bank card; you can check this by making sure that the sort code on the cheque is the same as the sort code on the bank card (except with a Barclays Bank bank card because the bank card can also be used as a credit card under certain circumstances at the time of writing)
   - the total of the bill does not exceed the guarantee figure on the bank card (if it does you must follow your establishment's procedure for dealing with the cheque).
3 Compare the bank card and cheque with the cancelled/invalid list, and make sure that it does not appear on it.
4 Write the card number on the back of the cheque (you may also be asked to write down other information but that will depend upon your establishment's procedures).
5 Place the cheque in the cash drawer.
6 Give the customer back their bank card, plus a copy of the bill, and a printed receipt if applicable.

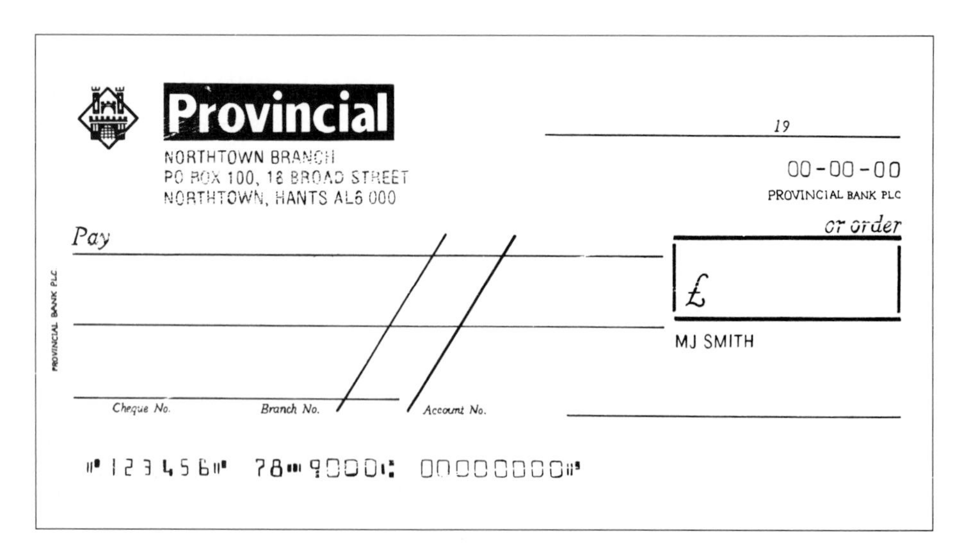
Provincial
NORTHTOWN BRANCH
PO BOX 100, 18 BROAD STREET
NORTHTOWN, HANTS AL6 000
19
00-00-00
PROVINCIAL BANK PLC
Pay
or order
£
MJ SMITH
PROVINCIAL BANK PLC
Cheque No. Branch No. Account No.
123456 78 9000 00000000

A blank cheque; compare this with the completed cheque on p. 76

If the bill total is for more than the amount guaranteed on the bank card your establishment will have a set of procedures for you to follow. This usually means that other information is entered on the back on the cheque, so that if the cheque is not *honoured* (paid) by the issuing company the customer can be traced and asked to pay by another method.

Your establishment will also have a set of procedures to follow if the cheque or bank card number shows up on the withdrawn list. Make sure that you are familiar with these and use them, always remembering to be as discreet and tactful as possible. If you accept payment by a cheque or bank card which has been withdrawn, the issuing company will not honour the cheque and your establishment, and perhaps you yourself, will lose money. If, on the other hand, you retain an invalid card correctly you may be financially rewarded.

In some restaurants cheques are not handwritten, but printed out by the billing machine. In this case the above procedures remain the same except for Point 1. This procedure would now be as follows:

- show the customer the totalled bill, and take a cheque from them. Print the cheque on the billing machine and return it to the customer for checking and signature.

Then continue as before.

Sterling travellers cheques

Before accepting a sterling travellers cheque you should note the following.

- An unauthorised travellers cheque is one on which the second signature is not yet filled in. The first one was filled in when the customer bought the travellers cheques.
- Travellers cheques are issued for standard amounts, i.e. £5, £20, £50, etc. This means that when a customer uses this method to pay, the amount on the travellers cheque is unlikely to be the same as the amount on the bill.
- If the value of the travellers cheque is greater than the value of the bill then you should give the customer change for the difference. For example, if the bill is for £79.50 and the customer gives you travellers cheques worth £80, they are entitled to 50p change. If, on the other hand, a customer's bill came to £55 and they gave the cashier £50 worth of travellers cheques, the difference would have to be made up, usually by the customer paying £5 in cash.
- Often a customer may use more than one travellers cheque to pay for one bill. For example, they may use two £50 cheques to pay for a £100 bill. This is an acceptable, standard practice.
- Customers who are entitled to change may only be given change in sterling. Only banks and other specifically licensed premises are legally allowed to issue foreign cash.

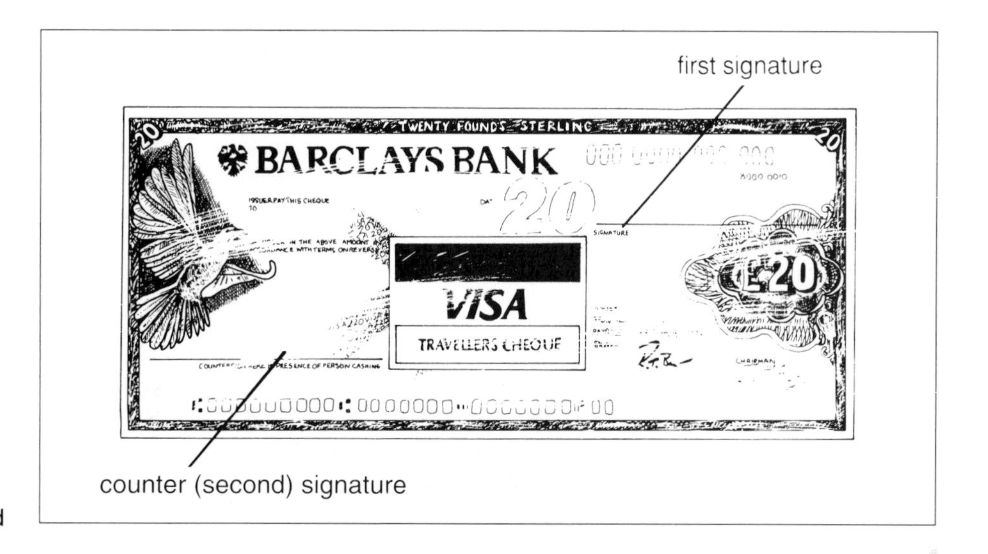

A sterling travellers cheque, not yet authorised

Accepting a sterling travellers cheque

1. Show the customer the totalled bill.
2. Accept from the customer unauthorised travellers cheque(s), usually for more than the total of the bill.
3. Accept from the customer an authorised form of identification, usually a passport or an official ID card.
4. Ask the customer to date the travellers cheque, and countersign it (that is, to enter the second signature). This second signature should only be entered in front of the person receiving the payment so that they can authenticate the signature.
5. Check this signature against the first signature and then check the photograph and signature in the passport or on the ID card against the signature and person in front of you.
6. If it is your establishment's procedure, write down the passport or ID card number on the back of the travellers cheque.
7. Receive the difference between the total of the travellers cheques being offered and the total of the bill, if applicable.
8. Give the correct change, the identification documents and a printed receipt to the customer.
9. Place the travellers cheque(s) safely and correctly in the cash drawer.

Credit cards and charge cards

Some cards are issued by banks, like Barclays, and others are issued by large financial institutions, like American Express. Some are only acceptable within the UK and some are acceptable internationally. Not all restaurants accept all credit and charge cards. This is because they have to pay commission to the issuing company. Your restaurant will have a list of those charge and credit cards which it accepts, and you should familiarise yourself with it so that you only accept the listed cards.

Credit cards

As far as accepting payment by credit or charge card is concerned, you will follow the same basic procedures. This is because the main difference in the type of card is how the establishment receives its final cash payment from the issuing company. Another difference that you will notice is that the internationally accepted cards, which tend to be charge cards, normally have a higher guarantee limit, and the restaurant will have a higher floor limit for this type of card.

A cheque is guaranteed by a bank card, and by its absence from the cancelled/invalid list. A charge card or credit card payment is guaranteed by the card's printed limit, by the floor limit of the restaurant, by an authorisation code and by its absence from the cancelled/invalid list.

Floor limits

- The *floor limit* is the restaurant's credit limit, i.e. the maximum amount that can be accepted without authorisation for a credit or charge card payment. Its purpose is to reduce the potential for fraud.
- Normally there is a different floor limit for each type of card that the establishment accepts.
- If the total of a bill exceeds the floor limit, an authorisation code must be obtained from the issuing company, otherwise they may not honour the payment.

Authorisation codes

An authorisation code is needed whenever the bill total is for more than either the card's stated limit, the restaurant's floor limit or both. In this case you must contact the issuing company by following the restaurant's procedure, which will normally involve telephoning a special number. You will need to give the issuing company the following information:

- the name of the restaurant
- the reference number of the restaurant
- the name, number and expiry date on the card
- the total of the bill.

The issuing company, if everything is in order, will then give you a number. This is the authorisation code. It guarantees that the issuing company will reimburse the restaurant for the total of that bill even if the customer should run out of money. Once an authorisation code has been obtained no adjustments may be made to the customer's bill. If even a single change has to be made, a new authorisation code for the new amount must be sought.

If there is a problem, you will be asked to retain the card and inform the customer why you are doing so. If this happens your restaurant will have a standard procedure to follow to help you do this. It will probably recommend that you contact your supervisor.

Always remember that when a card is cancelled, while it may be that the customer is trying to defraud your restaurant, it could also be that they are a genuine customer whose last payment simply got held up by something like a postal strike. If they are a genuine customer they will be deeply embarrassed, and would not want anyone else to know what has happened. Therefore you must be discreet. In all circumstances you must follow your restaurant's procedures, besides asking for another form of payment.

Basic procedure for accepting credit and charge cards

In some restaurants the method of accepting credit and charge cards is manual and in others it is incorporated into a computerised system. The procedures vary slightly from one another so both are described below. It may also be useful for your future career to learn both systems.

A manual acceptance system

1. Give the customer the totalled bill.
2. Accept the credit or charge card from the customer.
3. Check that this is a card which is accepted by your restaurant, and the floor limits for this type of card.

4 Check the following details on the card:
   - that it is still valid, i.e. the expiry date has not yet been reached
   - the cash guarantee limit of the card
   - that the signature is the original one. Do this by running your thumb over it; if a new paper strip has been added with a new signature written on it your thumb will catch on the edge of the new strip
   - if your restaurant has a validation machine, place the credit or debit card under the ultraviolet light to check that the hologram is real, not a two-dimensional fraud.

5 Take a blank voucher and the credit card, and run them through the imprinting machine.

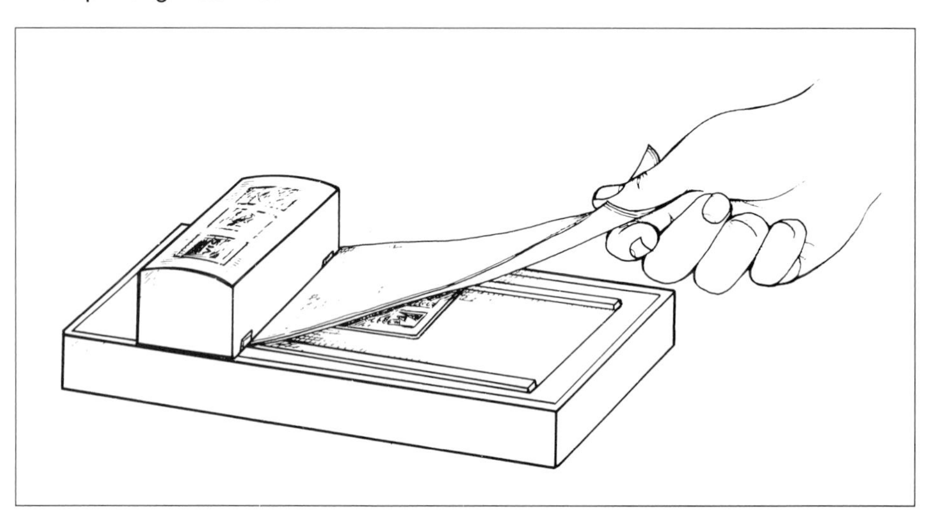

A credit card and voucher in an imprinter

6 Write the following information on the voucher:
   - date
   - department, if applicable
   - sales number, if applicable
   - your initials
   - a brief description of what is being paid for, e.g. 'meal'
   - the amount of the bill in the amount section and the total section
   - the authorisation code, if applicable.

7 Give the voucher back to the customer to sign.

8 Check the signature of the customer on the voucher against the signature on the card. (The card may be valid, but it may not be the owner of the card who has presented it to you.)

9 Give the customer the customer copy of the voucher, their card and a printed receipt.

10 Place the restaurant's copies of the vouchers in the correct place in the cash drawer.

A mechanised acceptance method

1 Give the customer the totalled bill.

2 Accept a charge or credit card from the customer.

3 Check that it is a card which is accepted by the restaurant.

4 Swipe the card through the appropriate machine (there will be a machine through which to swipe the card, or it will be incorporated as part of the billing machine). The machine will automatically check the card and provide an authorisation number. When the checks have been successfully completed the machine will print out a duplicate voucher.

5 Ask the customer to sign the voucher.

6 Check the signature on the voucher against that on the card. (The card may be valid, but it may not be the owner of the card who has presented it to you.)

7 Give the customer the customer copy of the voucher, their card and their copy of the bill.
8 Place the restaurant's copies of the voucher in the correct place within the cash drawer.

Combined systems

In some restaurants there may be a combined manual and mechanised system. Here the normal procedure would be for you to validate the card by swiping it through an authorising machine and entering the total of the bill. The machine would automatically show the authorisation code on a digital display, and you would complete processing the card via the manual system. This system is more popular now than an entirely manual system, because it saves time and all cards can be validated quickly and efficiently at any time of day or night.

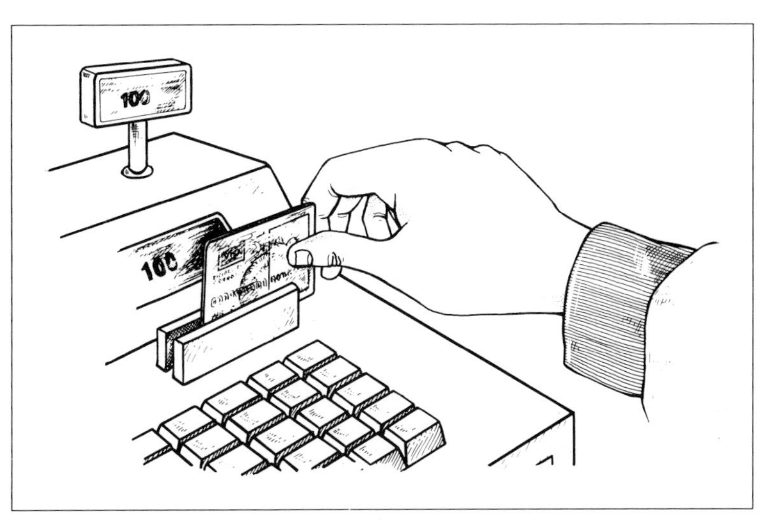

An authorisation machine

If at any stage you are not happy with the transaction, you cannot get an authorisation code, the signatures do not look the same (even after you have asked the customer to sign for the second time on the back), etc. you should not accept the payment, but, following the restaurant's procedures, should get assistance from another member of staff.

This is especially true if the payment point is very busy, because if you take a long time to deal with one customer others will be starting to ask where their bills are and become very frustrated. It is also very difficult to be discreet when there is a problem, with lots of other people around, such as customers and waiters, all trying to collect or pay bills, and therefore able to overhear any conversation that might be going on.

Direct debit cards

These are cards which directly debit the customer's bank account with the total of the bill, and place that amount into the restaurant's bank account. It is therefore similar to accepting cash, in that there is no waiting period for the payment. However, the procedure for accepting payment by this method is very like the mechanised credit or charge card system. The most common card of this type is a Switch card.

Many people choose to carry them in preference to cash, as a security measure. Restaurants are happy to accept them because as long as they are correctly accepted, the restaurant is guaranteed its money straightaway.

Basic procedures for accepting a direct debit card

1 Give the customer the totalled bill.
2 Accept the direct debit card from the customer.
3 Check that it is a card which is accepted by the restaurant.
4 Swipe the card through the appropriate machine (there will be a machine through which to swipe the card, or it will be incorporated as part of the billing machine). The machine will automatically check the card. When the checks have been successfully completed the machine will print out a duplicate voucher.
5 Ask the customer to sign the voucher.
6 Check the signature on the voucher against that on the card. (The card may be valid, but it may not be the owner of the card who has presented it to you.)
7 Give the customer the customer copy of the voucher, their card and their copy of the bill.

As with any other form of non-cash payment, if you are not happy with any part of the acceptance or validation procedure you should follow your restaurant's procedure for dealing with problems in a non-cash payment situation. This will normally involve explaining the problem to a more senior member of staff, in the first instance.

Dealing with errors or spoilt cheques or vouchers

From time to time, especially when you first start training, you will make errors. Your supervisors expect a few problems to occur, and there will be an establishment policy for dealing with them. However, when a cheque or voucher is spoilt or written incorrectly there are several basic steps to follow which will be part of your establishment's procedure. These are given below.

Cheques

1 If any part of the cheque is written out incorrectly (often it is the date), the customer can cross the error through, write down the correct information and initial the error.
2 As long as the cheque is still clearly legible it will not matter if there is more than one correction on it, but all the corrections must be initialled by the customer.
3 If there are a lot of corrections it is better to cancel the cheque by tearing it up in front of the customer so that they can see you doing it, and giving them the torn cheque if they require it. In this case a new cheque would be written out.

Credit or charge cards

Manual system

1 If there are any errors the voucher must be voided.
2 The voucher should be torn up, in front of or by the customer, and they should be given the torn voucher if they require it.
3 A new voucher should be written out.

Mechanised system
If you are using a mechanised method of accepting credit or charge cards and an error is made in the creation of the bill before it has been signed, there will be a method of cancelling the voucher immediately. Your establishment will have a procedure for this. There is probably a void key on the machine which will cancel the transaction. However you must always follow your establishment's procedure, keeping all paperwork that is generated by the error, i.e. the incorrect voucher and the cancellation slip. These should be placed in your cash drawer and handed over with the rest of the money at the end of your shift.

To do

- Write down the procedure for accepting a cheque if it is for more than the guaranteed cash limit on the card.
- Make a list of forms of ID other than a passport acceptable to your establishment when accepting sterling travellers cheques.
- Make a list of all the credit cards and charge cards that your restaurant accepts.
- Make a list of your establishment's floor limits for each card which is accepted.
- Find out where the cancelled/invalid lists are kept. Make sure that there is one beside the cash point.
- Write down exactly what you should do if you are at all worried about accepting a non-cash payment.
- Find out whether your restaurant uses a manual or mechanised credit and charge card authorisation system, and learn how to use it.
- Write down the procedure that your restaurant uses to cancel unusable cheques and vouchers.

Security of the payment point

Given that any form of payment is a temptation to dishonest people, it is obvious that security of the payment point is very important. If unauthorised persons gain access to a payment point they will be able to gain access to the customers' bills, as well as to cash and other forms of payment.

If a person gains access to the payment point they may be able to find out unauthorised information about various customers of the establishment. For example, if a celebrity is dining they may not want fans, press or other interested people to know that they are in the restaurant, as they would like to enjoy their meal uninterrupted. The information gained can also be used more seriously, perhaps in a legal situation such as a divorce court.

Unauthorised people may also behave in other dishonest ways, for example, they may alter the totals of the customers' bills, e.g. lowering their own. They may also simply steal, i.e. remove cash and other valuable items.

For these reasons payment points must be kept secure, and are sometimes physically separate from the other parts of the restaurant, even within a secure cubicle. In other establishments the payment point may be incorporated within the main service station.

If you are the person authorised to deal with payments during a shift it means that you are also responsible for the security and safety of the contents of your cash drawer and for the safety and confidentiality of the customers' bills.

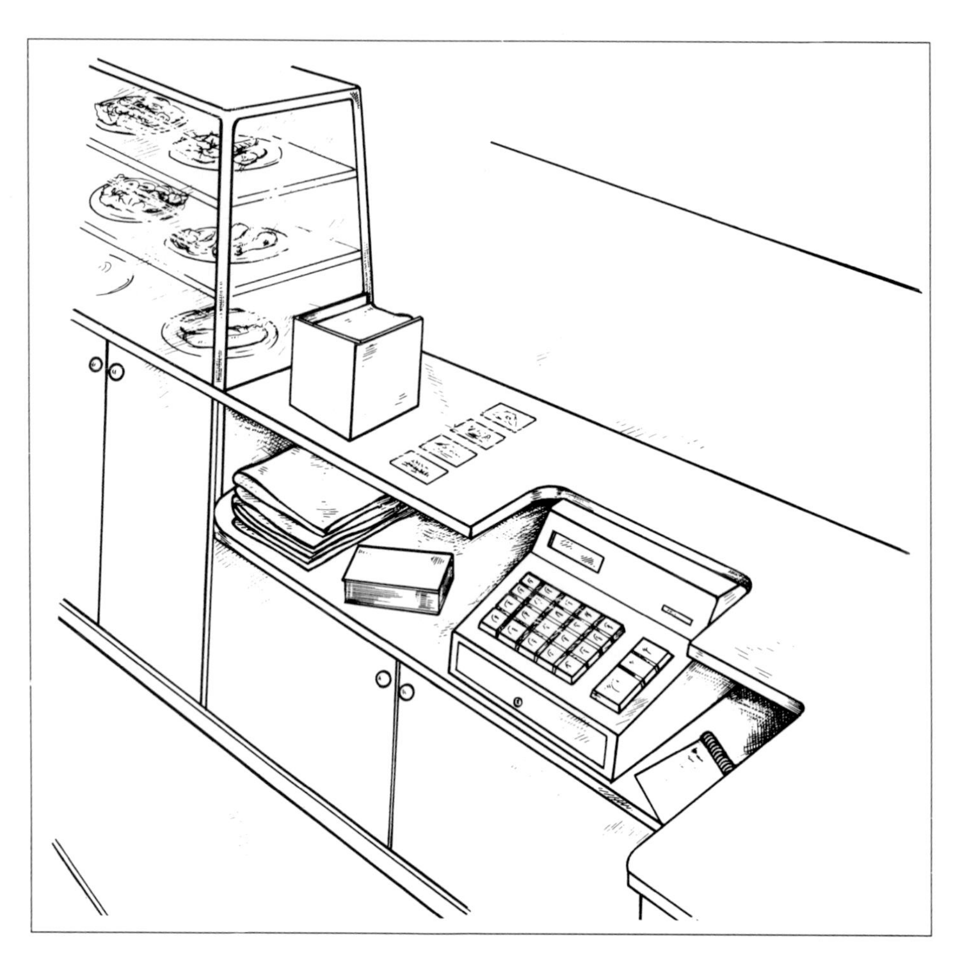

The cash machine should be positioned away from the access end of the service station

There are several golden rules which you should observe at all times.

- Never leave the open payment point unattended for any period of time.
- If you have to leave the payment point unattended, perhaps to serve a customer, make sure that it is securely locked.
- Never allow anyone except the customer or a properly authorised person to look at the customers' bills.
- Never allow anyone without proper authorisation into the area of the payment point.
- If you have to make an adjustment to a customer's bill, get the proper authorisation and signature before you do so.
- If you have to void a voucher or cheque, actually tear it up in front of the customer so that they can be certain that it has been destroyed.
- Whenever you have the smallest doubt about the honesty of anyone's actions immediately contact your supervisor.

Beyond this, each establishment will have a security procedure which has been set up to deal with each payment point's security needs. You must always follow this procedure.

Essential knowledge

It is essential that payment points are secured from unauthorised access:

- to prevent members of the public or members of staff stealing from the payment point
- to make sure unauthorised persons do not see customers' accounts
- to prevent anyone tampering with the payment point, for example, by making false charges or adjustments to customers' accounts
- to prevent damage to the payment points.

To do

- From time to time when you are in charge of a payment point you may need to leave it, to go to the toilet, for instance. Find out the procedure within your restaurant if this type of situation arises.
- Make a list of all those people who are authorised to have access to the customers' bills, and why they have that authorisation.
- Discuss with your supervisor and then make a list of when you should hand over any form of payment, to whom, why, and what the required authorisation is.

Dealing with customers and unexpected situations

Customers expect an efficient service at all times. This should be true but it is not always possible. If you are unable to assist a customer straightaway remember to remain polite and calm at all times, and if you are unable to deal with the customer at all, contact someone who can.

Anticipating customer needs will enable you to prevent most problems. If most people eat lunch between 12.00 noon and 2.00 p.m. make sure that all the documentation for creating bills is ready by 11.30 p.m. This is an example of being aware of a potential problem and defusing it before it occurs. The ability to do this comes through observation and experience.

You cannot, however, anticipate all potential problems. If a customer walks towards a payment point with a folded paper held in both hands, it may be that

A customer who may have criminal intentions

they have a gun or other weapon under the paper, as they intend to try to rob the establishment. It may also be a customer who has a strange way of holding their newspaper.

If someone comes into the restaurant and just orders a mineral water which they take a very long time to drink, while sitting and watching what is going on, it may be a person with dishonest intentions, or it may be a person who has arrived early for a meeting with a friend and who is merely killing time.

When you are responsible for a vulnerable area, like a payment point, you must learn to become aware of all unexpected behaviour, because of the potential trouble it could indicate. However you must not overreact, and possibly embarrass a genuine customer who happens to be behaving oddly. Bearing in mind that you must never leave an open payment point unattended, the following points are useful guidelines as to what you can do and what you should not do.

- If you have any reason to believe that there is something unusual going on you must immediately do something, such as contacting your supervisor, and not let it pass hoping that nothing will happen.
- You should always follow the establishment's policy in dealing with the situation. This would normally be to contact your supervisor, or the security department, if your establishment has one, and report your suspicions.
- Approaching a potentially suspect person by yourself may not be a wise thing to do, nor possible if you are alone at the payment point. It could also be dangerous.
- Being aware of suspect behaviour also means keeping an eye out for packages, etc. left lying unattended. These may have simply been forgotten, or they may be much more dangerous.

To do

- Find out your establishment's policy for reporting unusual or suspicious behaviour.
- Consciously try to become aware of anyone who is behaving in an unusual fashion when they enter a vulnerable area, like a payment point.
- Ask your supervisor and other members of staff about problem areas that frequently arise. Find out how they deal with them.
- Make a note of when you have a problem at a payment point. After a week or so look at your notes and see if some problems are occurring regularly. If they are, discuss with your supervisor how you could anticipate them, and so prevent them from happening.

What have you learned?

1 Why must the customer be allowed to check the total of their bill before paying it?

____

____

2 Why must the total of the customer's bill be correct when they pay it?

____

____

3 Why must the customer be given a printed receipt?

4 What do you need to guarantee a bank, giro cheque or Eurocheque?

5 What do you need in order to guarantee a sterling travellers cheque?

6 Which type of cheque can you give change to?

7 In what currency?

8 If an error is made on a credit or charge card voucher what is the most secure way of voiding it?

9 Which credit cards and charge cards are accepted by your restaurant?

10 How should all cheques and vouchers be held securely at a payment point?

11 Whom should cheques and vouchers be given to and why?

____

____

12 Why shouldn't unauthorised people have access to a payment point?

____

____

13 What should you do if you see an unusual occurrence within the restaurant?

____

____

ELEMENT 2: Handling and recording refunds

Dealing with customers requiring refunds

You may be the first person to hear about a problem for which a customer feels that they are entitled to a refund. This is because the payment point is where they settle their account. When dealing with such customers you should remember the following points.

- From time to time refunds either in cash or credit will need to be made by all establishments.
- Not *all* refunds are the results of errors or bad service, etc. but most are.
- A customer requiring a refund will usually be unhappy about something and therefore will require especially sympathetic handling.
- Applications for refunds are as open to abuse (such as fraud) as payments are.
- Because all applications for refunds are potentially fraudulent, all refunds must be appropriately authorised.
- The issuing of a refund must be authorised and recorded. If cash is handed over without being recorded, the person who handed it over is open to accusations of cash discrepancies, i.e. theft.
- All applications for refunds must be recorded so that management can take action to prevent the problem reoccurring.

There are three basic reasons why a customer may ask for a refund, but in each case they may be, or appear to be, very angry, and so need to be treated very politely and diplomatically. The reasons are as follows.

1 Something has gone wrong. For example, if the customer asked for chicken breast from a roast chicken and was served a drumstick, they are entitled to be angry. If they requested a birthday cake in advance, and it did not arrive at the end of the meal, they are caused great inconvenience. This means that when you are dealing with them you will have to be especially tactful.

2 A customer may be 'trying it on'. That is to say, seeing if they can get a price reduction even if they are not really entitled to it. In this case a senior member of staff will have to give authorisation, after they have become satisfied that the incident has occurred. The customer usually appears very angry in order to intimidate the establishment's staff. This is why a senior member of staff should investigate and deal with the problem.
3 A customer may have a problem, but they may have caused it themselves; for example when they ordered their meal they did not mention that they were allergic to bacon, but a hock was used in the preparation of the lentil soup, and the soup made them ill. As above, a senior member of staff will have to investigate the incident, and make a decision about whether or not the guest is entitled to some form of compensation.

In all these cases it is the food server who often gets the first blast of anger. Your restaurant will have a procedure to deal with this. If you follow it and remain calm the incident can be defused and remedies offered, but if you take the customer's anger personally and become angry in return the problem will get worse. For more information about how to deal with customer complaints, see Unit G3 (pp 48–52).

To do

- Find out your restaurant's procedure for dealing with applications for refunds.
- Ask your supervisor how they deal with very angry customers, and learn some techniques from them for handling people who are upset or angry.

Validating and issuing a refund

Your restaurant will have a procedure for validating and issuing refunds. You must never deviate from this procedure because it is designed to protect staff as well as the restaurant.

- Issuing a refund means giving money away from the business. It can only be done if a senior member of staff has authorised it.
- Giving money away means that the money in your cash drawer will be short. You must have documentation to justify the shortage.
- As a refund claim is as potentially open to fraud as any other payment transaction, the claim must be validated before the refund is issued.

Most establishments will follow the same basic rules and only the fine detail will vary from establishment to establishment. The basic procedure is as follows.

1 The restaurant becomes aware of a problem. This may happen in two ways.
   - In the first incident the restaurant's staff become aware of the problem, and alert the appropriate senior member of staff. For instance, a customer who has arranged a surprise party at the restaurant asked for flowers for the female guests to be available upon arrival, and paid in advance for them as it was an unusual request. The flowers have not arrived (they were sent elsewhere in error) and the florist has closed for the day. Here the management know that there is a genuine problem before the customer is aware of it and complains, and can work out the remedial action to take, i.e. arrange for champagne to be available upon the party's arrival and debit the cost of the flowers from the total of the bill.
   - In the second type of incident the customer becomes aware of the problem first. For instance they may have ordered one bottle of wine with their meal but the cost for two has been put on their bill. Your first action, after apologising, would be to contact the appropriate senior member of staff. The senior member of staff would quickly investigate the incident.

Mr Eaton			
V.A.T. reg no. 423 1654 39	Date 14-2-94		
Couverts 5 Dinners @ £8.50		42	50
Cafe 4 coffees @ £1.25		5	00
Wine 2 x 23 @ £11.50		23	00
Spirits —			
Liqueurs 1 Drambuie		2	50
1 Tia Maria		2	50
Beers —			
Minerals 1 Mineral Water		1	50
Cigars and tobacco	Sub Total:	77	00
Credit 1 x No. 23 wine		11	50
Table no. 4	Total £	65	50
No. covers 5			
04214			

A customer's restaurant bill with a reduction against the meal

2 Once the senior member of staff is sure that the incident happened, they will authorise you to make a refund. They will do this by writing up the incident in a Refund Book, which will be similar to the example given below.

Date	Details	Cash Refund	Credit Refund	Authorised By	Cashier

A page from an example Refund Book

Where there is a very simple manual or semi-mechanised payment system in operation, a cash refund may be authorised without the above paperwork, but simply by an authorised person initialling on the till/audit roll.

3 If the refund is a *cash refund* then cash is removed from the cash drawer and given to the customer. There will normally be a duplicate book for the customer to sign saying that they have received the cash, with the bottom copy going into the cash drawer to justify the reduction in cash. If the refund is a credit refund, that is to say that there is an adjustment made on the customer's bill, then no cash changes hands but when the customer comes to pay their bill there will be a reduction on it for the agreed amount.

4 If the refund is a *credit or charge card refund* you will have to fill in a voucher which is very similar to a credit or charge card voucher, but it will say *refund.* You will take an imprint of the customer's card, or run it through an authorisation machine, according to your restaurant's procedures. The customer will sign the voucher and retain their copy. However, when the customer eventually receives their statement from their credit or charge card company they will find that the refund amount has been deducted from their statement, not added on to it.
As previously mentioned, if your establishment has a mechanised method of accepting credit and charge card payments, and you make an error which you notice before the voucher is signed, there will be a method of voiding the voucher which you have just created. Always follow your establishment's procedure for doing this.
5 If the senior member of staff is not satisfied that the refund is justified then they will not authorise it, and will deal with the customer in private away from the public work areas. If there is no authorisation you must never give out a refund, even if it is only for a tiny sum like 50p, because you may not know the whole story.

In all restaurants the basic procedures will be as described above. However there will be variations in the documentation to be completed and in the members of staff who are authorised to issue refunds. You must learn the procedure for your bar.

To do

- Find out who is authorised to give refunds in your restaurant.
- Find out where the refund authorisation book is kept.
- Find out if there is a special key on your billing machine which is used to indicate that a credit refund has been given.
- Over a period of a month make a list of all the refunds which you are authorised to deal with. Analyse the list and see if any of the incidents occur regularly. Discuss them with your supervisor.

Dealing with unexpected situations

The ability to deal well with unexpected situations comes mainly through personal experience, and observing how others deal successfully with incidents. The restaurant's procedure for dealing with unexpected incidents has been set up to provide a set of guidelines to work within, but common sense is also required.

If a customer needs a refund because they have paid for a special function in advance, but has to leave halfway through because of illness, they will be upset. The restaurant will have a procedure, similar to the one above for issuing the refund, but you can do a lot to help the situation simply by remaining calm and being helpful. Perhaps you can arrange to call a cab for them to help with transport.

This would not mean, however, that you should forget about the security of the payment point and leave it unattended at any time. By following the establishment's procedure, using your own common sense and asking a senior member of staff for assistance each time you are unsure of what to do you should be able to deal with all unusual situations.

To do

- Find out your restaurant's procedure for reporting unexpected situations.
- Make a list of whom you should contact, and how you would do it if a situation you were unsure about arose.

What have you learned?

1 Why must all refunds be authorised?

2 Who is able to authorise refunds?

3 What should you do if a refund is not authorised?

4 Where should a refund be recorded if it is
a) a cash refund?

b) a credit refund?

5 Why must you remain calm and helpful all the time?

6 Why must you follow the establishment's procedures very carefully?

Extend your knowledge

- Find out why it is useful for management to have the details of all refunds recorded. What use do they make of this information?
- Find out the most common reasons for your senior staff to refuse to give a refund. What do they do when this type of situation occurs?
- Find out how much commission your restaurant pays for each type of credit or charge card it accepts.
- Find out why your restaurant accepts the cards they do.
- Find out how long it takes for the restaurant to actually receive the money in the bank if they accept payment by any non-cash method.
- Make a list of the most common ways that fraudsters are able to defraud restaurants using non-cash payment methods.
- Find out the legal position if confidential information about customers is given out to unauthorised persons by your restaurant.

UNIT 2C1

Preparing and clearing areas for table service

ELEMENTS 1–3: Preparing and clearing dining and service areas and equipment

What do you have to do?

- Plan and carry out your work to meet daily schedules in an organised and efficient manner, taking into account priorities and laid down procedures.
- Check that all service equipment, linen, and furniture is clean, free from damage, correctly prepared, stocked, stored and positioned ready for service.
- Prepare, store and clear correctly, in accordance with food hygiene regulations, all food condiments and accompaniments.
- Make sure that tables are correctly laid and ready for service.
- Check that the environmental (e.g. temperature, lighting) systems are correctly set in accordance with laid down procedures.
- Check all refuse and waste containers are clean and ready for service and that all waste is disposed of correctly after service.
- Deal with unexpected situations appropriately.
- Assemble all table items, service dishes and utensils used during food service for cleaning or storage.
- Ensure that the dining and service areas are left tidy and ready for cleaning, and that all service equipment is turned off or set in accordance to laid down procedures.

What do you need to know?

- How to maintain an efficient service, promoting customer satisfaction.
- Why a constant stock of food service items has to be maintained.
- Why it is important to handle and dispose of waste correctly.
- Why is important to check the menu before use.
- What factors affect room plans.
- Why dining and service areas must be left clean after service.
- Why certain electrical equipment should be turned off after service.
- How to prepare tables for table service.
- Why it is important to store food stuffs correctly.

Introduction

Restaurants need not only to attract potential customers but also to retain them as frequent customers. This can be done in a number of ways, such as through the type of menu, the name of the place or the atmosphere within the food service area.

The customers' first impressions of a restaurant are the most important, and these are largely determined by the professionalism of the service staff and their preparations prior to service. These pre-service preparations are known as *mise-en-place* and are vital in that they create the right environmental conditions by the setting and controlling of temperature, lighting and equipment.

What is *table service*?

The definition for table service is 'service where the customer is seated at a table, their order taken and the food brought to them and served'. There are several ways in which this can be done:

- silver service
- plated service
- family service
- French service
- Russian service
- guéridon service
- banquet service.

Banqueting is a term used to describe the service of special functions within an establishment, such as conferences, luncheons, wedding breakfasts and dinner dances. There is no real difference between restaurant table service or banquet service preparation other than the number of customers to be catered for at one time. For this reason, large establishments often have rooms set aside for these functions with a separate administration and staffing. Smaller establishments might use a room adjacent to the restaurant covered by the regular service staff and, perhaps, a couple of part-time staff.

Whatever the situation, each establishment has to consider these points:

- the type of clientele expected
- the restaurant's location
- the food and beverage service layout
- the type of service offered
- the funds available.

Once these are established the restaurant's environment can be decided, and considerations in turn given to:

1. service equipment
2. condiments and accompaniments
3. cover lay-ups
4. table items and table linen
5. environmental systems
6. food service areas
7. health and safety
8. establishment standards and procedures
9. food hygiene.

ELEMENT 1: Preparing service equipment and areas for table service

Health, safety and hygiene

Before starting any sort of work, you need to be aware of the fact that all service staff are responsible for health, safety and hygiene standards within their working areas. The following list gives you some brief points to remember (additional information can be found in Units G1 and G2, pp. 1–37).

Hygiene points

- Cover all food to avoid contamination by dust, insects, coughing, etc.
- Refrigerate cold food stuffs until required at a temperature of 4 °C (40 °F).
- Remember that hot plates are for keeping hot food hot, not for heating it up.
- Serve food as soon as possible after preparation.
- Clean up any spillages immediately.
- Avoid cross-contamination: use a clean set of service equipment for each individual food item.
- Hold cutlery by the handles, crockery by the rim and glasses by the stem or base to prevent contamination.
- Never re-use food which has been served to customers and left uneaten (e.g. butter).
- Pay attention to personal hygiene; prevent food contamination in preparation and service areas by not spitting, smoking, etc. Always wash your hands after coughing, sneezing, going to the toilet, etc.

Safety points

- Comply with all work procedures.
- Keep work areas clean and in a safe condition, i.e. remove any waste or dirty equipment.
- Report any faults or problems as soon possible to your supervisor.
- Report all incidents and accidents to your supervisor.

Preventing accidents

Most accidents can be avoided by practising some simple rules:

1. treat hotplates, gas or spirit lamps with care
2. keep any handles turned inward, away from people passing
3. use dry cloths to hold or carry hot items
4. keep floors clean and dry
5. remove potential hazards; e.g. trailing electrical wires

The knives and forks protruding from this table are a potential hazard

6 walk, never run
7 wear the correct clothing and footwear
8 take care when using knives
9 clear broken glass and crockery straight away: wrap it in paper, place it in a box and mark the box clearly; do not put it in a bin liner
10 when using electrical equipment make sure your hands are dry
11 switch off and unplug electrical equipment when not in use.

Unavoidable accidents and incidents

No matter what precautions have been taken, accidents sometimes happen. It is therefore wise to be prepared:

- learn the basic first-aid procedures
- make sure you know the name of your establishment's first aider and how to contact them
- be aware of all establishment procedures for dealing with accidents and incidents (including how to record them)
- be aware of fire procedures
- find out where the the first aid box and fire extinguishers are kept
- be aware of your role in the event of an unexpected situation.

Planning your work

In order to maintain efficiency and speed when preparing, using and clearing work areas, work needs to be planned and allocated to meet daily requirements. The restaurant supervisor is normally responsible for drawing up work plans to help the smooth running of service.

The order of preparation varies from one establishment to another and the tasks involved may be allocated under a rota system, where various tasks are completed by individual staff members in rotation. As there are so many different types and styles of food service establishments it is impossible to give a specific order of preparation or rota, but the following example may give a guide as to the principles of a work rota in a hotel restaurant.

Two week duty rota

Food Server	Sat	Sun	Mon	Tue	Wed	Thu	Fri	Sat	Sun	Mon	Tue	Wed	Thu	Fri
A	1	11	*	10	9	8	7	6	5	*	4	3	2	1
B	2	1	*	11	10	9	8	7	6	*	5	4	3	2
C	3	2	*	1	11	10	9	8	7	*	6	5	4	3
D	4	3	*	2	1	11	10	9	8	*	7	6	5	4
E	5	4	*	3	2	1	11	10	9	*	8	7	6	5
F	6	5	*	4	3	2	1	11	10	*	9	8	7	6
G	7	6	*	5	4	3	2	1	11	*	10	9	8	7
H	8	7	*	6	5	4	3	2	1	*	11	10	9	8
I	9	8	*	7	6	5	4	3	2	*	1	11	10	9
J	10	9	*	8	7	6	5	4	3	*	2	1	11	10
K	11	10	*	9	8	7	6	5	4	*	3	2	1	11

Key to tasks

1 Dusting
2 Vacuuming
3 Polishing
4 Linen
5 Stillroom
6 Sideboards and trolleys
7 Accompaniments
8 Silver cleaning
9 Hotplate
10 Table and chair arranging
11 Miscellaneous

Whatever the size of establishment, the staff's approach to tasks will affect the overall standard of preparation, service and clearing. Consider ways in which you can save both time and effort while maintaining standards, such as those given below:

- make journeys worthwhile; never go empty-handed between wash-up and hotplate, or hotplate to restaurant
- stock sideboards with equipment that is polished ready for service and has been checked for chips and cracks
- always count the required cutlery, crockery, etc. needed for service; never try to guess
- while customers are eating one course, prepare the service equipment for the next
- avoid wastage by: turning off appliances when not in use; making small quantities only of perishables (e.g. mustards, butter and rolls) when the number of customers is unknown; return any left-over food items on trolleys to the kitchen as soon as service finishes.

Cleaning and preparing the service and dining area

The general 'light' cleaning of dining areas can be carried out by service staff, but the more 'heavy' cleaning is better done by trained specialist personnel. Light cleaning includes such tasks as the regular cleaning and polishing of restaurant chairs, tables, sideboards, mirrors, glassware, silverware, cruets and exposed surfaces.

Daily duties

Every day the restaurant supervisor checks the daily bookings for a restaurant, making out the seating plans, allocating 'stations', checking the menus and monitoring the carrying out of tasks. Each task area can be broken into daily duties, to be carried out by the restaurant team (*brigade*).

The following list gives an idea of how this may be carried out.

Everyday tasks

- vacuum carpet and brush surrounds
- clean and polish doors and glass
- empty waste bins

Tasks on rota

- Tuesday: polish brasses
- Wednesday: brush and dust tables and chairs
- Thursday: clean and polish reception area
- Friday: clean and polish sideboards
- Saturday: clean window ledges and skirting

The service area

Most of the work of mise-en-place starts in the service area. In large establishments this area is found between the kitchen and the food service areas and is one of the busiest areas, especially at service time. The whole area can be broken down into five specific sections:

- silver (or *plate*) room
- wash-up
- stillroom
- hotplate
- spare linen room.

Throughout this unit we will make references to each of these areas and the work carried out within them.

Why is hygiene important?
It is important that all preparation and storage areas and equipment are kept clean and in a hygienic condition in order to:
- prevent any transfer of food poisoning
- comply with health and safety requirements
- maintain the highest standards of cleanliness
- prevent the risk of accidents or fire
- prevent a build up of waste and unpleasant odours which will then attract pest infestation.

The silver (or *plate*) room

In very large establishments the silver and the plate room may be two separate units, but in the majority of places they are combined and in some cases, are a part of the wash-up.

The silver room holds the stock of silver required for the service of meals. The various types of silver are kept here on labelled shelves, with all the service flats of one size stacked together. Cutlery, flatware, holloware and other smaller items are usually stored in draws lined with baize, as this helps to reduce noise, slipping and scratching. Note that silver used for banquets may have a different design to the silver in everyday use.

For details on the silverware itself, see pp. 109–10.

The wash-up

At service time especially, the wash-up area is one of the busiest sections. It must be correctly sited to allow a smooth flow of work, promoting a fast and efficient service. There are two methods of washing:
- *the tank method.* Using this method, items of equipment are first washed in a sink of hot water containing detergent and then placed into racks and

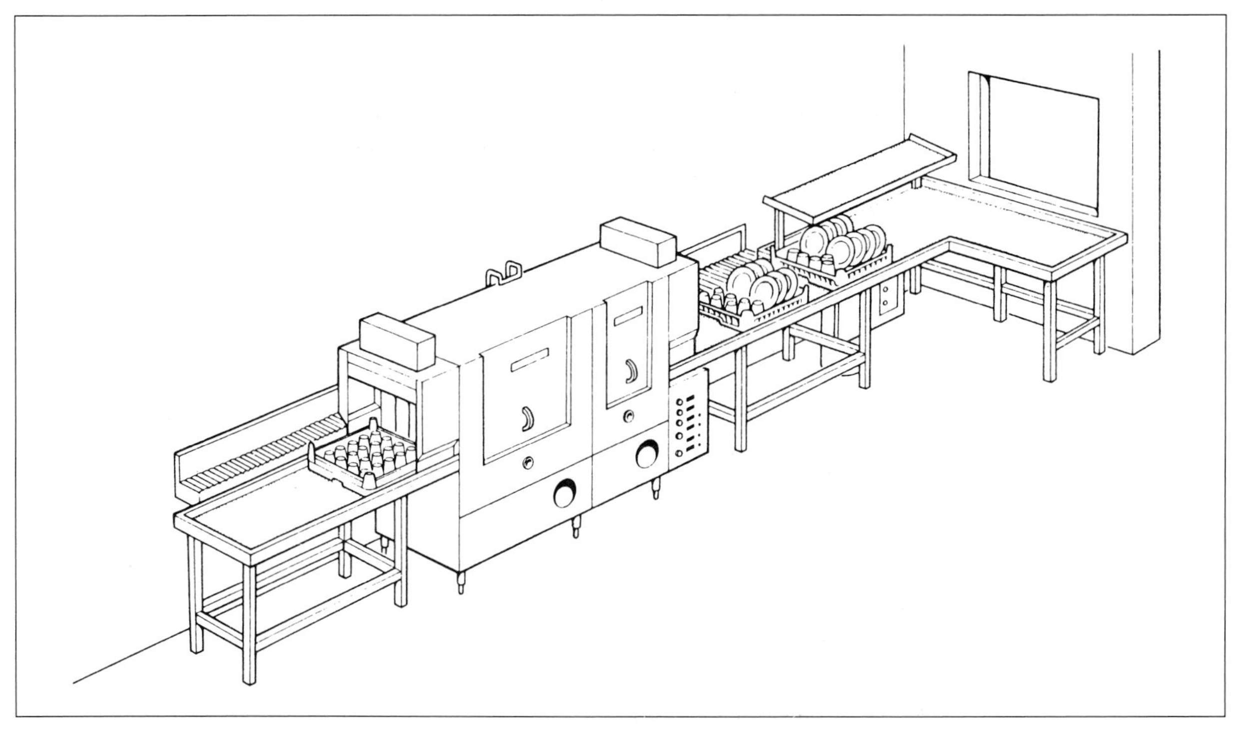

A commercial dishwasher

dipped into another sink. This second sink is known as a *sterilising tank*; the water temperature is very high, at approximately 75 °C (170 °F). The items need to be left in here for a few minutes then lifted out. As the water is so hot, the items, especially crockery, will air dry, making this a more hygienic method (no cloths are needed). The crockery can then be stacked and put away as required.

- *the machine method*. In principle the machine method is no different to the tank method except that the whole system is automated and therefore labour saving. It is essential here to follow the manufacturer's instructions.

The stillroom

The main function of the stillroom is to prepare and provide food items and equipment which are not catered for in any other department (such as the kitchen or larder). The actual daily work carried out in here will vary from one establishment to another according to the type of meals offered and the size of the establishment.

The stillroom has to produce a wide variety of food items, so it normally contains a considerable food stock as well as (possibly) a large amount of equipment for storage, preparation and presentation.

The equipment that may be found includes:

- bread slicing machine
- coffee grinding machines
- coffee machines
- general storage space, shelves and cupboards
- hot cupboard
- refrigerators for the storage of milk, cream, butter, cheese and fruit juices
- salamander
- sinks and washing machine
- steamer and hot water boiler.

Provisions from the stillroom

The list below gives the type of items that could be obtained from a stillroom:

- beverages such as: coffee, tea, horlicks, hot chocolate, etc.
- butter: pre-wrapped, curled or passed through a butter pat machine
- sliced and buttered bread (white, brown or malt) and toast
- rolls, croissants, brioches and breakfast toast
- Melba toast, gristicks and biscuits for cheese
- scones and tea-cakes
- sandwiches, assorted savouries and small cakes.

Hotplates and hot cupboards

The hotplate is the contact point between the kitchen and the service staff. It is the point at which both areas must cooperate and communicate effectively so that the customer gets the quick and efficient service expected.

Hot cupboards can be used for either food or plates, but when you are using it for plates make sure the temperature is not too high or the plates will become to hot to handle, the glaze may be damaged and any food items placed onto the plates will burn.

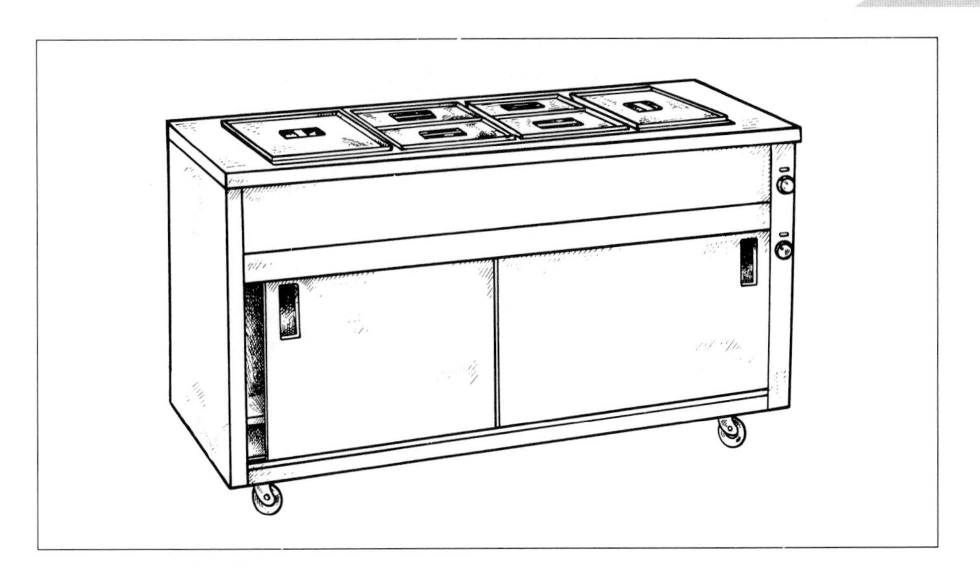

A bain-marie hot cupboard

Units as a whole are usually made up of a hot cupboard with sliding doors, topped by a heated serving surface. The top may also house containers acting as dry or wet heated bain-maries. *Dry-heat* keeps the food hot by electric elements or gas flame. The *wet-heat* method provides heat via an open tank of water, which itself is heated by gas-fired burners or by an electric immersion heater.

The hotplate or hot cupboard needs to be stocked with all the china and crockery needed for service, e.g. soup plates, fish plates, consommé cups, platters, soup cups, tea cups and demitasse.

Other heating/chilling equipment

Plate warmers

This piece of equipment is specially designed to warm plates. Before loading the plates are checked to make sure they are clean and unchipped, then they are loaded into the top of the plate warmer and the machine turned on. The top section houses a spring which has been especially tensioned to carry plates; as plates are removed from the plate warmer the spring pushes the rest of the plates up, nearer to the top.

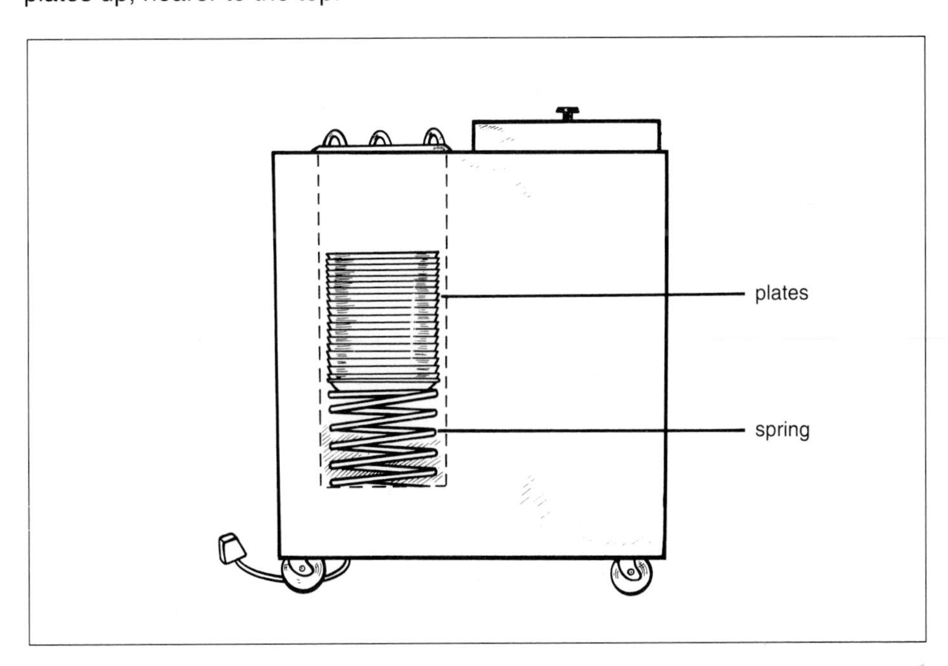

A plate warmer

Chiller cabinets

Chiller cabinets are used to keep food stuffs at a cool temperature. The items stored might include food items such as salads, sandwiches, sweets and beverages, all of which are generally displayed behind glass or perspex. Chiller cabinets may be situated in the restaurant or in the service preparation area. They can be mobile or static, and have either a motorised rotating display (which stops when the door is opened) or fixed, individually-chilled shelves.

Other refrigerated units such as a standard refrigerator may be used to store milk, cream and butter, etc. in the preparation area.

Temperature control

As refrigerated and heated units are used to store food items, they must be cleaned and turned on *before* service. This allows the units to reach the correct temperatures by service time. The following temperatures may be used as a guide:

- chiller cabinets should be at a temperature of approximately 4 °C (40 °F)
- hotplates are used for keeping food hot and the temperatures should be 75–88 °C (170–190 °F)
- plate warmers should be kept at 65 °C (150 °F).

Sideboards

Food service staff may either work directly from the kitchen to dining room, or use sideboards as a base from which to work within the dining room. Where a sideboard is used, it needs to be fully stocked, containing items such as cutlery, crockery, linen and accompaniments in numbers adequate to service a number of tables. Having these items to hand helps maintain an efficient service and reduce service time.

Before any sideboard can be stocked it must be cleaned and prepared. Sideboard tops are generally heat resistant and may have a hotplate fitted; if so, take care

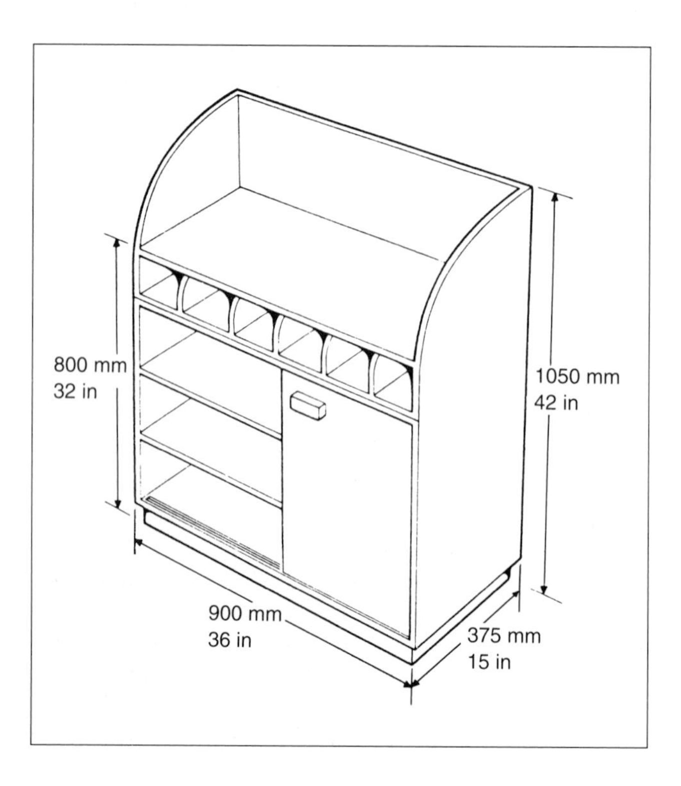

A typical sideboard

when cleaning this, and always remove or disconnect the heat/power supply. Choose your cleaning materials carefully, as strong-smelling, lingering or scented cleaning and polishing agents should not be used; remember that cutlery, crockery and food items will be stored on and in the sideboard.

The actual layout of a sideboard depends on its construction and the establishment requirements. Whatever the type or style of sideboard, all sideboards within an establishment should be stocked the same way so that any food server can approach any sideboard knowing the position of particular items. This saves time and therefore provides the customer with an efficient and speedy service.

Always store cutlery carefully into drawers or racks placing the handles in the same direction; this will make handling safer and more hygienic. Sideboard shelves may be lined with clean cloths on which to store crockery.

How a sideboard may be stocked

Left to right in the drawer section:	First shelf:	Lower shelf:	Side cupboard:
• Service spoon and forks • Dessert spoon and forks • Tea and coffee spoons • Fish knives and forks • Joint knives • Side knives and soup spoon	• Joint plates • Fish plates • Side plates • Sweet plates • Coffee saucers	• Service salvers • Spirit or electric heaters • Bread/roll baskets • Check pads, service cloths, menus • Service plates	• Clean linen (tablecloths and napkins etc.)

To do

- Find out where your establishment uses sideboards.
- Check whether they are all stocked in the same way. If not, ask your supervisor to explain why they differ.
- Draw up a plan to show how one of your sideboards is stocked.

Drink dispensers

There is a wide range of drink dispensing machines for both hot and cold drinks; the one chosen by your establishment will depend on the type of service offered. The main types include: pour and serve, espresso, bulk systems, water boilers, Cona systems and cold drink dispensers.

Pour and serve

Here cold water is poured into a machine which brings the water to the boil before filtering it through coffee into a jug. The coffee can then be kept hot on the machine hotplate until needed.

Espresso

This is where a machine uses an internal pressure boiler to force steam through a small amount of coffee to make one or two strong cups of coffee. Other hot drinks can also be made this way.

Bulk systems

In this system the water is boiled in the centre of a machine and then fed into two containers (urns) either side by a swinging arm tap. The water passes through a filter which may contain either tea or coffee and the temperature of the container is then controlled by thermostat. To dispense the beverage, each urn has a tap to release the hot liquid; one cup or a pot can be poured depending on the selection button pressed.

Water boilers

Water boilers allow service staff to make drinks to customers' individual requirements. The boiler can be a single kettle, a wall mounted unit or a large bulk boiler or pressure boiler.

A Cona coffee maker

Cona system

This method of making coffee is often considered eye-catching. The system consists of two containers (a bottom flask and a top bowl) connected by a glass tube holding both the coffee and a filter. The bottom flask is heated, and as the water heats it passes up through the connecting tube, infusing the coffee, and fills the top bowl. As the liquid cools slightly it falls back through the connecting tube via the filter and into the bottom flask ready for service.

Cold drink dispensers

Most cold drink dispensers use either liquid or powder concentrates. There are two main types: pre-mix and post-mix dispensers. *Pre-mix dispensers* contain ready-prepared drinks, e.g. still orange. *Post-mix dispensers* mix concentrates with water at the point of service; the water can be carbonated if the unit is fixed up to a carbon dioxide cylinder, so making for example, lemonade.

Milk can be bought in bulk (one gallon boxes), with a plastic inner which is placed within a refrigerated unit then connected to a tap or lever via a plastic pipe. Fruit juices can be dispensed in much the same way although fresh juices can also be bought frozen, fresh or dehydrated, canned or bottled. Juices can also be served by lines, much like draught coke or beers. Care must be taken however, in the monitoring of storage and rotation. The majority of bulk juices have been through a form of preservation process, the most common being pasteurisation.

Key points to remember

1. Follow the manufacturer's instructions carefully for all types of dispensers. This relates especially to mixing preparations, the quantity and dispense settings and operational procedures. Following instructions correctly will:
   - reduce waste
   - prevent accidents
   - maintain speed and efficiency in service, so maintaining customer satisfaction.
2. Do not overload electrical circuits by putting two appliances on the same plug.
3. Keep all equipment spotlessly clean.
4. Report faulty electrical equipment and have it removed immediately so that it cannot be used until repaired. This will prevent further damage to equipment or injury to staff or customers.

Service equipment

Trays

Trays used for food service are normally rectangular and flat with only a slight lip. They should ideally be:

- heat resistant
- easily cleaned (with few or no mouldings)
- lightweight yet strong
- non-slip
- stackable.

Glassware

Glasses on restaurant tables contribute towards the table presentation and vary in shape and size depending on what drink is to be served. The majority of restaurants use plain, clear glasses although certain high-class restaurants use cut glass and traditional glasses for particular wines (e.g. hock wine glasses with brown stems and Moselle wine glasses with green stems). Whatever type or style of glass is used, glasses must be washed correctly (either by hand or machine), rinsed and dried then checked that they are not smeared, cracked or chipped.

Cleaning and polishing glasses

Ideally, glasses should be washed in a glass washing machine. If you are operating one of these, read the machine manufacturer's instructions carefully; it is important to carry out the correct operating procedures and set the machine to the right temperatures. Remember to empty the machine at the end of service periods and do not wash any items other than glass as this is likely to leave smears on the glasses.

The polishing of glassware is very important. Dirty or smeared glasses are unhygienic and will spoil the customer's enjoyment of the drink.

To polish glasses:

1. assemble the necessary equipment, i.e. a jug or pot of boiling water and a clean, dry glass cloth
2. holding the base of the glass, upturn it over the pot of boiling water and rotate it in the steam, allowing the steam to enter and circle the glass. Take care not to scald yourself
3. remove the glass from the steam
4. hold the base of the glass in one hand with a corner of the cloth then fill the bowl of the glass with the opposite corner of the cloth
5. place the thumb of your free hand inside the bowl with your fingers on the outside of the glass, making sure the cloth is in between
6. holding the glass firmly yet gently, use the hand holding the base to rotate the glass slowly so that the cloth is drawn around the bowl
7. check that the glass is polished and sparkling clean by holding it up to the light and looking through it. If it still appears to be smeared or dull do not breathe on it; return it to be washed again.

Carrying empty glasses

When carrying glasses, such as during mise-en-place or when transferring glasses from one point to another, carry stemmed glasses upside down between your fingers. Upturn your hand and pick up the glasses by their stems, lacing the stems between alternate fingers. Do not try to carry too many. Alternatively, carry them upside down on a tray or salver.

Types of glasses

The list below gives some of the more common types:

- brandy balloon — a large balloon-shaped bowl on a small stem
- burgundy balloon — a large distinguished glass for fine burgundy wines
- champagne coupe — a wide shallow glass
- champagne tulip — a tall slender glass
- claret glass — 175 ml (6 fl oz)
- fruit juice glass — 125 ml (5 fl oz)
- general glass — 250 ml (9 fl oz)
- lager glass — 285 ml ($\frac{1}{2}$ pt)
- liqueur glass — a small single-measure glass
- port glass — 100 ml (4 fl oz)
- sherry glass — 75–100 ml (3–4 fl oz)
- water or wine goblet — 225 ml (8 fl oz)

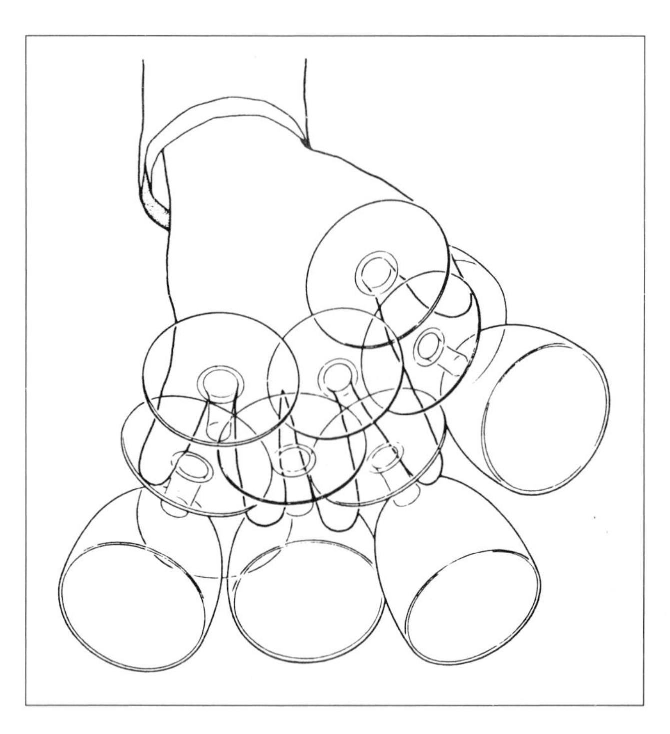

Carrying glasses

The number and type of glasses used in an establishment will vary but as a guide to quantity, the number of glasses required is approximately one and a half times the number of restaurant seats.

To do

- Using the equation suggested above, calculate how many glasses of one type your restaurant would require.
- Compare the cost of buying this number of glasses in a plain design of glass to that of buying a cut glass design.

China or crockery

China is a term used for crockery whether bone china (i.e. fine and expensive), earthenware (opaque and cheaper) or vitrified (metallised). Most catering crockery used these days tends to be vitrified earthenware, which is very durable, having been strengthened. Crockery is also usually given rolled edges to make it more chip resistant.

One fairly recent development is the use of stackable crockery, including cups and even tea and coffee pots (sunken knobs on lids allow stacking). All the lids for the pots are the same size and are therefore inter-changeable. Another development is in ovenproof ware, which has in many cases replaced silver serving dishes. This type of crockery consists of enamelled, cast-iron, ovenproof dishes such as casserole and cocotte dishes which allow food to be brought straight from the oven to the table.

Whatever quality of crockery or china is used, the most important thing to ensure is that it is washed, rinsed and dried correctly to ensure that no dirt, stains or streaks appear. Never use chipped or cracked crockery: chipped and cracked items harbour germs and should therefore be disposed of carefully.

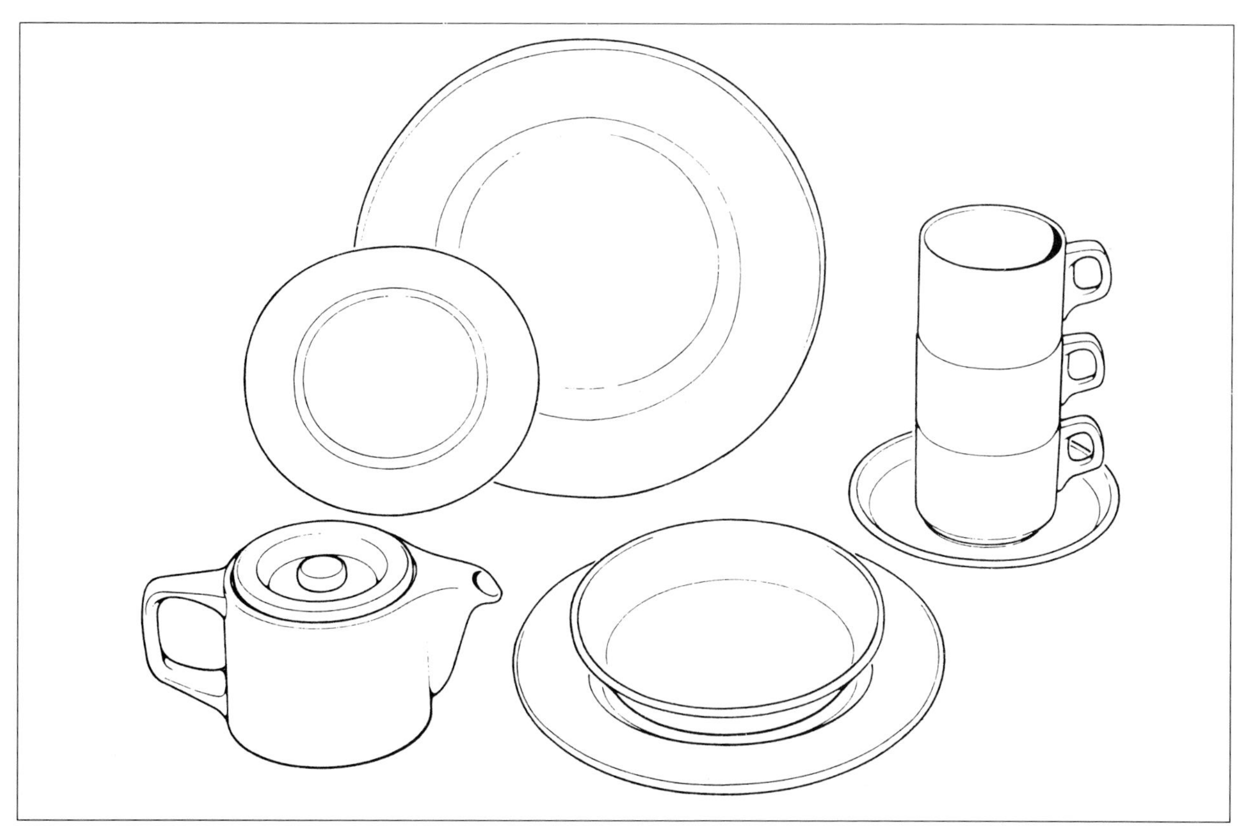

Stackable crockery

Plates

Plates come in a variety of shapes, sizes and designs depending on the type and style of service offered.

Plate types: their sizes and uses

Cereal plate	19 cm ($7\frac{1}{2}$ in)	deep plate used for all cereals and porridge also for compôtes and milk puddings etc.
Entrée plate	21.5 cm ($8\frac{1}{2}$ in)	hors d'oeuvres,fish/entrees when not the main course, underliners, cover/service plates
Meat/fish plate	25.5 cm (10 in)	main course service
Salad plate		crescent/half moon shaped
Side plate	17.5 cm (7 in)	cheese and bread roles
Soup plate	23 cm (9 in)	thick soups, mussels, oysters, goulash and Irish stews
Sweet plate	21.5 cm ($8\frac{1}{2}$ in)	sweets and puddings
Tea plate	19 cm ($7\frac{1}{2}$ in)	bread and butter, cakes

Cups

Cups, like plates, come in various shapes and sizes but there are four main types used:

- soup cup 300 ml ($\frac{1}{2}$ pt)
- breakfast cup 300 ml ($\frac{1}{2}$ pt)
- tea cup 150 ml (5–6 fl oz)
- coffee cup 75 or 125 ml (3 or 5 fl oz).

Storing crockery

In the mise-en-place period you need to place crockery into various storage places ready for service such as:
- on sideboards
- in/on hot cupboards and plate warmers
- on trolleys
- in chiller units
- on a service point (as underplates).

Handling crockery hygienically

For reasons of hygiene the following points need to be remembered when handling crockery:
- always hold cutlery by the handles
- hold glasses by the stem
- hold crockery by the rim
- always use a clean service cloth or disposable towels to polish glasses and cutlery.

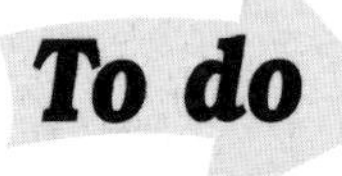

- Look through your restaurant crockery stock and identify the types of plates and cups stored.
- Check with your supervisor which pieces of crockery are needed for today's menu and find out where and how it is to be stored ready for service.

Table linen

The term *linen* is used to describe tablecloths, napkins and any other cloth or textile items used in the presentation of tables whether made from linen or not. Actual linen could be used, but it is expensive and difficult to launder. Table linen today is generally recognised as being made up of cotton, man-made fibres, mixed linen and cotton, or any combination of the these. White tablecloths and napkins are the most commonly used, although various pastel colours and even, in some theme restaurants, bolder colours may now be used.

Not all restaurants use tablecloths. They may choose instead to place mats on polished, marble or finely-textured tables. However, where cloths are used, the tables underneath are often baized or felt-topped to help soften the noise of the plates, crockery and cutlery being placed on the table. This type of table also prevents the cloth from slipping and provides the customer with a softer support for their wrists. Tablecloths also provide a background for crockery, cutlery and glassware, while at the same time showing up dirt: this ensures the frequent changing of cloths, so enforcing high standards of hygiene.

Supplies of linen and laundering can be done by three means. An establishment may:
- buy all its own linen, then launder and iron it itself on site
- buy its own linen and then send it to a company to launder and iron
- hire linen from a company who will supply, launder and iron it as required.

Types of table linen

The list below shows some standard sizes of linen:

Square tablecloths	137 × 137 cm (54 × 54 in) 183 × 183 cm (72 × 72 in) 285 × 285 cm (90 × 90 in) (All square cloths can be used on round tables)
Rectangular tablecloths	137 × 183 cm (54 × 72 in) 137 × 274 cm (54 × 108 in) 183 × 244 cm (72 × 96 in)
Buffet cloths	2 × 4 m (6 × 12 ft) is the minimum size to cover a buffet table
Napkins	Vary in size: tea napkins 30 cm (12 in) square, dinner napkins 46–50 cm (18–20 in) square
Slip cloths	Designed to be laid over the main tablecloth to protect it from spoilages – cheaper to launder due to its size, at least 1 m (3 ft) square maximum, 122 cm (48 in) square
Tea and glass cloths	Best made of linen and cotton. Nowadays being replaced by washing machines which dry as well or by the use of paper disposable towels. Tea and glass towels can be unhygienic if not spotlessly clean
Trolley and sideboard cloths	Often made up from tablecloths which may have been repaired or cut down to fit their purpose

Linen storage

Cloths should be stored neatly stacked on shelves or in a cupboard lined with paper or old, worn, clean tablecloths. They should be stacked in sizes with the central fold outwards to aid counting and handling, then covered with paper or cloths. The requisition of linen differs from one place to another, but in larger establishments where a housekeeping department exists, a system of exchanging dirty for clean is an effective means of control. Under this system the food server counts out the dirty laundry, enters it into a duplicate book, and has this checked by the housekeeper. The housekeeper is then able to issue clean laundry, sign the book and retain the top copy leaving the second copy in the book. The system is sometimes known as *one for one* or *clean for dirty.*

The spare linen room

This refers to a cupboard or room near to the service area where a supply of linen is kept. It is kept locked and the linen used for emergencies only. The day-to-day linen supply is always drawn from the housekeeping department.

Handling linen

Linen needs to be handled correctly or the items become creased and dirty, so increasing laundry costs. There are several ways you can prevent unnecessary costs:

- make sure all surfaces are clean before placing linen on them
- dust and vacuum before laying tablecloths
- check you have the right size of tablecloth before you unfold it
- wash and dry your hands before handling linen; this will keep the cloth visibly clean and reduce the risk of cross-contamination.

See also p. 122 on laying a tablecloth.

Disposable cloths

A combination of linen and disposable cloths are often used. Disposable cloths come in all the regular sizes or can be purchased in long rolls and cut to the required length. Paper napkins and slip cloths can also be purchased in many different qualities of paper, from thin single-ply to three and four-ply, some napkins having a linen feel to them. All of these disposables can be printed with the establishment's logo or advertisement.

There are some advantages to using disposable cloths and linen:
- the cost generally works out to be less than laundry or hire costs
- there is a large range of colours and designs to suit different occasions
- labour time is saved, as there is no need to sort and bundle laundry
- disposables are more hygienic, as dirty laundry does not accumulate in service or preparation areas (disposables are thrown away when dirty).

Service cloths

A service cloth is a very important part of service equipment as well being part of the food server's uniform. It must be kept clean and ironed at all times and only used as a service cloth for certain activities, such as:
- carrying hot plates
- final polishing of plates
- wiping small spills
- brushing crumbs onto a service plate
- wiping the undersides of plates before placing plates on the table.

A cruet set

Condiments and accompaniments

The term *accompaniments* includes a range of sauces, seasoning and breads which are offered with certain dishes. The term *condiments* refers to any spice or sauce such as salt, pepper, or mustard which may be offered at the table. Accompaniments and condiments are offered so that the customer can alter the flavour or counteract the richness of dishes to suit their personal taste or to provide a contrast of texture. They can be dry, fresh, preserved, or reconstituted prior to service (e.g. mustard), and they may be served hot or cold.

Accompaniments are served with all kinds of dishes throughout the menu, including savouries, sweets, desserts and cheeses.

Preparing accompaniments and condiments

Some accompaniments are prepared in the kitchen and sent to the restaurant with the dish they accompany. Others, especially dry and cold types, may be prepared by the service staff. Accompaniments can be served in sauce boats, in small bowls, on plates or from jars and bottles.

The same accompaniment may be served differently in different establishments, for example:
- salad dressings may be made to order at the table or served made-up in bottles or jars
- sauce may be offered from a sauce boat on a doily covered plate or from a jar
- toast may have the crusts removed and then be arranged in a toast rack on a doily covered plate or wrapped in a linen napkin.

Always use clean utensils for each item being prepared, store food items correctly (see p. 117) and thoroughly clean down and dispose of waste carefully when finished. This will reduce the risks of contamination, fire, accidents, pest infestation and unpleasant odours.

Storing accompaniments

If accompaniments are prepared some time before service they will need to be stored correctly. The storage of hot accompaniments is normally undertaken by the kitchen staff, but any cold and dry types may be the server's responsibility. If you are responsible for this, store cold accompaniments in a refrigerator and cover them to prevent transfer of smell and taste onto other stored food items. Store dry ones by covering them and keeping them in a cool, dry place until needed. Avoid waste: make only small quantities if the numbers for the meal are unknown.

Standard accompaniments

Hors d'oeuvres/appetisers	Hors d'oeuvres variés: oil and vinegar Grapefruit: caster sugar Melon: caster sugar and ground ginger Tomato juice: Worcester sauce Prawns: mayonnaise, brown bread and butter Pâté: hot toast
Soups	Minestroni soup: Parmesan, grilled cheese flutes Cream of tomato soup: croûtons
Pasta	Spaghetti: Parmesan
Fish	Whitebait: cayenne pepper, peppermill, segments of lemon, brown bread and butter Poached salmon, hot: hollandaise, cold: mayonnaise Fish fried in batter: tomato sauce Fish fried in breadcrumbs: sauce tartare Grilled fish: segments of lemon and cold sauce, e.g. tartare, remoulade, Gribiche or hot sauce, e.g. bearnaise or tyrolienne
Meat and poultry	Curry: poppadums, Bombay duck, mango chutney, chopped apple, sultanas, sliced bananas and desiccated coconut etc. Roast beef: horseradish sauce, Yorkshire pudding, English and French mustard Roast lamb: mint sauce Roast pork: apple sauce, sage and onion stuffing Roast chicken: bread sauce, bacon rolls, game chips, stuffing and watercress

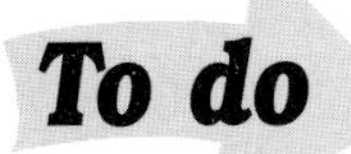

- Check the menu or find out from your restaurant supervisor what cruets and accompaniments will be required for service.
- Empty, clean, polish and refill: any cruets, peppermills and cayenne pepper pots, oil and vinegar sets, sugar basins and dredgers required.
- Prepare any other accompaniments, putting them into their appropriate dishes or dispensers.
- Distribute cruets to the tables and accompaniments to the sideboards or store as otherwise required.
- Check different types of menus and find out which accompaniments would be served with them. List them under the following headings according to how they are served: dry, cold, hot, reconstituted.

Disposing of waste

To prevent the risks of accidents, fire, contamination, pest infestation and unpleasant odours:

- do not let waste build up within your work area
- clean up as you work
- make sure that waste is disposed of cleanly and efficiently
- keep all storage areas clean and tidy
- dispose of broken or chipped glass and crockery carefully; if possible wrap in paper or place in a box and mark the package clearly.

Essential knowledge

Waste must be handled and disposed of correctly in order to:

- prevent accidents
- prevent risk of fire
- prevent contamination of food and food areas
- prevent pest infestation and unpleasant odours from arising
- comply with the law
- comply with establishment procedures.

What have you learned?

1 What three points of hygiene need to be observed when handling cutlery, crockery and glasses?

___

___

2 Why should manufacturers' instructions be followed carefully?

___

___

3 What five quality points should be looked for in a service tray?

___

___

4 Why must waste be handled and disposed of correctly?

___

___

5 Why do you need to maintain a constant stock of food service items?

___

___

6 What six points need to be taken into consideration when preparing and loading trolleys ready for service?

______

______

______

7 Why must linen be handled carefully?

______

______

8 How should you store accompaniments prior to service?

______

______

ELEMENT 2: Preparing customer dining areas for table service

Planning your time

Consideration of the following points will help to make preparation time short, efficient and effective:

- identify the task
- know how it is to be done
- collect all the equipment needed before you start
- complete your work tasks to meet the required schedules
- work as a team.

Health, safety and hygiene

As with any kind of work involving food, contamination can occur if national and establishment standards are not met. Remember:

- keep all work areas and surfaces clear of rubbish, waste and other obstructions
- use protective clothing as required
- store all food items correctly
- practise good personal hygiene
- comply with all health and safety regulations.

To prevent the risks of accidents, fire or injury to yourself and others:

- always follow safety procedures when using machinery and electrical appliances
- do not carry lighted candles, oil, spirit or gas lamps
- if refilling oil, gas or spirit lamps, do so in a well-ventilated area away from food items and naked flames
- dispose of all waste and empty fuel canisters carefully.

The restaurant environment

Arranging the furniture

The way in which furniture is arranged in a food service area influences the atmosphere and mood. For instance, soft, luxurious seating relaxes customers and produces a leisurely dining mood; round tables are associated with sociability and communication. In contrast, if you were to seat customers in large parties at long narrow tables you would only generate communication between people sitting side by side or opposite one another. It is also worth noting that rows of rectangular tables give an image of authority, conjuring up school meals, etc.

Tables which are packed closely together can make customers feel uncomfortable; they may feel that other tables can overhear their conversations. This arrangement also increases the likelihood of service staff knocking customers when passing.

Table plans

The organisation of table plans depends on a number of factors and could include some of the following:

- organisers' requests
- the type of meal or occasion
- the size and shape of the room
- the number of people being catered for.

For banqueting, either 'U' or 'T'-shaped table plans can be used or a top table could be flanked by several round or rectangular tables. Banqueting requires very careful use of space; as a guide the minimum space between *sprigs* (rows) is 2 m/6 ft (table edge to table edge), and between two chairs 46 cm (18 in) with a gangway of 1 m (3 ft). A table to wall space would therefore be 1.4 m (4 ft 6 in), i.e. one chair with a 1 m (3 ft) gangway. The space required for each cover width is 50–60 cm (20–24 in) depending on the type of cover to be laid.

In normal restaurant situations it is not unusual to find a mixture of table sizes, shapes and positioning. The space between tables should be enough to allow customer privacy and ease of movement for staff, with room for trolleys to pass between tables. A mixture of round and square tables may be used to allow maximum flexibility: people like to sit in rounds with their friends, but square tables are more economical as they can be used for small parties yet easily pushed together to accommodate larger parties. Some designs of tables are inter-locking or adaptable with various extensions to suit requirements.

You may work in an restaurant that uses fixed seating. Here, tables and chairs either come fixed together, or the tables might be free while the seating is fixed (e.g. to the wall). Where chairs and tables are fixed together they are usually also fixed to the floor, and are therefore static.

Chair positions

The position of the chair at a table is quite important. So as not to discomfort customers, chairs should be placed between table legs. This is relatively easy to achieve on rectangular tables, but can become a problem when seating more than four people on round ones. The standard round table has four legs although occasionally one centre leg may be found. In the case of four legs the following options can be adopted:

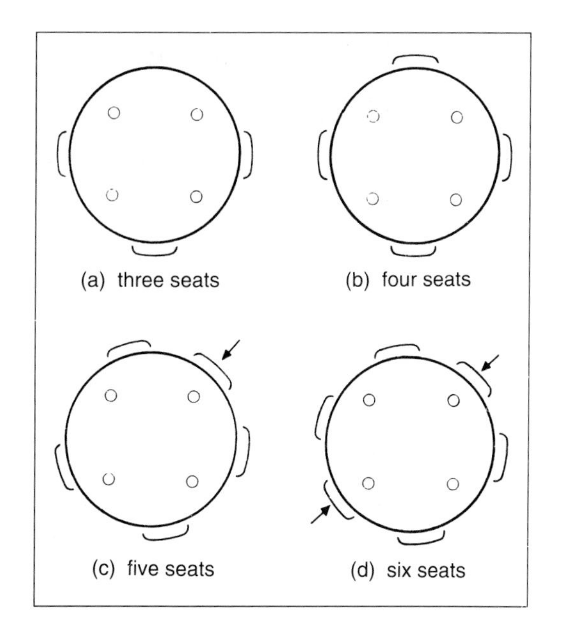

Arranging seats at round tables

Arranging furniture safely

- Remove and report any faulty or damaged furniture immediately; this will prevent any unnecessary accidents or injuries to staff or customers.
- Take care not to block any fire exit doors or escape routes with tables, chairs, spare furniture, laundry, other equipment or rubbish and waste.

Ventilation and temperature

It is important to keep the dining room free of stale smells (i.e. of food and tobacco) from any previous meals. This can be done by the use of extractor fans, by opening windows or with air conditioning systems. Ideally, the temperature should be comfortable for customers (who are sitting still) as well as for the staff (who are moving about). The generally accepted temperature is 18 °C (65 °F). This can be set on timers or thermostats; it is worth noting that the temperature will start to rise once service starts and fall as it comes to an end, so the flexibility of a thermostat may be more efficient. Air conditioning systems can be set to monitor the air quality and temperatures in a room and adjust themselves accordingly.

Lighting

Before opening the restaurant to customers, always check that all light bulbs are in working order; all candlesticks are clean and candles renewed; and all oil lamps are cleaned, refilled and have trimmed wicks. As a general rule, lunches need to be well lit with as much natural light as possible, while evening meals need a more subdued, soft lighting. Consideration also needs to be given to the fact that coloured lighting reflects onto food items.

Music

Check that where music is provided, the equipment is in working order and that the selection of music is appropriate. The volume should be such that it does not interfere with the customers' conversations while at the same time provides background ambience.

Laying tables

The tablecloth

Tablecloths provide an excellent backdrop to a lay-up although not all restaurants use them (see p. 114). Where cloths are used they may be changed every service session or at least once every day. In order to prolong the life of tablecloths some establishments use slip cloths. These are slightly smaller than tablecloths (so are cheaper to launder), and can be placed over the top of slight blemishes.

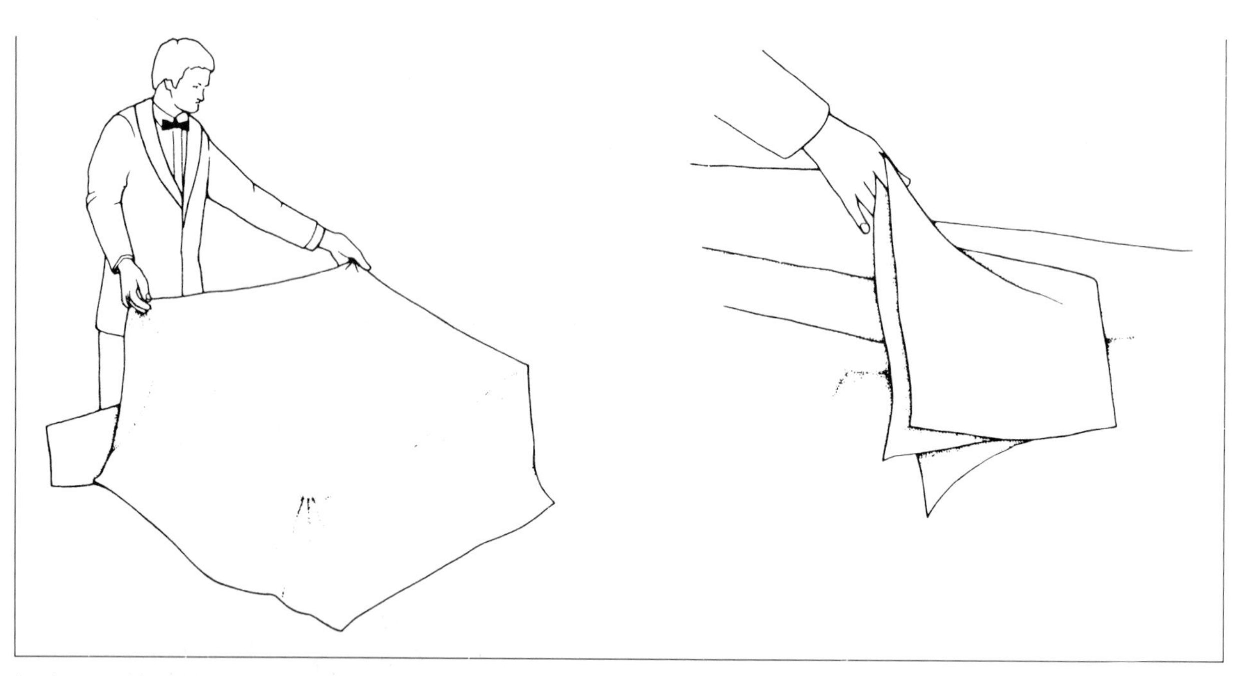

Laying a tablecloth

When placing a tablecloth on a table, make sure the centre of the cloth is in the centre of the tables with the corner points hanging down the table legs. The correct way of laying a cloth is as follows:

1 stand between two legs of the table
2 open the cloth so that the edges of the tablecloth are underneath the folded centre of the cloth
3 hold the top loose edge between your first finger and thumb, and the second edge between your first and second finger
4 lift the cloth across to the far edge of the table and let the lower edge drop
5 as you bring the cloth back towards you, release the centre crease covering the table as you come back
6 check the cloth is clean, in good repair, has an even drop all round and that the corners of the cloth drop down the table legs
7 if more than one cloth is used on a table, make sure that the overlaps run away from the entrance door and that all the main creases run together.

The term used to describe a lay-up on a table is a *cover*, although it does have two meanings:

1 the number of customers expected
2 a place setting on the table.

Types of lay-up

There are two basic lay-ups:
- *table d'hôte*; used for a fixed price menu of three or more courses with limited choice on each course
- *à la carte*; used for a menu with a selection of individually priced dishes.

The cover for each type of menu differs as given below:
- *table d'hôte*: joint fork, joint knife, fish fork, fish knife, soup spoon, side plate, side knife, napkin, dessert spoon, dessert fork, wine glass
- *à la carte*: cover plate (if used), napkin, fish knife, fish fork (or meat knife, meat fork), side plate, side knife, wine glass.

Laying up procedures

The items laid on a cover may differ slightly depending on menu requirements and establishment standards, but the basic procedures are the same whether laying up on tablecloths, place mats or other surfaces:
- collect all the equipment needed (e.g. cutlery, crockery) from either the sideboard or cutlery and flatware trolleys
- collect a service cloth
- place a cover plate or a napkin in the centre position of the cover space (where the customer will be seated)
- lay the cover from the inside out. This will help you to achieve even spacing and prevent over-handling, which can leave finger marks. Start with the items which the customer will need last, so that when the cover is fully laid the items to be used first are on the outside of the cover
- place the side plate to the left of the place setting
- place a side knife on the side plate
- place a folded napkin either on the cover plate (if used), in the glass or under the side knife depending on your establishment standard
- lay all cutlery and flatware so that the base of each item is 1.25 cm ($\frac{1}{2}$ in) away from the table edge; this will prevent the items of equipment being knocked when the customer sits down
- if the equipment has a badge or logo on it, make sure this is face up
- place any glasses at the top of the cover (above the joint knife) and upside down until just before service starts (if this is your establishment standard). This will prevent dust or other contaminating items from falling into the glasses. It is especially used where tables are set several hours before service
- give all equipment to be laid on the table a final check and polish with your service cloth
- lastly, place any condiments (e.g. butter) onto the table.

A basic table d'hôte cover. Note the position of the wine/water glass at the top of the meat knife

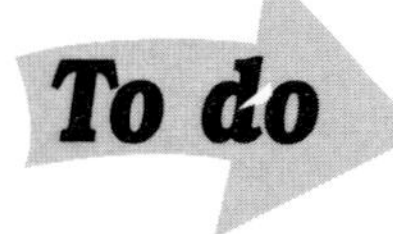

- Find out how the temperature is controlled in your restaurant.
- Note the furniture used. If possible, find out why this type and arrangement was chosen.
- Collect the equipment needed for one à la carte and one table d'hôte cover, or the cover used in your establishment, and practise the laying up procedure for each.

Laying up functions (e.g. banquets)

The procedures used are generally as given as above, the only difference being that there is likely to be more cutlery, flatware and glassware to lay per cover (this will be determined by the establishment standard, the menu and the wines chosen).

If there are a number of service staff laying-up it is not unusual for one to lay a particular piece of equipment throughout the room while another staff member follows, laying another item. If a long function table is used and the equipment is laid clean, systematically and symmetrically, the room can be checked by looking down the table and seeing that all the glasses, cruets and napkins, etc. are in a line.

On smaller tables laid for an even number of covers (e.g. for two or four people) the accompaniments should be placed centrally; while tables laid for an uneven number (e.g. three people) should have them placed in such a way as to make them accessible yet balance the table. As a guide, place one set of cruets per four place settings.

Placing glasses on the table

If the wine has been ordered in advance, the number of glasses required will be known and can be placed on the table prior to service. If the choice is unknown, then one or two glasses can be placed on the table, one for water and the other for wine. They should be highly polished and arranged neatly to the right of each cover.

Napkins

Napkins are usually folded into decorative shapes, but it must be remembered that the same rules apply to the handling of napkins as to other linen (see p. 115). When deciding on a napkin fold, consideration should also be given to the amount of handling, as over-handling and folding is unhygienic and time-consuming and may leave the eventual open napkin creased; simple folds reduce these problems.

Additional table items

Accompaniments

Table accompaniments are usually the same for both à la carte or table d'hôte menus, although they may vary from one establishment to another. In most cases, the additional items would be as follows:

- cruet (salt, pepper, mustard and mustard spoon)
- ashtray
- decoration; e.g. flowers (fresh or dry), candles, lamp (spirit or oil)
- table number.

Extras on sideboard or near to hand, may include:
- roll basket
- Melba toast
- gristicks
- peppermill
- cayenne pepper
- butter.

Other accompaniments are stored in the refrigerator or on the sideboard and they accompany specific dishes when served.

Table decorations

Table decorations such as a vase of flowers, a candle stick or a lamp can give an attractive finish to a well-laid table. The following needs to be noted:
- each decoration should be in keeping with the theme and not interfere with the meal presentation
- no decoration should be so large that it obstructs the customer's view
- any candles and lamps (spirit or oil) should be odourless and smokeless
- flowers need to be checked for insects (which must be removed), and the strength of their perfume (it must not be too strong).

Ashtrays

It is commonplace these days to find that ashtrays are not put on the tables, but kept on the sideboard or near to hand until it is apparent that a customer requires one.

Menus

Menus are one of the most important items in a restaurant. As well as showing the dishes available, they are the link between restaurant and kitchen, and in a way determine the order of work. They are also a link between the customer and restaurant, showing the standard and skills of the establishment. They must be checked prior to service to ensure that:
- the correct type and number of service items are prepared
- the appropriate accompaniments can be prepared
- the menu is the correct one on offer for that day
- they are clean and presentable with no misleading information
- there are enough for that day's service
- any promotional information is included and correct.

Legal requirements for menus

There are certain legal requirements that need to be observed when using menus:
- under the *Price Marking Order (Food and Drink on Premises 1979)*, a restaurant must display their menu where it can be easily read by prospective customers
- the displayed menu must show and state the prices charged (inclusive of VAT), whether a service or cover charge will be added, and what, if any, is the minimum charge.

However, there are some exceptions:
- restaurants with large menus and wine lists need not show all items, but must give a fair selection. This 'fair' selection is clearly defined in the *Price Marking Order (Food and Drink on Premises 1979)*

- establishments that only serve their members, e.g. clubs, schools, office canteens and colleges are exempt
- pubs, wine bars and other establishments offering food and drink from a self service counter must have their menus visible to customers before they make their selection. If the menu and prices are behind the counter, but cannot be seen from the service entrance, they must be displayed there as well.

BREADS

Garlic Foccacia bread 1.25
A selection of Rustic breads 1.25
Ciabatta (olive oil bread) served with niçoise olives and pesto mayonnaise 1.65
Bruschetta (grilled Italian bread with tomato, basil and olives) 1.95

STARTERS & SALADS

Roasted peppers, baby artichokes and goat's cheese 4.40
Freshly made soup 2.95
Caesar salad – Cos lettuce, garlic croutons, anchovies and parmesan 3.95/5.95
Chargrilled prawns wrapped in parma ham and basil with an avocado dip 4.95/10.50
Smoked salmon and warm new potato on a bed of mixed salad leaves with a dill and horseradish dressing 6.95/9.95
Crostini of Mediterranean flavours 3.95
Hot chicken and duck marinated in soy and honey on french beans 4.75/7.75
Wild mushrooms pan fried on a bed of salad leaves and smoked mozzarella 4.75/7.75

PASTAS

Gnocchi with spinach and three cheeses 3.85/5.85
Spaghetti carbonara with smoked ham, egg, and parmesan 3.95/5.95
Spaghetti with red basil pesto and courgettes 3.95/5.95
Fusilli with roasted peppers, rocket, olives and sun dried tomato 3.85/5.85
Angelhair with king prawns, mangetout, lemon grass and coriander 4.65/6.65
Rigatoni with a tomato and meatball sauce 3.85/5.85

All pastas available starter size

SIDE SALADS

Rocket 1.75
Tomato and red onion 1.45
Mixed leaf 1.45

MAIN COURSES

All the below are served with salad or mixed vegetables and a choice of mash, new potatoes or chips.

Baby chicken marinated in rosemary, garlic and lemons served with garlic mayonnaise 7.95
Calves' liver with thyme and balsamic vinegar 11.95
Crispy duck confit on a stew of white beans 8.95
Roast rabbit with mustard, thyme and cream 8.65
Fillet steak with Bearnaise 12.95
Rack of lamb with a herb crust and onion confit 9.75
Chopped steak burger with Swiss cheese (optional) served on ciabatta bread fully garnished 6.75
Chargrilled vegetables served with polenta, pesto and tomato sauces 7.25
Spicy crabcakes with a tomato and coriander salsa 8.50
Salmon steak with lime and dill butter 8.75
Lemon sole with herb vinaigrette 10.95
Fresh fish from the market fully garnished
Sunday roast, rib of beef served in the traditional way– from 12.30 pm onwards 9.95

PUDDINGS

Chocolate and Raspberry cake with cream or vanilla ice cream 3.95
White and dark chocolate mousse with pistachio nuts 3.25
Creme Brulee 2.95
Fresh fruit bowl with yoghurt 4.50
Apple tarte Tatin with creme fraiche 3.75
Choice of sorbet and ice cream 2.95
Tiramisu 3.65
Iced mango parfait with raspberry coulis 3.25
Grilled goats cheese and poached pear 3.95
Plate of assorted cheeses with walnut bread and biscuits 3.95
Vin santo and cantucci biscuits 3.45

BRUNCH & LIGHT LUNCH

Ham and Cheese Croute with eggs 3.95
Traditional English breakfast 5.45
Eggs Benedict with ham or smoked salmon 5.25
Scrambled eggs with smoked salmon 5.25
Minute Steak, wild mushrooms and salad 5.45
Omelettes: Herb, Wild mushroom, Goat's cheese and sun dried tomatoes, Parma ham 4.45
French toast with strawberries and maple syrup 3.75
Muesli, nuts, yoghurt and honey 2.95
Fresh fruit with yoghurt 3.75

Brunch Saturday and Sunday 10.30am – 12.00noon

Children's Menu available on request.
10% service charge on parties of five or more.
Private parties and Weddings, please ask for details.

Gee's BRASSERIE

MONDAY FRIDAY
12noon- 2.30 pm
6.00 pm - 11.30 pm
SATURDAY
10.30 am - 11.30 pm
SUNDAY
10.30 am - 11.00 pm
61 Banbury Road, Oxford OX2 6PE
Telephone Oxford 53540

An example menu

Essential knowledge

Menus should be checked before use in order to:

- ensure that the information is correct and clear, to prevent the customer from being misled
- ensure menus are clean and presentable
- ensure that the correct quantity are ready for use
- ensure that the table lay-up is correct
- comply with the law.

Final preparations for service

Certain mise-en-place tasks can be left until just before service, as dictated by establishment procedures. Butter, Melba toast and other bread items may be brought into the dining area, along with sugars, accompaniments and display trolleys.

If display trolleys or cabinets are to be used, they should be switched on in time to achieve the correct temperature before the items are placed on or in them.

What have you learned?

1 How can you create a relaxed, leisurely dining area when table planning?

2 What factors contribute to table planning?

3 Why should menus be checked before use?

4 What procedures should be followed for faulty or damaged furniture?

5 How can hygiene and appearance problems be reduced in napkin folding?

6 What five points need to be observed when using table decorations?

7 What legal requirements have to be observed concerning menu presentation?

8 How can ventilation and temperature be controlled in a service area?

ELEMENT 3: Clear dining and service areas after food service

Why is clearing important?

People who work within the food industry have a legal and moral responsibility to their colleagues and customers, so it is up to you to prevent outbreaks of food poisoning. This can be achieved by:

- complying with the law
- removing food debris on which bacteria can grow
- removing food which may attract pests
- clearing and storing items correctly.

Working efficiently and safely

At the end of service all food items which have not been served to customers must be returned to the kitchen or service preparation areas for refrigeration or other hygienic storage. Do not re-use food items which have been returned from customers' tables.

In order to ensure that the clearing procedure is effective and efficient, you need to consider the possible methods of working and select the most appropriate, where clearing can be done in a methodical and systematic way. The clearing procedures must also at all times follow health, safety and hygiene regulations (see Units G1 and G2, pp. 1–37).

Essential knowledge

Dining and service areas should be left clean after service in order to:

- prevent accidents
- maintain establishment standards
- prevent pest infestation
- prevent unpleasant odours developing
- provide a clean and organised environment for staff on the following shift
- comply with the law
- maintain customer satisfaction and expectations.

Heating, ventilation, music and lighting

If the heating system is on a control timer it should be self regulating, although it is wise to check that it has turned itself off at the correct time. Ventilation is important as the smells of the last meal need to be cleared before they go stale; either open windows or (where appropriate) check that the air conditioning system is working correctly. Music needs to be turned off and the system unplugged if possible. Clear under full lighting, but make sure all lighting is turned off once clearing is finished (except any security lighting).

Clearing electrical or heating equipment

Before clearing or cleaning any electrical or heating equipment:

- turn it off and disconnect it from its power source
- allow it to cool.

Doing this will prevent the risk of injury or fire.

Hotplates, bain-maries and plate warmers

1 Turn off or disconnect the power supply; if wet, drain.
2 Allow to cool.
3 Remove any extra equipment and food debris.
4 Clean with detergent and a damp cloth.
5 If cleaning a wet bain-marie, clean out with detergent then rinse thoroughly and refill.

Refrigeration units

1 Switch off and disconnect.
2 Return unused food items to the kitchen.
3 Clean with detergent and disinfectants which do not taint food then rinse well with hot water.

Hot and cold beverage dispensers

All types of drink dispensers need to be switched off and disconnected, with the exception of certain types of chilled drinks dispensers. Whichever type of dispenser is used, check the manufacturer's instructions to find out what procedures need to be followed once service has finished; this prevents damage to equipment or products.

Certain types of electrical equipment should be turned off after service in order to:
- prevent injury to yourself, colleagues and customers
- eliminate risk of fire.

Clearing sideboards

Sideboards can either be emptied at the end of service or restocked ready for the next service period. In both cases:
- if a hot plate is fitted, switch it off and unplug from the mains
- empty any stock still held in the sideboard and return any food items to the kitchen
- using a damp cloth lightly impregnated with an anti-bacterial cleaner, wipe out the cutlery draws; make sure the cloth is not too wet (this would damage any baize lining)
- remove and exchange any shelf cloths then wipe each shelf with a damp cloth
- clean the hotplate once it has cooled.

Clearing trolleys

Before cleaning a trolley, switch off the heat or power supply and return any unserved food items to the kitchen then:
- remove any service equipment and crockery
- remove any cloths
- wash/wipe down with a anti-bacterial cleaner
- return the trolley to its normal storage area.

- Make a list of the clearing and cleaning tasks that need to be carried out in your service area and ask your supervisor to explain the establishment procedures for completing them.
- Check the manufacturer's instructions for the beverage dispensers in your establishment.
- Ask your supervisor to show you the establishment procedures for laundry supplies. If you do not use laundry, arrange a visit to a hotel nearby which uses linen, asking to study their laundry system.

Clearing tables

Tables need to be cleared of all food debris and equipment. Depending on the establishment procedure, tablecloths can either be taken off and sent to the laundry or base cloths left on and the slip cloths changed.

If the tables are polished or texture-finished, they need to be wiped down with a damp cloth impregnated with a anti-bacterial cleaner. If the tables were used for a function they may need careful storing or stacking (this also applies to any side tables).

Linen

The methods of laundering in establishments will vary, but the main principle of exchange must occur. The method of laundering depends on the system used by the establishment (see *Table linen* on pp. 114–16). To make the exchange easier and quicker, the tablecloths can be bundled into fives or tens, depending on size, while napkins can be bundled into tens or twenties.

Cutlery and crockery

All dirty crockery and cutlery needs to be sent through to the wash-up area where food debris should be cleared off and the crockery and cutlery stacked for cleaning. The clean equipment should be returned to its original storage area or set for the next service session (depending on establishment procedures).

Silverware

Care needs to be taken with silverware. If it is not cleaned, washed and dried immediately after use its appearance will be damaged. It should also be stored very carefully; items which are only used for special occasions and then returned to storage need to be polished and ideally wrapped for protection.

Ashtrays

Empty ashtrays with great care: a smouldering cigarette can easily be missed when clearing, but if thrown into a waste bin along with flammable materials (such as paper), a fire can easily start. Ideally, ashtrays should be emptied into metal bins or containers with lids and left until there is no risk of fire.

Wash ashtrays separately to all other items then return to storage area.

Glassware

Glasses are best washed in glass-washing machines as they are time-saving and hygienic. If you are using a glass-washing machine, read the manufacturer's instructions carefully; it is important to use the correct operating procedures and temperatures.

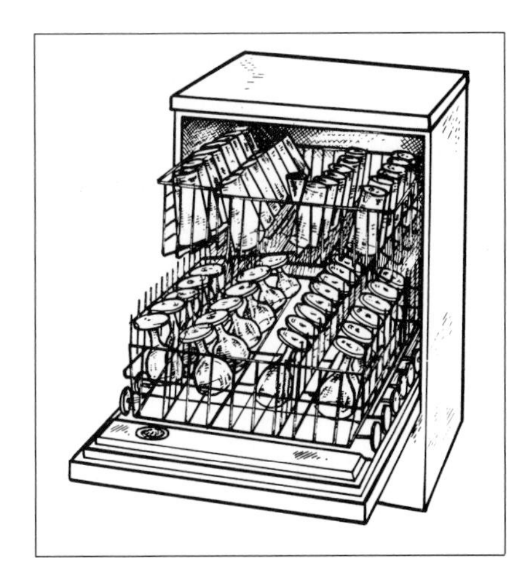

A glass washer

If washing by hand, wash the glasses in hot water with a detergent, then rinse in hot water (82 °C/180 °C), dry and store upside-down on shelves lined with glass storage matting.

Menus and holders
Collect all the menus and wipe down any folders. If new menus are to be used for the next service period, make sure that all of this period's menus are removed.

Table decorations
All table decorations need to be collected together, checked, and stored according to requirements. If they include lamps or candles, extinguish these and allow to cool before moving.

Condiments and accompaniments
As with food items, return to the kitchen or service preparation area, where those items which have not been used can be stored and used again or disposed of.

Dealing with waste

All food waste must be disposed of carefully, either through waste disposal units or into containers with tight fitting lids. When handling waste:

- empty bins regularly
- do not allow bins to become full or over-full
- wash the bins, lids and surrounding areas thoroughly with detergent or disinfectant before or after every service session or whenever they become full
- wash your hands after handling rubbish bins
- store waste in designated areas away from fire exits, preparation areas and corridors.

Essential knowledge

Waste must be handled and disposed of correctly in order to:

- prevent accidents
- prevent the risk of fire
- prevent the contamination of service and preparation areas
- prevent pest infestation and unpleasant odours from arising
- comply with the law and all establishment procedures.

What have you learned?

1 Why should all dining and service areas be left clean after service?

2 What should be done with left-over food at the end of service?

3 Why should certain types of electrical equipment be turned off after service?

4 What two points of safety need to be observed before clearing heated and electrical equipment?

5 Why must waste be handled and disposed of correctly?

6 Why must care be taken when emptying ashtrays?

Extend your knowledge

1 Study the work carried out within your food service and dining areas to see if any tasks or service procedures can be improved to provide a more efficient service.
2 Look through a catering supplier's equipment brochure to see if there are any pieces of equipment which would help with these improvements. Be prepared to justify the purchases of these pieces of equipment.
3 Design a long-term maintenance programme for your restaurant, to include re-decoration, furnishing and equipment replacement.

UNIT 2C2

Providing a table service

ELEMENTS 1–3: Greet customers and take orders. Serve orders and maintain dining and service areas

What do you have to do?

- Deal with customers in a polite and welcoming manner at all times.
- Identify customer requirements and check booking records.
- Escort customers to an appropriate table or waiting area and assist with coats and bags as required.
- Present the correct menus and translate them where appropriate, giving customers accurate information on individual dishes.
- Guide customers to an appropriate menu choice, then identify and record customer orders.
- Work in an organised and efficient manner, planning your time to meet daily schedules.
- Provide customers with the correct table items.
- Serve the correct type, quality and quantity of food in accordance with laid down procedures.
- Clear customer tables of soiled and unrequired table items at appropriate times.
- Remove soiled table linen, left-over food items and accompaniments from tables as appropriate.
- Maintain sufficient stocks of clean table and service items, condiments and accompaniments throughout service.
- Carry out all work causing minimum disturbance to customers.

What do you need to know?

- Why menus should be checked before use.
- Why information given to customers should be accurate.
- Why care has to be taken to serve and arrange food correctly.
- Why waste must be handled and disposed of correctly.
- Why a constant stock of linen, table items and accompaniments must be maintained.
- Why dining and service areas must be kept tidy and free from rubbish and food debris.
- How to deal with unexpected situations.

Professional table service leads to satisfied customers

Introduction

The term *table service* applies to any situation where the food is served at a table; e.g. Little Chefs, Beefeaters, ethnic restaurants, five-star hotels. This type of service gives food service staff the opportunity to use their knowledge and skills to help provide an enjoyable and satisfying meal experience for customers, who come to a restaurant for relaxation and pleasure as well as nourishment. A professional waiter or waitress providing table service therefore requires not only technical expertise, but also sales and social skills to fulfill his or her role as a representative of the establishment in direct contact with the customer.

ELEMENT 1: Greeting customers and taking orders

Greeting customers is often the job of the receptionist, head waiter or supervisor, but in smaller establishments it could be the responsibility of anyone, so it is important that all restaurant staff know how to greet customers in an appropriate manner since this can determine their first impressions of the restaurant. It is important for all restaurant staff to develop a sound knowledge of dishes on the menu so that they can offer assistance to the customer if necessary, while taking orders in an organised and efficient manner.

It must be noted that practices and policies may vary in different establishments. The practices described here are those generally accepted, but remember that different styles of restaurant, e.g. a Beefeater, a Little Chef or an Italian restaurant, will adopt different procedures and standards, so you should use the following text in conjunction with the methods used in your own establishment.

Greeting customers

As a member of staff involved in food service, you will come into regular contact with customers. This is an important link; if you are able to ensure that customers leave with pleasant memories of the restaurant, they are more likely to make a return visit. Establishments are often judged by the standards of service and staff as well as the quality of food served, so professional personal appearance and presentation are very important.

- As customers arrive at the restaurant, greet them in a polite but friendly way, by addressing them either as 'Sir' or 'Madam' or, preferably, by their name if known. This has the effect of making them feel more welcome. Children should be warmly welcomed and spoken to in a manner appropriate to their age.
- Offer your assistance in removing their coats, hats, etc. to the cloakroom.
- Check if the party has a booking; if not, find out whether there is a suitable table available.
- Many restaurants seat guests in a bar area when they first arrive, where they may be offered an aperitif. However, if the customers' table is ready you may offer them the alternative of going straight to their table.
- Customers' needs vary greatly: some may need extra attention and assistance from the staff, for instance, if they are suffering from mobility or communication difficulties. Be aware of your customers' special requirements and offer assistance in a polite but unintrusive way.
- Most importantly, remember that during this time it is essential that a welcoming and efficient image is conveyed to the guests.

Seating guests

Identifying the host

As the head waiter or supervisor approaches the table with the guests, the waiter should greet them and identify the host of the party. This can be done in a number of ways:

- the head waiter may tell the waiter which member of the party is the host
- the name the table is booked in is usually that of the host
- the host generally takes control when guests are sitting down or deciding what to order
- the host may enquire about the special dish of the day or ask for the wine list.

Assisting the guests in seating

As a waiter, you will need to assist guests in taking their seats.

1. Pull out each chair slightly, then push it in again carefully as the guest sits down. Offer this assistance to female guests first, followed by male guests and lastly, the host.
2. While seating the guests, engage them in light conversation, creating a friendly atmosphere. It is important to ensure that each table has the correct number of place settings and that if applicable, these have been arranged in accordance with any special customer requirements.
3. In a traditional restaurant, the station waiter may unfold each guest's serviette or napkin and place it on their lap once the customers are seated (this is sometimes known as *breaking the serviette*). The station waiter may then also turn the glasses up the right way if this has not been done beforehand.
4. At this point it is appropriate for the waiter or wine waiter (*sommelier*) to approach the table and offer an aperitif to the customers.
5. In some restaurants it may be necessary for the waiter to offer the guests bread rolls and/or Melba toast, followed by water (some establishments place jugs of iced water on the table for guests to help themselves).
6. If the menu is not already on the table, it should now be presented to the guests. Give them information on any specials or dishes of the day and be ready to answer any enquiries about dishes suitable for specific dietary requirements, e.g. vegetarian. Allow a short time for guests to make their choice.

Essential knowledge

Menus should be checked before use in order to:
- ensure accuracy of ingredients, availability and pricing
- ensure the inclusion of promotional items.

To do

- Ask your supervisor who is responsible for greeting customers when they first arrive in your restaurant.
- Find out how bookings are taken in your establishment.
- Check that you know where customers can leave their hats and coats.
- Find out the procedures for seating guests in your establishment.

Taking the order

1 The waiter normally takes the order for the entire table through the host. Stand to the host's left and be ready to offer suggestions, advice and explanations of dishes on the menu. You may need to translate the foreign names of certain dishes. This point represents an ideal opportunity to promote sales.

2 Food checks (written copies of the order) should be written in the language of the menu and orders are usually taken up to and including the main course. It is a good idea at this stage to establish a permanent point for yourself at the table; i.e. a point at which you will always stand when approaching the table for the rest of the meal. If you then list the dishes ordered following a clockwise direction around the table from this point, you will be able to deliver the correct dish to the correct guest when serving the order without having to ask the guests what they ordered. This creates a more professional impression.

Table No. 2 Coverts 3

1 Crème de tomate
2 Cocktail de crevettes

---

1 Dinde rôti
2 Boenf stroganoff
2 Riz
1 Pommes roties
1 Haricots verts

Date 20/9/94 Signed S Tomley

A check written out for the first two courses of a meal

3 Record all the dishes ordered accurately and clearly on the food check, together with any additional information necessary: e.g. the degree of cooking required for a steak.

4 Record any other important information on the food check. Most restaurants would require you to record:
- the date
- the table number
- the number of covers
- the waiter's initials.

Essential knowledge

Information given to customers should be accurate in order to:
- ensure an efficient service is maintained.
- ensure customer satisfaction.

Methods of taking orders

There are two traditional methods for taking orders, as given below.

1 **Triplicate checking system**
This is a control system used in many medium-sized and large establishments. Here the food check consists of three copies, which are divided as follows:
- the top copy goes to the kitchen and is handed to a member of the kitchen brigade at the hotplate
- the duplicate (bottom) copy goes to the cashier who will make out the guests' bill
- the flimsy (middle) copy is kept by the waiter as a means of reference (you may need to hold this copy against a white background to make it easier to read).

2 **Duplicate checking system**
This control system is more likely to be used in a smaller establishment. It is generally used where a table d'hôte menu is in operation. Here the food check consist of two copies, which are divided as follows:
- the top copy goes to the kitchen
- the second copy is used for service and billing purposes (the waiter may carry out the billing).

Table No. 2 **Coverts** 3

Suivant

2 Crème caramel
1 Profiteroles.

Date 20/9/94 **Signed** S Tomley

An example check for an additional order

Other points to note

- Additional checks may be written out later for sweets and coffees.
- If an à la carte menu is in use, record the time the order was taken and the individual dish prices on the check. Abbreviations may be used when taking orders as long as they are understood by everyone and cannot be misinterpreted by the kitchen, causing subsequent delay in service.
- Even the most sophisticated electronic system is based on the duplicate or triplicate system, even though the actual checks may not be written but communicated electronically to VDUs or print-out machines.

To do

- Find out what system is used for taking orders in your establishment.
- Check with your supervisor which type of menus are used.
- Ask your supervisor who is responsible for taking orders.

What have you learned?

1 Why is it important that customers are greeted correctly?

2 Why should menus be checked before use?

3 In what order should you assist guests to sit down?

4 How may you be able to identify the host of a party?

5 Why must information given to guests always be accurate?

6 What information should be recorded on a food check?

7 When using the triplicate system, where do the three copies go?

____

____

ELEMENT 2: Serving customers' orders

Types of food service

There are a variety of styles of food service; the type used in any establishment will depend on a number of factors:

- the policy of the establishment
- the type, size and site of the establishment
- the time available
- the type and number of customers
- the type of menu and its cost.

For most types of food service customers are seated at a laid table and served by one (or a combination) of the service methods listed in the table below.

Service Methods

Silver/English	The waiting staff present and serve food to the customer from a flat or dish (see Unit 2C5: *Providing a silver service*, pp. 192–206)
Family	Main courses are plated with dishes of vegetables placed on the table for customers to help themselves; e.g. ethnic restaurants
Plate/American	This type of service is found in a wide variety of catering establishments and is probably the most common style of food service. Food is pre-plated and served to the customers, sometimes under cloche/plate covers which are removed in front of the guests. The advantages of this type of service include the maintenance of food presentation and portions, and the possibility of a faster turnover of customers
Butler/French	Food service staff present the food on dishes or flats to each customer and they help themselves
Russian	The table is laid with food and the customers help themselves
Guéridon	Food is served onto the customer's plate from a side table or trolley. This style of service can also include the preparation of salads and their dressing, the filleting of fish, carving, cooking and *flambage* (flaming of dishes at the table)

Serving the customer

After you have taken the customers' order you will probably need to change the cover according to the dishes ordered. If this is the case, carry the cutlery to and from the table on a salver or plate with a serviette on it to help deaden the noise. If a table d'hôte menu is in operation the covers are usually changed up to and including the main course. If an à la carte menu is in operation the cutlery for each course should be placed on the table before the service of each course. Any accompaniments may also be placed on the table at this time.

In order to comply with current food safety and trade description legislation, it is important to ensure that the food served is of good quality and meets the customers' expectations.

General accompaniments and covers

Covers

Many items on the menu will require alternative cutlery to that which is already on the table, and you may also need extra service equipment. Make sure that these items are kept on the sideboard for easy access.

Accompaniments

Accompaniments are often highly flavoured seasonings of various kinds offered with certain dishes to improve the flavour of the food or to counteract its richness. There are standard accompaniments for some dishes and it is important for you to have a thorough knowledge of these, so that you can automatically offer the correct accompaniments.

Although there are traditional accompaniments for specific dishes, in certain parts of the country alternative accompaniments may be acceptable. Note also that if a customer requests an unusual accompaniment to be served with a specific dish this should be undertaken without question.

All accompaniments for the menu should be placed on the sideboard or on a service table ready for service.

Hors d'oeuvres

The first course of a meal can consist of either an hors d'oeuvres variés or a single hors d'oeuvres.

Hors d'oeuvres variés

This usually consists of a selection of foods and salads which are either plated in the kitchen or served from a table, trolley or tray so that customers may select for themselves. If served in the restaurant, the salads are usually presented in dishes called *raviers* with a clean spoon and fork for each variety.

When serving from a trolley: place the trolley between the table and yourself and rotate it away from the guest so that he or she can see everything on the trolley and so make a choice.

When serving from a tray: rotate the tray on your hand so that the item being served is in the ravier closest to the customer's plate.

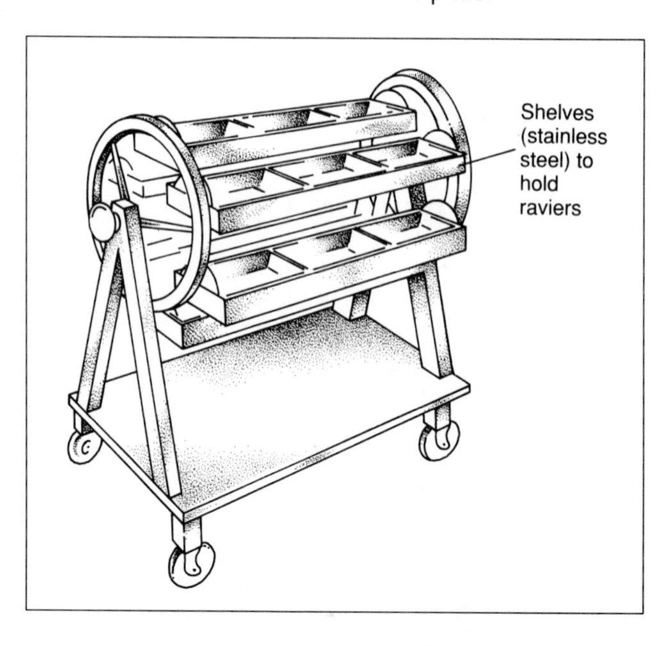

An hors d'oeuvres trolley

Single hors d'oeuvres

This consists of one item or dish such as avocado pear, melon, fruit cocktail, pâté, smoked salmon or oysters.

Hors d'oeuvres: their accompaniments and covers

Dish	Cover	Accompaniments
Potted shrimps	Fish knife and fork; cold fish plate	Cayenne pepper; pepper mill; lemon segment; hot toast or brown bread and butter
Smoked eel/trout/ mackerel	Fish knife and fork; cold fish plate	Cayenne pepper; pepper mill; lemon segment; brown bread and butter; horseradish sauce
Fresh prawns	Prawns are placed over the rim of a wine goblet filled with crushed ice on an underplate with doiley. Fish knife and fork; cold fish plate (for debris); finger-bowl (with warm water and a slice of lemon, placed at the head of the cover); spare serviette	Brown bread and butter; horseradish sauce
Gulls' eggs	Small knife and fork; cold fish plate; fingerbowl; spare serviette; sideplate for shell	Brown bread and butter; Oriental salt (4 parts salt to 1 part cayenne pepper)
Hors d'oeuvres variés	Fish plate; fish knife and fork	Brown bread and butter; oil and vinegar
Grapefruit cocktail	Coupe or goblet on sideplate with doiley; grapefruit spoon or teaspoon	Caster sugar
Fruit juices (orange, pineapple or grapefruit)	Goblet or small tumbler on a sideplate with doiley	None
Chilled melon (*melon frappé*)	Dessert spoon and fork; fish plate	Ground ginger, caster sugar
Pâté maison	Side knife and dessert fork; cold fish plate	Hot toast without crust, cut into triangles and served on a sideplate
Corn on the cob	Hot fish plate; corn-on-the-cob holders either inserted into each each of the cob or placed on a sideplate at the head of the cover	Melted butter

Essential knowledge

Care must be taken to serve and arrange food correctly in order to:
- comply with costing considerations
- maintain a professional appearance
- maintain customer satisfaction.

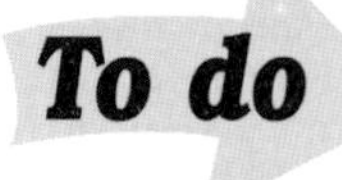

- Find out what service methods are used in your establishment.
- Ask your supervisor what hors d'oeuvres are usually offered in your restaurant and check what covers and accompaniments are used.
- Find out what covers and accompaniments are standard for the following dishes:
  - Avocado pear
  - Asparagus
  - Escargots
  - Smoked salmon
  - Seafood cocktail
  - Oysters
  - Globe artichoke.

Soups

Soup may either be served as the first course or the second, following the hors d'oeuvres. It may be plated in the kitchen or served from a tureen. Most thick soups, purées, creams and broths are served in soup plates on underplates. Clear soups (consommés) are served into a consommé cup on a saucer and underplate. These are usually eaten with a dessert spoon.

Soups: their accompaniments and covers

Dish	Cover	Accompaniments
Purée or ungarnished soups	Soup plate; underplate; soup spoon	Croûtons
Minestrone	Soup plate; underplate; soup spoon	Grated Parmesan cheese; toasted flute
French onion soup	Soup plate; underplate; soup spoon	Grated Parmesan cheese; toasted flute
Petite marmite	Special earthenware dish called a *petite marmite*; underplate and doiley; dessert spoon	Grated cheese; toasted flute

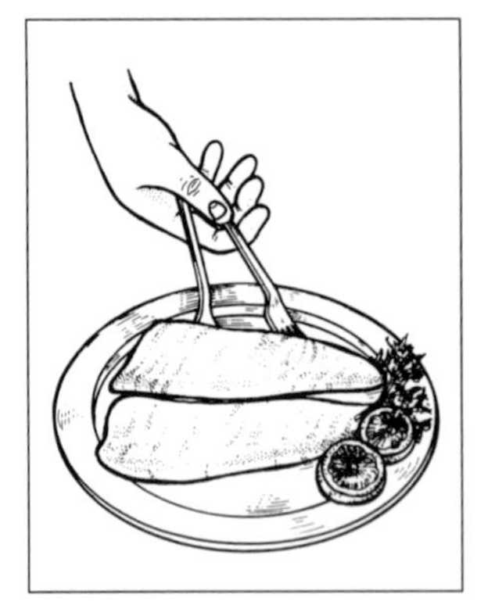

Serving fish

Fish

Fish can be served as a course on its own or as a main course with vegetables and potatoes. The accompaniments are the same in both cases and the cutlery is normally a fish knife and fork. Some fish can be filleted at the table (e.g. Dover sole) while other fish (e.g. trout) should have the head and tail removed by the waiter. Fillets of fish may be served by using two service forks or two fish knives: these are fanned out and slid under the fish to be served (see illustration opposite).

When fish is served as a main course it should always be served on a hot joint plate. However, some establishments serve fish on an oval platter.

Fish dishes: their accompaniments and covers

Dish	Cover	Accompaniments
Deep-fried scampi	Fish knife and fork; hot fish plate	Tartare sauce; lemon segment
Cold lobster	Fish knife and fork; lobster pick; debris plate, fingerbowl; spare serviette	Mayonnaise; lemon segment
Fish fried in batter	Fish knife and fork; hot fish plate	Hot tomato sauce; lemon segment
Fish fried in breadcrumbs	Fish knife and fork; hot fish plate	Tartare sauce; lemon segment; parsley
Grilled fish	Fish knife and fork; hot fish plate	Parsley butter; lemon segment
Blue trout	Fish knife and fork; hot fish plate	Hollandaise sauce; lemon segment; melted butter

- Ask your supervisor how soups are served in your establishment.
- Find out what covers and accompaniments are standard for: Bouillabaisse (Mediterranean fish stew); Bortsch; Consommé.
- Find out what covers and accompaniments are standard for: Whitebait; Hot poached salmon; Grilled herring; Mussels; Cold salmon.

Farinaceous dishes

This category includes all pasta (e.g. spaghetti, macaroni and ravioli), rice dishes (e.g. pilaf and risotto) and gnocchi (little dumplings) when served as a course on their own. All of these dishes except spaghetti are served on a fish plate and eaten with a dessert spoon and fork. Spaghetti is served into a soup plate with an underplate and a dessert spoon and joint fork.

Farinaceous dishes: their accompaniments and covers

Dish	Cover	Accompaniments
Spaghetti	Joint fork (on the right); dessert spoon (on left); hot soup plate on underplate	Parmesan cheese
Others	Dessert spoon (on the right); dessert fork (on left); hot fish plate	Parmesan cheese

Egg Dishes

These can be served as various courses during a meal, i.e. as a starter, main course, intermediate course or dessert.

Egg dishes: their accompaniments and covers

Dish	Cover	Accompaniments
Oeuf sur le plat	Sur le plat dish; underplate and doiley; dessert spoon and fork; (small knife depending on garnish)	
Oeuf en cocotte	Cocotte dish on underplate and doiley; teaspoon	
Omelettes	Hot fish plate; joint fork (on the right)	
Main course omelettes	Hot joint plate; joint knife and fork	
Sweet omelette	Hot fish plate; dessert spoon and fork	

Meat, poultry and game

These dishes are usually served as main courses. When you are serving meat dishes, particularly joints of meat, offer their traditional accompaniments.

Meat, poultry and game dishes: their accompaniments and covers

Dish	Cover	Accompaniments
Roast beef	Hot joint plate; joint knife and fork	Roast gravy; French and English mustard; horseradish sauce; Yorkshire pudding
Roast lamb	Hot joint plate; joint knife and fork	Roast gravy; mint sauce
Boiled mutton	Hot joint plate; joint knife and fork	Caper sauce
Boiled fresh beef	Hot joint plate; joint knife and fork	Rock salt; grated horseradish; gherkins
Grilled steak, mixed grill	Hot joint plate; joint knife and fork	French and English mustard; parsley butter
Roast chicken	Hot joint plate; joint knife and fork	Roast gravy; bread sauce; parsley and thyme stuffing; bacon rolls; game chips; watercress
Roast duck	Hot joint plate; joint knife and fork	Roast gravy; sage and onion stuffing; apple sauce
Hare	Hot joint plate; joint knife and fork	Heart-shaped croûton; redcurrant jelly

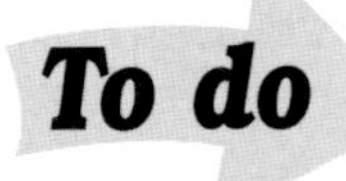

- Find out what *sur le plat* and *cocotte* dishes are.
- Find an example of a sweet omelette.
- Ask your supervisor whether accompaniments are ever served with omelettes.
- Find out what covers and accompaniments are standard for the following dishes:
  - Curry
  - Roast pork
  - Irish stew
  - Roast mutton
  - Lancashire hotpot
  - Roast goose
  - Roast game birds
  - Boiled salt beef.
- Ask your supervisor to tell you of any speciality meat dishes that are served in your establishment and find out what covers and accompaniments are used.

Vegetables and salads

Some vegetables are served as a course on their own (such as Asparagus and Corn on the cob); these have already been mentioned in the hors d'oeuvres section (page 140). Many other vegetables are served with sauces which form part of the actual dish.

Vegetables and salads: their accompaniments and covers

Dish	Cover	Accompaniments
Baked (jacket) potato	Hot sideplate; dessert fork (on sideplate, placed at top left of cover)	Butter pat; pepper mill
Side salad	Salad crescent, sideplate or bowl; dessert fork (placed on crescent at top left of cover)	Vinaigrette or other salad dressing

Cheese

The cheese course is normally offered towards the end of a meal, as an alternative or an extra to the sweet. Some restaurants may adopt the continental custom, where the cheese is offered before the sweet. A restaurant will usually offer a selection of cheese from a trolley or a cheeseboard; the cheeses should be arranged attractively. Make sure you are familiar with all the cheese offered so you are able to help the customers with their choice.

When serving a cheese course, lay the cover first. This consists of a sideplate, side knife and sometimes a small fork. Present the cheeseboard or trolley to the customer and offer assistance or information as required. Once the customers have made their choice, cut a portion of each cheese chosen (using a clean knife for each variety) and place the portion on the sideplate. Two factors are particularly important when cutting cheese: make sure you cut the correct portion size and take care to maintain the attractive appearance of the cheeseboard.

Note that Stilton should no longer be served in the traditional manner of scooping out (which creates a large amount of wastage), but by cutting out thin wedges across the surface of the cheese.

From left: two ways of cutting hard cheese; portioning soft cheese; an economical way to cut Stilton

After the cheese has been served, you may offer the following accompaniments:

- cruet (salt, pepper and mustard)
- butter (in a dish on an underplate with doiley, with a butter knife)
- celery (served in a celery glass half-filled with either crushed ice or cold water)
- radishes when in season (placed in a glass bowl on an underplate with a teaspoon)
- caster sugar (for cream cheeses)
- apples, grapes and pickles
- assorted cheese biscuits.

Sweets

Restaurants may offer their customers either a sweet menu or a sweet trolley, or a combination of both, since some sweets such as ice cream and hot sweets are unsuitable for serving from a trolley.

When using a trolley, make sure that sweets are attractively presented and arranged at all times so that customers have a clear view when making their choice. Once a sweet has been selected, hold the plate or bowl in your left hand and serve the sweet using a spoon and fork or a gâteau slice (in your right hand). Offer cream as an accompaniment.

Most sweets are served onto a plate or into a pudding bowl on an underplate. Bowls are usually used when a sauce is served with the sweet (e.g. custard). Certain sweets, such as mousses, fruit fools and syllabubs may be served in a glass or coupe on an underplate. Most ice cream sweets are served in coupes.

Sweets are generally eaten with a dessert spoon and fork, although some ice creams and mousses may be eaten with a teaspoon or sundae spoon. Note that sorbets are often served as a sweet but occasionally they are served in the middle of a large banquet to cleanse the palate for the next course.

To do

- Find out which cheeses are normally offered in your establishment.
- Check which service methods and accompaniments are used when serving the cheese course in your establishment.
- Find out what type of dishes Sundaes and Banana splits are normally served in.

Fresh fruit and nuts

These may be served as an alternative to a sweet or as an extra course at the end of a meal. Lay the cover as follows:

- dessert plate
- dessert knife and fork
- spare sideplate for shells or peel
- spare serviette
- fingerbowl
- nut crackers and grape scissors (to be placed on the fruit basket).

If nuts are chosen, place some nutcrackers on the table next to the dessert knife or on a sideplate at the head of the cover. If grapes are chosen, cut off the selected portion of grapes using grape scissors.

Accompaniments would consist of caster sugar (in a holder on a sideplate) and salt (for nuts). You may offer cream to accompany fruit; it may be served in a cream jug placed on the table, or from a sauceboat and offered to the guest, using a sauce ladle or dessert spoon.

Savouries

Savouries may be served at the end of a meal either as well as or as an alternative to a sweet. Items such as hot canapés or croûtes, bouchées, savoury soufflés or fritters may be offered.

The cover for savouries consists of a hot fish plate and a small knife and fork. Savoury soufflés may be eaten from an individual soufflé dish presented on an underplate with a teaspoon, dessert fork or fish fork. Set the following accompaniments:

- cruet to be replaced
- cayenne pepper (placed on a sideplate on the table)
- pepper mill (on a sideplate on the table)
- Worcester sauce (placed on a sideplate on the table but only offered with a meat savoury).

Serving coffee

Coffee is normally served from the right. Place coffee cups, saucers and spoons on the table for each customer with the cup handle on the right and the spoon underneath.

There are many ways of serving coffee, including silver service. Other methods include:

- cups of coffee taken straight to the table
- jugs of coffee, cream or hot/cold milk placed on the table for guests to help themselves
- service of milk or cream and coffee from pots, one held in either of the waiter's hands. The sugar is placed on the table for customers to help themselves.

General food service points

- Always use a waiter's cloth when carrying hot plates to help protect against burns and scalds.
- Serve cold foods before hot foods. This ensures that when the hot food is served, the customer may eat it immediately without having to wait for other food to be served to the table.

- In general, food should always be served from the left. However, this may vary according to establishment practices; check with your supervisor on whether this applies to your establishment.
- Serve guests in the following order: female guests, male guests, host.
- When carrying items to and from the table, place them on a salver, underflat or service plate.
- Always ensure that sufficient accompaniments, bread items and seasonings are available to customers throughout their meal.
- Make sure that all crockery and cutlery used is clean, polished and free from damage in order to maintain customer satisfaction.

Finally, remember that the practices and methods given in this element are those generally accepted within the catering trade, but these may vary depending on establishment style and customer requirements.

Presenting the bill

At the end of the meal, usually when the customer requests, you will need to collect the bill from the cashier. When doing this, fold the bill to conceal the figures and then present it to the host on a sideplate. When payment has been made, take it to the cashier and then return the receipt and change to the customer on the sideplate.

Guest departure

When customers are ready to leave, be ready to assist them with chairs, hats and coats making sure that nothing has been left behind. You may then thank the customers and say goodbye.

What have you learned?

1 Name three different service methods and describe them.

____

____

____

2 Why must care be taken to serve and arrange food correctly?

____

____

____

3 Why is it important to ensure that food served is of good quality and meets customer expectations?

____

____

____

4 What are the cover and accompaniments for French onion soup?

5 What are the possible accompaniments for cheese?

ELEMENT 3: Maintaining dining and service areas

Clearing tables

Clearing should only begin when all guests at the table have finished eating. It is important to learn how to clear tables correctly for a number of reasons:

- it ensures speed and efficiency
- it avoids the possibility of accidents
- it creates minimum disturbance to the guests
- it allows dirty dishes to be stacked neatly and correctly on the sideboard with minimum delay
- more can be cleared, in less time and in fewer journeys between sideboard and table. This helps to speed up the eating process, allowing for greater turnover.

Essential knowledge

Dining and service areas must be kept tidy and free from rubbish and food debris in order to:

- prevent contamination of food and food areas
- prevent accidents
- maintain customer satisfaction
- comply with the law.

Clearing techniques

All clearing techniques stem from two main hand positions but also depend on what is being cleared from the table. The following principles should be maintained whenever possible.

1 Clear plates from the right-hand side of the customer.
2 Position yourself so that you are standing sideways-on to the table.
3 Collect any plates with your right hand and then transfer them to your left. Remember to turn away from the guests while you clear the plates.
4 Hold a joint plate by placing your thumb on top of the plate and your first two fingers underneath; the remaining two fingers should stand upright to help balance and support further plates.

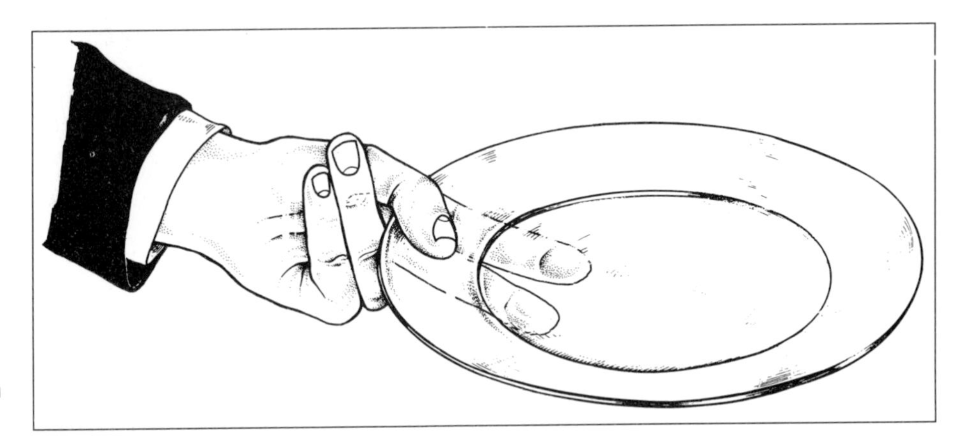

Holding the first plate when clearing

5 Secure the fork under your thumb and slide the knife underneath the fork. This prevents the cutlery sliding about or falling to the floor.
6 Balance the next plate on your left forearm, thumb and two upright fingers.
7 Scrape any food debris from the second to the first plate and place the dirty cutlery onto the first plate.
8 Continue to clear the remaining plates following this method.
9 If clearing the main course, remove the sideplates, butter dish and cruet.

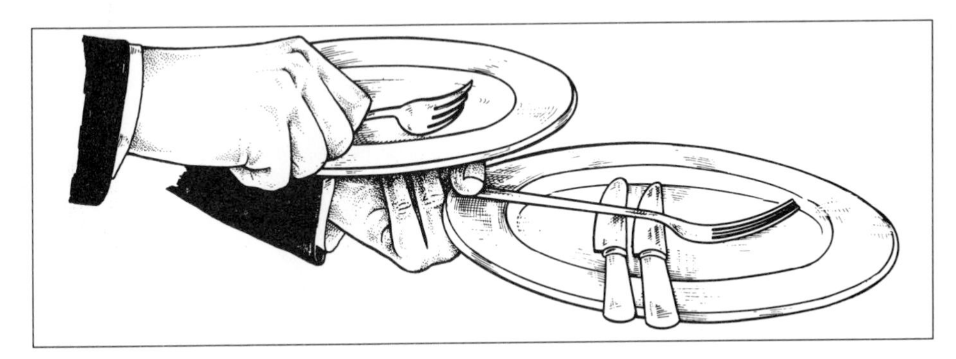

Clearing the debris from the second plate

Clearing soup plates

1 Collect the first bowl and underplate, positioning the underplate as for a joint plate (see Step 4 above).
2 Collect the second bowl and underplate, positioning it on the forearm, thumb and fingers of your left hand.
3 Transfer the spoons from the first bowl to the second bowl.
4 Place the second bowl into the first bowl, so that a clear underplate remains, allowing you to continue the process.

Clearing soup plates

Clearing accompaniments

Cruets should be removed after the main course but should remain available nearby for service with cheese if required. Mustards, sauces, dressings, etc. should be cleared away at the end of each appropriate course.

Crumbing down

Crumbing down usually takes place after the main course has been cleared and before the sweet order is taken. The process is carried out to remove any crumbs or debris left on the tablecloth. If a table d'hôte cover has been laid, the dessert spoon and fork will normally have been laid at the head of the cover (see Steps 2 and 3 below); if an à la carte menu has been laid there should not be any cutlery remaining on the table when you come to crumb down (the cutlery is not laid until after the dessert order has been taken).

Crumbing down

1. Working from the left-hand side of the customer, place a service plate just slightly beneath the edge of the table. Brush any crumbs towards the plate using a neatly folded napkin or waiters' cloth.
2. Move the dessert fork (where necessary) from the head of the cover to the left-hand side.
3. Move round to the right-hand side of the same guest and complete the crumbing down procedure for that place setting. Then move the dessert spoon from the head of the cover to the right-hand side.
4. After completing the crumbing down for that place setting, you are now in the correct position for crumbing down the next place setting.

Essential knowledge

A constant stock of linen, table items and accompaniments must be maintained in order to maintain:

- speed and efficiency of service
- customer expectations and satisfaction.

Changing an ashtray

This may be carried out at any stage of the meal if necessary.

1 Carry two clean ashtrays to the table; place one onto the table for use and place the second upside down over the dirty ashtray already on the table.
2 Remove the covered, dirty ashtray from the table, preventing any cigarette ash from being blown onto the tablecloth.

Clearing glasses

Used, dirty glasses need to be cleared at regular intervals throughout the meal (preferably at the end of each course). Place them on a napkin-covered salver and return them to the bar or wash-up area. Clear any water glasses at the end of the main course unless the customer requests otherwise.

Carrying dirty glasses from a cleared table

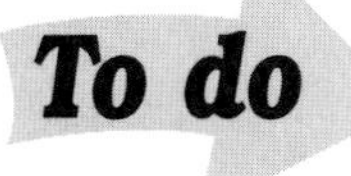

- Ask your supervisor what your establishment's policy is on smoking in the restaurant.
- Practise clearing plates from a table (when the restaurant is empty).

An example order of service for a four-course à la carte meal

The following order of service should be read as an example only. Note that practices and policies may vary in different establishments; the procedures listed below are the generally accepted procedures for restaurant table service.

1 The guests enter and are greeted and seated.
2 The station waiter unfolds each serviette and places it over the guest's lap.
3 Aperitifs may be offered by the sommelier (wine waiter).
4 Bread rolls/Melba toast and water are served.
5 Menus are presented, allowing time for guests to make their choice.
6 The station waiter takes the food order through the host.
7 The sommelier takes the wine order.

8 Covers are changed for the first course and any accompaniments are placed on the table.
9 The first course is served.
10 Once all the guests have finished the plates are cleared.
11 The cover is laid for the fish course and all accompaniments are placed on the table.
12 The fish course is served.
13 Once all the guests have finished the plates are cleared.
14 The cover is laid for the main course and all accompaniments are placed on the table.
15 The main course is served. The meat should be served first on that part of the plate which is nearest the guest or at the bottom of the cover, i.e. at 'six o'clock'. This should be followed by potatoes, vegetables and any hot sauces and accompaniments which have to be offered.
16 The station waiter may offer more rolls, Melba toast and butter if required.
17 When all the guests have finished, the main course plates, sideplates, sideknives, cruets, butter dishes and any accompaniments are cleared.
18 Each place setting is crumbed down and any ashtrays changed if necessary.
19 The sweet menu is offered and the order taken.
20 The sweet covers are laid and any accompaniments brought to the table.
21 The sweet course is served.
22 Once the sweet course is finished, the plates are cleared when all guests have finished.
23 The coffee order is taken.
24 The sommelier may offer liqueurs.
25 Coffee cups are placed on the table and coffee is served. More coffee is served as required.
26 The bill is presented to the host.
27 Payment is taken from the host to the cashier; then receipt and change returned to the host.
28 The station waiter sees the guests out of the restaurant.
29 The table is cleared down and re-laid if necessary.

Essential knowledge

Waste must be handled and disposed of correctly in order to:
- prevent accidents
- prevent the risk of fire
- prevent contamination of food and food areas
- prevent pest infestation
- avoid pollution of the environment
- comply with the law.

Unexpected situations

When an unforeseen incident occurs it should be dealt with promptly and efficiently, causing the minimum of disturbance to any of the guests. Quick action will often soothe an irate customer and ensure a return visit to your establishment.

In the case of accidents or spillages, a report of the incident must be kept and signed by those involved, and your supervisor must always be informed of the incident.

Dealing with spillages

Slight spillages

If the accident involves a slight spillage on the table, the following procedure is generally acceptable.

1 Check to make sure that none of the spillage has fallen on the guest being served. Apologise to the guest.
2 Remove any items of equipment which may have been soiled or are in the way of cleaning up the spillage.
3 Clean the spillage with either a clean, damp cloth or a knife onto a service plate.
4 If tablecloths are being used, place an old menu card under and over the spillage to prevent marking the table and the clean cloth.
5 Unfold a clean serviette over the soiled area.
6 Replace any items as necessary.
7 Return any meals to the table that had been taken to the hotplate.

More serious spillages

More serious spillages may require the table to be completely cleared and re-laid.

1 If possible re-seat the customers at another table. If there are no tables available, follow Steps 2–6 below.
2 Clear all items from the table using a salver. Hot food should be placed in the hotplate.
3 Seat the customers slightly back from the table so you have more room to work.
4 Mop up as much spillage as possible with a clean absorbent cloth.
5 Change the tablecloth without showing the table top:
   - place the partly unfolded clean cloth across the table
   - drop the bottom fold of the clean cloth over the far edge of the table
   - take hold of the soiled cloth and lay the clean cloth, while at the same time drawing the soiled cloth towards you (see below)
   - the table will now be covered with the clean cloth and the soiled cloth can be taken away.
6 Re-lay the table and return the customers' food to the table from the hotplate.

Changing a tablecloth

Spillages onto guests

If some spillage falls onto a guest's clothing it will need to be dealt with immediately to avoid staining. Apologise to the guest and check that he or she has not been burned or scalded. Provide the guest with a clean, damp cloth to remove the worst of the spillage.

If the guest has to retire to the cloakroom, remove his or her meal to the hotplate. Depending on the nature of the spillage, the establishment may offer to have the garment concerned cleaned.

What have you learned?

1 Why must a constant stock of linen be maintained?

____

____

2 Why must the dining and service areas be kept tidy and free from rubbish at all times?

____

____

3 Describe how to *crumb down.*

____

____

4 Why must waste be handled and disposed of correctly?

____

____

5 Describe how you would deal with a small spillage.

____

____

Extend your knowledge

1 Visit other establishments and investigate the different methods of service used.
2 Carry out some research into table service for banquets, breakfasts and afternoon teas.
3 Find out more about guéridon service; what techniques and equipment are used? What sort of dishes are often served this way?
4 Find out how to carve certain meat dishes and fillet fish dishes at the table. Watch this being carried out.

UNIT 2C3

Providing a table drink service

The work of serving alcoholic drinks in the restaurant is often the work of a wine waiter or *sommelier*. However, many establishments may not have a member of staff who specialises in the service of wines and other drinks and, as a member of the restaurant's staff, you may be required to serve alcoholic and non-alcoholic drinks to guests at their table.

ELEMENT 1: Providing a table drink service

What do you have to do?

- Deal with customers in a polite and helpful way at all times.
- Serve alcoholic drinks only to those people whom you are permitted to serve by law.
- Give customers accurate information about any drink offered by the establishment.
- Promote certain drinks to customers at the appropriate times.
- Make sure that all service equipment is clean and free from damage at all times.
- Make sure that you take down customers' orders clearly and accurately to avoid misunderstandings.
- Serve a variety of drinks in the correct glassware, at the correct temperature and with the appropriate accompaniments.
- Carry out your duties in an organised and efficient manner.
- Deal with unexpected situations.

What do you need to know?

- The appropriate ways of dealing with customers.
- Who you may or may not serve with alcoholic drinks.
- Why customers must be given accurate information about the drinks being served.
- Why your service equipment should be clean and free from damage.
- How to promote certain types of drinks.
- Why it is important that you correctly identify the drinks your customers require.
- How to serve a range of alcoholic and non-alcoholic drinks.
- How to carry out your work in an organised and efficient manner, taking account of priorities and laid down procedures.
- How to deal with unexpected situations.

Providing a professional service

Re-read Units 2G2 and 2G3 to refresh your memory about the need for a professional appearance and how to deal with customers.

A skilled waiter/waitress must also have a thorough knowledge of the beverages that he or she sells. Without good product knowledge, you cannot:

- advise customers when asked
- discuss customers' requirements with them
- promote products to customers
- suggest suitable alternatives when necessary
- serve drinks correctly
- maintain a professional standard of service.

Serving staff and the law

There are a number of laws related to serving alcoholic drinks that you should be aware of. The main ones are:

- the Licensing Acts
- the Weights and Measures Acts
- the Trade Descriptions Act and other consumer protection acts
- the Food Safety Act and Food Hygiene Regulations
- the Health and Safety at Work Act.

The main points related to table service are given below.

Licensing laws

The licensing laws set down who may or may not be served alcoholic drinks, and the hours of opening (called *permitted hours*) allowed by the law.

There are two types of licence:

1. an *On-Licence*, which allows the sale of alcoholic drinks to be drunk either on or off the premises
2. an *Off-Licence*, which only allows the sale of alcoholic drinks to be consumed off the premises.

Most licensed restaurants have an On-Licence, but the types of alcoholic drinks they can sell may be restricted.

The type of licence your establishment holds will depend on whether:

- the establishment is a restaurant only and not part of any other (larger) premises
- the restaurant is part of a hotel; in which case the licence would be a *Residential and Restaurant Licence*
- the restaurant is part of a public house; in which case the licence would be a *Full On-Licence* with the possible additions of a *Supper Hour Certificate* or a *Special Hours Certificate*.

When can you serve alcoholic drinks?

The following types of On-Licences may be granted to restaurants; note that their effect is to determine when drinks may be served. The opening hours for the restaurant itself are the same as for all premises with an On-Licence.

You may only serve alcoholic drinks during the permitted hours; it is illegal to sell such drinks either before or after these hours.

- *Restaurant Licence.* This type of licence allows the sale of alcoholic drinks only as part of a 'table meal' at midday or in the evening, or both. Drinking-up-time is 30 minutes after the end of the permitted hours.

- *Supper-Hour Certificate*. In premises where a table meal is supplied, this certificate allows the supply of alcoholic drinks for one hour after the end of general licensing hours at night.
- *Special Hours Certificate*. If the restaurant is adapted to provide music and dancing as well as meals, this certificate allows the supply of alcoholic drinks up to 2.00 a.m. (3.00 a.m. in London). However, this may be restricted to certain days of the week.

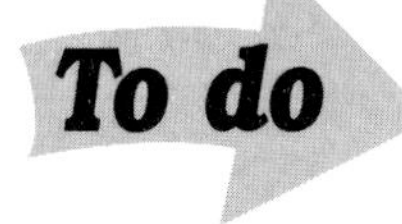

- Find out what type of licence your establishment has.
  Is it a:
  – Full On-licence?
  – Restaurant licence?
  – Residential and Restaurant licence?
  What are the permitted hours?
- Are there any restrictions on the type of alcoholic drinks the establishment is allowed to sell?
- Find out if your establishment has any of the following:
  - a Supper-hour Certificate
  - an Extended Hours Order
  - a Special Hours Certificate.

Whom may you serve?

The law does not allow you to serve the following people:

1. *Young persons under 18 years of age*, except under certain conditions. The licensing laws separate the *sale* of alcoholic drink from the *consumption* of alcoholic drink in the restaurant.
   Sale
   - You may sell beer, stout, cider or perry (and wine in some parts of the United Kingdom) to a person over 16 years of age to be drunk with a meal.

   Consumption
   - Young persons between the ages of 16 and 18 years can consume any alcoholic drink, including spirits and liqueurs, provided it has been purchased by a person over 18 years of age if it is to be drunk as part of a meal.
   - Young persons under the age of 16 and over 5 years of age may consume beer, stout, cider or perry as part of a meal if it is bought by a person over 16 years of age.

   However, even though the law allows consumption by persons under 16 years of age as part of a meal in a restaurant, you should follow the procedures operated in your establishment on this matter.
2. *Drunken customers*. It is an offence against the Licensing Acts to sell alcoholic drink to a person who is already drunk or to someone attempting to buy drink for them to be drunk on the premises.
3. *Persons behaving in a violent or disorderly manner*. It is an offence to allow people acting in a drunken, violent or disorderly manner to remain on licensed premises. Such people should not be served alcoholic drinks or encouraged in any way to remain in the establishment.
4. *Persons under an exclusion order*. Any customer who has been barred from the premises or who is known to be subject to a court order forbidding them from entering licensed premises should not be served.

If you suspect that a customer falls into any of these categories, refer the matter to your supervisor or employer immediately.

Essential knowledge

In order to make sure you do not commit an offence against the current licensing laws, you should not sell alcoholic drinks to:

- any person at the bar that you suspect is under 18 years of age or any person attempting to buy a drink for them
- any person in a restaurant or area put aside for table meals who you suspect is under sixteen years of age
- a customer who is obviously drunk or any person attempting to buy more drink for that customer to drink on the premises
- any customer behaving in a violent or disorderly manner or who is under an exclusion order
- any customer requesting service outside licensing hours.

Weights and Measures Laws

The *Weights and Measures Acts* set out the legal measures that must be used when selling draught beers and cider, some spirits and wine by the glass.

Draught beers and ciders

Draught beers and ciders must be sold in quantities of one-third of a pint (rarely used now), half a pint or a multiple of a half a pint (such as the pint itself).

Spirits

Gin, rum, vodka and whisky must be sold *in most cases* in legal (imperial) measures of $\frac{1}{4}$, $\frac{1}{5}$, or $\frac{1}{6}$ of a gill, or a (metric) measure of 25 millilitres (ml), or in multiples such as doubles or trebles. Note that after 1 January 1995 all spirit sales will have to be in metric quantities.

Wine

The sale of wine by the glass is not covered by Weights and Measures Laws unless a giver. quantity is advertised; the measures are largely set by a Voluntary Code of Practice. However, on 1 January 1995, the law will require still table wine to be sold in quantities of either 125 or 175 ml or in multiples of these amounts.

Suggested wine measures

Imperial	*Metric*
10 fl oz	250 ml
8 fl oz	200 ml
$6\frac{2}{3}$ fl oz ($\frac{1}{3}$ pint)	175 ml
6 fl oz	150 ml
5 fl oz (gill, $\frac{1}{4}$ pint)	125 ml
4 fl oz	100 ml

Suggested measures for wine

Until 1 January 1995, there is no legal requirement for licensed premises to serve a fixed amount of wine when selling it by the glass. Unless a restaurant has advertised the quantity of wine sold it may sell wine by the glass in any quantity it wishes.

However, the Weights and Measures Act has suggested 'appropriate' measures as given in the table opposite.

Many licensed premises, restaurants and hotels have adopted the Voluntary Code of Practice for selling still table wines by the glass. If so:

1. the quantity served must be one of those listed opposite and must be displayed where customers can see it
2. a lined glass, optic or thimble bearing a government or manufacturer's stamp must be used to dispense the wine
3. the Weights and Measures, Trade Descriptions and Price Marking Laws must be complied with.

No laws apply to the quantities to be sold if the wine is sparkling, fortified or aromatised.

Carafes

'House' wines are often bought in large 1.5 litre bottles or 2–3 litres 'bag-in-a-box' containers and then transferred to open glass containers called *carafes* for service.

Note the following points concerning measurement:

- wine in carafes must be sold in quantities of 25 cl, 50 cl, 75 cl (standard bottle size) or one litre. It may also be sold in half pint (10 fl oz) or one pint (20 fl oz) carafes
- a carafe may or may not have a line showing the correct *fill height* and should be shaped so that all the wine is poured out when the neck of the carafe is tilted about 30° downwards
- the quantities of wine sold in carafes must be clearly stated on the restaurant's Wine List.

Exceptions to legal measures

There are some exceptions you should be aware of:

- the Weights and Measures Laws do not apply to alcoholic drinks which are pre-packaged (such as those sold in bottles, cans or boxes)
- if beer or cider is sold as part of a mixture of two or more liquids (for example, in a shandy or lager and lime) a legal measure is not necessary
- when serving spirits, you do not have to use legal measures if:
  1 the customer requests a different quantity, or
  2 the drink is a mixture of three or more liquids (e.g. a cocktail).

Consumer Protection Laws

The Trade Descriptions Act

The Trade Descriptions Act operates alongside other laws such as the Weights and Measures Acts and the Price Marking Order.

Essentially, the Act states that there should be a price list available in any establishment where food and drink are sold for consumption on the premises. The price list may be displayed in the form of a notice or may be part of a wine list or menu.

- It is an offence to serve less than the advertised quantity of any drink (you would be guilty of overcharging) or to suggest that the price is lower than it actually is.
- You must supply the advertised product and not a cheaper substitute.

Food Safety Act and Food Hygiene Regulations

The Food Safety Act defines *food* as *any article used for food or drink for human consumption* and the regulations cover a wide range of activities. The main points of concern to the waiter/waitress are as follows:

- it is an offence to sell any food or drink that is unfit for human consumption, contaminated, or not of the nature or quality demanded by the customer
- any article or equipment likely to come into contact with food or drink must be in good condition and clean. This includes furniture (e.g. tables) and service equipment (e.g. linen, trays and glassware)
- many of the points relating to personal hygiene in Unit 2G2, *Maintaining a professional and hygienic appearance*, must be observed to comply with these laws.

Health and Safety at Work Act (HASAWA)

This Act requires employers to provide a safe and healthy working environment for their employees as far as possible. At the same time, it states that it is the duty of every employee to take reasonable care for the health and safety of him/herself and other members of staff.

Re-read Unit 2G1, *Maintaining a safe and secure working environment*, to refresh your memory if necessary.

Establishment procedures

Besides acting in ways which enable you to comply with the Acts above, you also need to take into account (and act on) any rules or procedures laid down by your employer.

To do

- Discuss with your employer or supervisor what you should do:
  - if a young person between 16 and 18 years orders beer with a meal
  - if a customer becomes drunk on your premises
  - if a person who has been barred from the premises comes in for a drink or meal.
- Examine any beverage list used in your establishment or any notices displayed concerning the drinks offered to your customers.
  - Is the list up to date or are some brands unavailable?
  - Are the prices correct?
  - What information is given about the quantities (measures) used to serve spirits and wine by the glass?
- Make a copy of six entries on the establishment's price list. Try to choose different types of drinks.

Providing customers with accurate information

The Trade Descriptions Act (mentioned in the last section) makes it an offence to give a false or misleading description of any drink you serve, in either measure or price.

It is important to give customers the correct information, both to comply with the law and to avoid offending customers, who may feel that:
- they have been overcharged
- they have been given a short measure
- they have been misled, misinformed or cheated.

A dissatisfied customer may leave and not return. They may also tell other people and the establishment might acquire a bad reputation.

What do you need to know?

One of the professional skills a good food server needs to possess is a thorough knowledge of the products being sold. Not only should you be completely familiar with the beverage list and know the range of drinks available, but also be able to provide customers with information on the price and alcoholic content of drinks.

Prices

Make sure you are familiar with the price of each of the drinks you sell. The prices of mixed drinks (such as lager and lime, gin and tonic or brandy and soda) should be calculated by *adding together the cost of each part*, unless a separate price for the mixed drink is displayed on the price list.

Relative strength

Many customers are now more conscious of the amount of alcohol they drink, especially in relation to driving. You need to be able to advise them on the alcoholic strength of the drinks you serve if asked.

The Food Labelling Regulations require that the alcoholic strength of drinks above 1.2% alcohol by volume should be stated on all pre-packaged drinks such as those in bottles, cans and boxes. The Regulations also require that *strength markings* should be given for a representative sample of dispensed drinks sold in bars and restaurants. The strength marking is often indicated along with the prices on the beverage list.

There are several points you should be aware of when advising your customers.

- While the strength of a drink like Scotch whisky varies very little depending on brand, the amount of alcohol your customer consumes will depend *on the size of the measure used to dispense it.*
- There is approximately the same amount of alcohol in a glass of wine, a half pint of normal strength beer, a $\frac{1}{6}$ gill measure of a spirit and a small glass of sherry or port.

If you have any doubts about the strength of an alcoholic drink, either check the label or consult your supervisor.

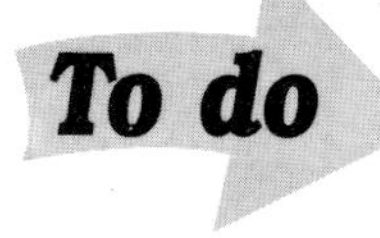

- Examine the stock of alcoholic drinks sold in your establishment Compare the alcoholic strength of:
  - a bottle of ordinary beer and a lager
  - a bottle of dry vermouth and of sherry
  - a bottle of whisky and of vodka.

  Make a note of them.
- Examine the stock of liqueurs held by your establishment. Make a list giving the name and the alcoholic strength of each type you find. Note the differences you find.

The ingredients of drinks

Most customers will be familiar with the main types of alcoholic and non-alcoholic drinks. However, they may be unfamiliar with the ingredients of most liqueurs, even though they may know their name.

Spirits and liqueurs

Try to learn about the flavour and ingredients of the more unusual spirits and liqueurs. When serving spirits or liqueurs at the table from a tray or trolley, follow establishment procedures. Note that there is, as yet, no legal measure for the service of liqueurs.

Cocktails and mixed drinks

Cocktails can be served before or after meals. Many of the pre-dinner or aperitif cocktails are based on wine-based drinks, while the after-dinner cocktails tend to be based on spirits, such as brandy and whisky. However, there are no hard and fast rules about what type of cocktails should be served at a particular time. The customer is always right.

You will need to know how cocktails are made and the ingredients of some of the more common cocktails. There are four main methods of making cocktails, as given below.

1. *Stirring*
   Stirred cocktails are made in a mixing glass using a bar spoon or *muddler.* Stirring is used when the cocktail to be made is clear, such as a Dry Martini.
2. *Shaking*
   Shaking is generally used when the cocktail to be made is not clear, but opaque, and contains ingredients such as fruit juices, egg white or cream. A *Boston* or *standard shaker* is commonly used.
3. *Building*
   Built cocktails are made in the glass in which they are served. The ingredients may be left in layers (such as for a Pousse Cafe), or mixed with the bar spoon.
4. *Blending*
   Some cocktails, especially those containing fresh fruit, such as the Banana Daiquiri, are made using a cocktail blender (a machine similar to a liquidiser).

Making cocktails is a trained bar person's job, but the food server should be aware of ingredients in order to advise customers or to promote cocktails at the appropriate times. Study any lists available in your establishment or find out about the ingredients from the bar staff when they are not busy.

Speciality coffees

You need to be aware of the ingredients of the main types of speciality coffees such as Irish coffee and Calypso coffee. Check with your bar staff for details.

Recommending substitutes or alternatives

It is not practical for any licensed premises to stock a complete range of every brand of alcoholic and non-alcoholic drink. Even those establishments with a well-stocked bar and cellar will not be able to provide every drink that is likely to be requested.

Substitutes

A *substitute* is something which is similar to the item ordered. If a customer requests Satzenbrau Pils and you do not stock this brand, you should suggest a suitable substitute brand. For example:

- apologise; e.g. 'I'm sorry, Madam, but we don't stock that brand'
- offer a substitute; e.g. 'However, we do stock Holsten Pils, which is quite similar'
- do *not* suggest that the substitute is in some way of a lesser quality by saying, 'I'm sorry, but we *only* stock Holsten Pils.'

Alternatives

An *alternative* is something different from the item ordered which serves the same purpose. If a customer requests a drink for which you have no substitute brand available, you should suggest an alternative. For example:

Customer (ordering aperitif): 'I'd like a chilled white port, please.'

Food server (apologising): 'I'm sorry, Madam, but we don't stock white port.' *Then going on to offer an alternative:* 'However, perhaps you would like a dry sherry or a glass of chilled white wine instead.'

You should never attempt to pass off a substitute or alternative as the brand or drink a customer has requested. Always consult the customer.

To do

- Ask your head waiter or bar manager what cocktails are available to be offered to customers. Find out:
  - if there is a list and if there is, does it give the ingredients?
  - what you should do if a customer asks for details of cocktails and no list is available.
- Find out what you could offer a customer who requests:
  - a brand of lager you do not stock
  - a brand of Scotch whisky which is not available
  - an orange-flavoured liqueur
  - a herb-flavoured liqueur.
- Over a period of one week, make a note of any drink that you are asked for which is not available. Discuss the situation with your supervisor. What action could be taken?

Essential knowledge

It is important that you give your customers accurate information about the drinks you serve them:

- to comply with the Trade Descriptions laws
- to prevent customers becoming dissatisfied, feeling cheated or misled
- to ensure that customers receive an efficient and high-quality service.

Promoting and selling drinks

A skilled waiter/waitress is both an advisor and a salesperson, selling the customer products (food and drink) and offering a professional service. Remember: a satisfied customer will stay longer in the restaurant, come back again and recommend the establishment to other people.

Like a salesperson in any other type of business, you must have a positive approach to selling your products and be alert for opportunities to promote and sell drinks.

Use promotional materials

Any materials used to promote products must be accurate, helpful and clean.

- Wine and beverage lists should be up to date. If a product is not available, you should inform the customer when you present the list.
- Tabletop items such as tent cards, dripmats and coasters should be clean and unmarked. Soiled items should not be reused.

Use a positive selling approach

Positive selling requires you to take the initiative when dealing with the customer. Compare the three approaches below:

Waiter A: 'I don't suppose you will want a drink before your meal, Sir?'
Waiter B: 'Do you want to order a drink before your meal, Sir?'
Waiter C: (Presenting beverage list) 'May I suggest a drink before your meal, Sir. I'll come back and take your order in a few minutes.'

The difference between these three approaches is:

1. Waiter A has a negative approach and discourages the customer from ordering.
2. The customer can quite easily refuse Waiter B and not order.
3. Waiter C is using a positive selling approach. By presenting the customer with the beverage list and giving him time to look at it and perhaps discuss whether or not to order with his companions, Waiter C has made it more likely that the customer will buy. This is an example of positive selling.

The main aim of the positive approach is to encourage customers to buy at times when they might not have intended to or to buy a better quality (and more expensive) product. It is *not* to make customers drunk.

When using a positive approach, your technique should be what is called the *soft sell* approach. At no time should customers feel that they are being pressured into buying. Care should also be taken not to embarrass the customer into ordering more than he or she wants to buy or can afford.

Promote selected drinks at appropriate times

Some types of drink are more suitable at one time than at another. Part of positive selling is to recommend drinks to your customers.

- *Aperitifs* are taken before a meal. You can recommend/suggest:
  wine or wine-based cocktails
  sparkling wines like champagne
  sherry or chilled white port.
- *After a meal* you can recommend/suggest:
  liqueurs or cognac
  certain cocktails, some based on brandy
  speciality coffees.
- *In cold weather* you can recommend/suggest warming drinks such as:
  hot toddies
  mulled wine or punches.
- *In hot weather* you can recommend long, cool drinks such as:
  well-chilled premium beers, e.g. Budweiser, Schlitz, Sol, Rolling Rock
  long mixed drinks/cocktails, e.g. slings, juleps, Pimms and spritzers.

Promotions and special offers

Occasionally, suppliers will run promotions for a limited period on a certain brand when either launching a new brand or trying to increase sales of a particular product.

- Make sure all promotional materials are clean and displayed in the correct position.
- Watch for 'buying signals' such as customers reading the promotional material or asking questions about the product.
- Use positive selling, e.g. 'You must try . . . Everyone who has tried it so far really likes it.'
- Tell your customers about any reduced prices or any offers available to them if they purchase the product.

Be alert for 'buying signals'

You should be alert for openings to offer customers another drink.

- As you walk around the tables, look for customers who have almost finished their drink. A polite, 'May I freshen your drink, Sir?' often brings a repeat order.
- A casual question to a customer about a drink you have served them such as, 'Did you enjoy your cocktail?' or 'Was there enough tonic (soda, lime, etc.) in your drink, Madam?' may also lead to a repeat order.

Liqueur trolleys

Some restaurants use a trolley as a method of dispensing brandy and liqueurs after a meal.

- One method of promoting these drinks is to position the trolley close to customers while they are taking their dessert, so attracting their attention; or to bring the trolley to their table while coffee is being ordered.
- You might also ask customers if they would like brandy or liqueurs served with their coffee. Present the beverage list if one is available.

To do

- Find out how drinks are promoted in your establishment. Look for:
  - tent cards
  - sections on wine lists, menu holders and menu cards
  - coasters and drink decorations, e.g. stirrers.
- Ask an experienced waiter/waitress about the 'buying signals' they look for in customers.
- Ask experienced staff about any positive selling techniques that they have used successfully. Make a note of any which you think you could use.
- Find out from your supervisor/employer if the establishment has a policy for promoting certain types of drinks and what you should do to help promote them.

Preparing for service

There are a number of activities and checks that you should complete before you begin service. It is important that you organise your time to allow completion of these activities before service starts.

Check your tray coverings

It is important to use the appropriate tray coverings, in order to provide a professional service and clean up any spillages. Make sure you have a supply of clean linen or paper napkins to use on trays or salvers and clean, lint-free glass cloths for polishing glassware as well as the normal service linen.

- Handle clean linen carefully, as it is easy to crease or soil.
- Check that you have a sufficient supply for performing any cleaning operations and to replace soiled coverings as necessary during service.
- Make sure that all linen is in good condition and suitable for use during service.

A cloth or paper-covered salver/tray prevents glasses slipping and can absorb spillages. The covering can be replaced if it becomes soiled or stained. Some establishments use cork-lined trays for table drink service and these can serve the same purpose.

Check your glassware

It is important that all the equipment that you use is clean and in good condition. This is especially true of glassware as it comes into contact with the customer's mouth.

If a liqueur trolley is used, check the condition of the glassware before service. Glassware received from a dispense or other bar should be examined before any drink is poured into it.

Before using glassware:

- look carefully for lipstick and other grease smears. Check carefully for cracks in glasses and examine the rim for signs of chipping
- polish the glass using a clean, dry, linen glass cloth. Small glasses used to serve spirits and liqueurs can be polished by:
  1. lifting the base of the glass with a clean, dry glass cloth
  2. placing the bowl of the glass over a bowl of hot water until the steam condenses on the glass. *Never* breathe on a glass to polish it.
  3. polishing the bowl with the other end of the glass cloth. Use a new, dry cloth whenever the first one becomes damp. A wet cloth will not be effective in removing smears and may lead to the glass being damaged.

Check your trays or salvers

Trays or salvers are made of various materials and used for the service of drinks in glasses and for clearing dirty glasses from tables. The trays are round and are usually found in different sizes. The smaller sizes are used to serve a small order of drinks; the larger sizes are used for large orders or for clearing tables. The rim of the tray is usually raised or lipped. All trays should be clean and polished:

- stainless steel trays should be washed in warm water and detergent and polished with a dry cloth
- metal trays should be cleaned with metal polish
- silver salvers should be cleaned with plate powder or an appropriate silver cleaning product
- wooden or plastic trays should be wiped with a damp cloth soaked in a sterilant and polished with a dry cloth.

Metal, wooden or plastic trays and salvers are often covered with a clean napkin or circular tray cloth, but cork-topped trays require no covering. Always follow establishment procedures regarding tray coverings.

Check your equipment

If drinks are to be served at the table, check that you have all the necessary items of equipment and that they are clean and free from damage.

These include:

- openers
- measures
- driptrays
- ice buckets and tongs
- chopping board and fruit knife
- a supply of fresh fruit (e.g. lemons and oranges and bottled fruits such as cherries, onions and olives)
- sugar, cream and spices (e.g. cloves, nutmeg and cinnamon)
- a cigarette lighter or matches.

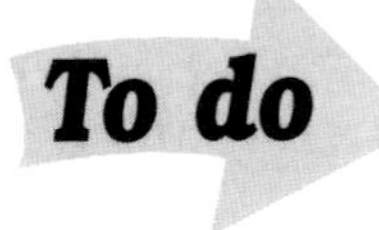

- Find out the procedure for obtaining clean napkins and clean cloths in your establishment. Are there circular tray cloths for use with salvers? Does the establishment use paper or linen types?
- If a trolley is used to serve brandy and liqueurs in your establishment, make a list of the types of glasses on the trolley and the drinks served in them.
- Make a list of the trays and salvers used in your establishment. You should note:
  - what they are made of
  - the sizes available
  - how they are cleaned
  - where they are stored when not in use.

Taking orders at the table

Taking orders from customers in the restaurant or in a lounge area while they wait to be seated can be simple and straightforward when there are only two or three people but quite complicated if large parties are involved.

When taking the order, three points should be kept in mind:

1 each order should be recorded accurately

2 you should be able to serve the drinks (in the best condition possible) without asking each customer what they ordered
3 if the customer is a resident in a hotel, a record of the order may have to be passed to the financial control point (cashier's or receptionist's desk) so that the amount can be added to the customer's bill.

The procedures involved will vary from one establishment to another depending on its size. Follow the establishment's procedures carefully.

Writing the order

The order is normally recorded on a pad which may be either duplicate or triplicate depending on the establishment's size and procedures for stock and cash control.

The check should record all of the following information:

- date
- table number
- number of covers
- room number (if the customer is a resident)
- name, quantity (large, double) and price of each drink ordered
- initials of waiter/waitress or sommelier.

If the customer is a resident of a hotel of which the restaurant is a part, the customer's signature is usually obtained after the drinks have been served.

If you are not familiar with the prices of the drinks ordered, write them on the check when the drinks are being dispensed. An example of a completed order is given below.

Table No. 6 Covers 10

1 x Cointreau	1.75
1 x Drambuie	1.75
2 x Tia Maria	3.50
1 x Hennessy X.O.	5.00
1 x LBV Port	2.50
1 x Irish coffee	2.25
1 x Calypso coffee	2.75
TOTAL:	£19.50

Date 28 Feb 94 Signed EB

An example drinks order

Techniques for recording the order

As you should be able to serve the drinks to the customers without asking them what they ordered, develop a technique which will allow you to record orders in a way which can be used to serve the drinks later. A number of techniques are useful, especially table diagrams and remembering distinctive features.

Table diagrams

This technique involves sketching a diagram of the seating arrangement and recording each drink ordered against the relevant seat.

- Identify the host on the seating arrangement as they are usually served *after* their guests. The host usually asks you to take the order.
- On your diagram, indicate *all seats* even if no order is given for a seat, or you may serve a drink to a customer who has not ordered.

An example of this technique is given below.

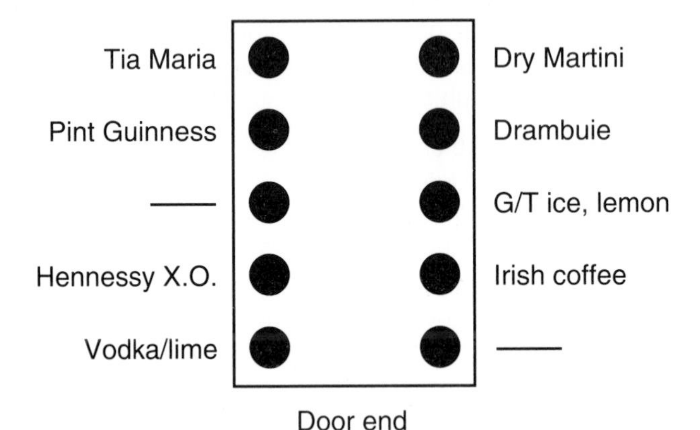

An example table diagram

Distinctive features

This technique involves using some feature of each customer to identify them. The feature is usually some aspect of dress or jewellery. For example: red blouse – Cointreau; gold brooch – Benedictine.

This technique is especially useful when orders are placed at the table, but served in a different area, e.g. the lounge.

Orders using these techniques are not usually written on the check pad – remember, the customer may be signing it – but on a separate pad. The order can then be transferred to the check pad for dispense and customer billing.

Recording accompaniments

Check which accompaniments your customers require with their drinks. Examples of the most common ones are given in the table below.

Drinks and their accompaniments

Spirit/liqueur	*Accompaniments*
White spirits (gin, vodka, rum, tequila)	Offer ice and enquire about cordials (orange, lime, blackcurrant) *With clear mixers* (e.g. tonic or soda water): offer lemon slices *With tequila*: offer lime wedge and salt *With cola mixers*: offer orange slices
Whiskies and brandy	Offer ice Enquire about mixers (water, soda water, dry ginger ale)
Golden and dark rums	Offer ice and enquire about cordials (blackcurrant, peppermint) *With cola mixers*: offer orange slices
Liqueurs	Offer ice, asking whether cubes or crushed ice (frappé) is preferred *Coffee-flavoured liqueurs*: enquire about cream
Pure juices, fizzy fruit drinks and mineral water	Offer ice Offer lemon or orange slices as appropriate *With tomato juices*: offer Worcestershire and Tabasco sauces

Some customers may request additional service features like warming or flaming. For instance, when ordering brandy, a customer may ask for the glass to be warmed, while a liqueur like Sambuca is served with a coffee bean and *flamed*, i.e. the alcohol is warmed and lit with a match or lighter. This can be done with any liqueur.

Recording cocktail orders

The majority of cocktails are made to a standard recipe and the price charged is based on the ingredients and measures used.

- If a customer requests a cocktail you are unfamiliar with, check the list of cocktails available or consult your supervisor.
- If a customer requests different proportions of the ingredients in a cocktail, e.g. in a Dry Martini, make a note of the changes and consult your supervisor about any change in the price.

Follow the establishment's procedures as far as possible.

Check for accuracy

After you have recorded a large or complicated order, repeat the order back to the customer:

- to check that all the drinks have been included, and
- to check that all the required accompaniments have been included.

There are several reasons why you should make sure that you take down customers' orders accurately.

1. The customer will not be happy if they are given the wrong drink. Some may suffer in silence; others may complain after tasting the drink and ask for the correct drink.
2. It will not be possible to recover any part of an incorrect drink if the customer has drunk from the glass or you have added a second liquid, like a mineral or cordial, or ice and lemon.
3. Time will be lost in replacing an incorrect drink and having to readjust the till and change.
4. Having to dispose of an incorrect drink affects your employer's profit.

Wastages and spillages

Details of any drink that cannot be recovered either because the customer has drunk from the glass, the drink has been mixed or because of a fault in the drink (such as a flat beer or mineral) should be recorded into a *spillages or wastage book* which is usually kept at the point of dispense.

- Normally, you would enter the date, the drink, the price, the reason for the wastage and your name.
- You should find out and follow the establishment's procedures regarding wastages or spillages.

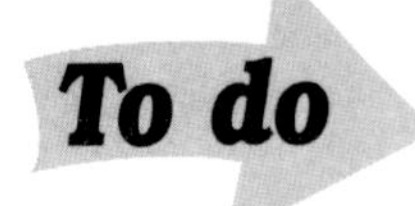

- Find out from an experienced waiter/waitress how they take down large orders. Do they use a 'shorthand' like TM for Tia Maria or DOM for Benedictine?
- Find out how experienced staff take orders at tables. Do they take orders in a clockwise or anti-clockwise direction? What techniques do they use to remember what each customer has ordered?
- Ask your supervisor/employer what you should do if you order an incorrect drink or spill a drink while carrying it or serving it. Ask about a wastage or spillage book.

Obtaining the drinks

Having obtained your customers' orders and recorded these on a check, take the order to the issuing point for drinks in your establishment.

This may be either:

- a dispense bar close to the pantry area of the kitchen
- a bar in the restaurant area
- a banqueting bar
- a bar outside the restaurant area serving, for example, a hotel lounge.

Normally, the top copy of the order on the check pad is given to the barperson who will issue the drinks. However, other systems include orders being recorded in the bar on a separate coloured pad, call-order systems and computer/machine-based systems.

Ordering/dispensing mixed orders of drinks

1. Order/begin dispense of highly carbonated draught products like lagers or Guinness first. The head on these drinks needs time to settle before the glass is topped up.
2. Order/dispense spirits, liqueurs and still wines next. These are not carbonated.
3. Order/pour bottled beers, soft drinks and open mixers like tonic water. These are quite highly carbonated and will lose their head or sparkle quite slowly.
4. Add ice to spirits and other drinks, top up highly carbonated draught products.
5. Order/dispense low carbonated draught products last. These lose their head quickly and you should aim to serve them with as good a head as possible.

Your intention should be to serve drinks to your customers in the best condition possible.

Ordering cocktails

When ordering cocktails, follow the general rules given below:

- if cocktails are included in a mixed order for drinks, the cocktails should be made after the other drinks have been poured. Cocktails should be served as freshly made as possible
- if you have a mixed order for cocktails, you should order the long drinks over ice to be made first and the short, cold cocktails served without ice to be made last. A little melted ice in a long drink is less noticeable than a warm or separated short drink
- glasses should not be filled to the brim. This can make them difficult to carry and serve and could stain the customer's clothing
- remember that a cocktail is a *mixture* of ingredients, so the parts will begin to separate if the drink is left standing too long.

Serving a range of drinks

It is important to know how to carry and load a tray or salver correctly.

- The tray or salver is balanced on the palm and outspread fingers of the left hand, because drinks are normally served and cleared from the right-hand side of the customer. When loading the tray, try to keep the tray in balance.
- Do not load all the glasses and bottles on one side of the tray or it will be difficult to balance.

- Place the heaviest items (e.g. bottles of liqueurs and spirits) above your wrist or close to your body where your arm can give the tray some support.
- When loading a tray of poured drinks at the bar, place the heaviest items (e.g. pints of draught beer) in the centre over the balance point and lighter items around the edges.
- When distributing drinks from the tray, lift the heaviest items first. Do not unload all the drinks from one side only. Keep the tray balanced by lifting drinks from different sides alternately. See the diagrams below.

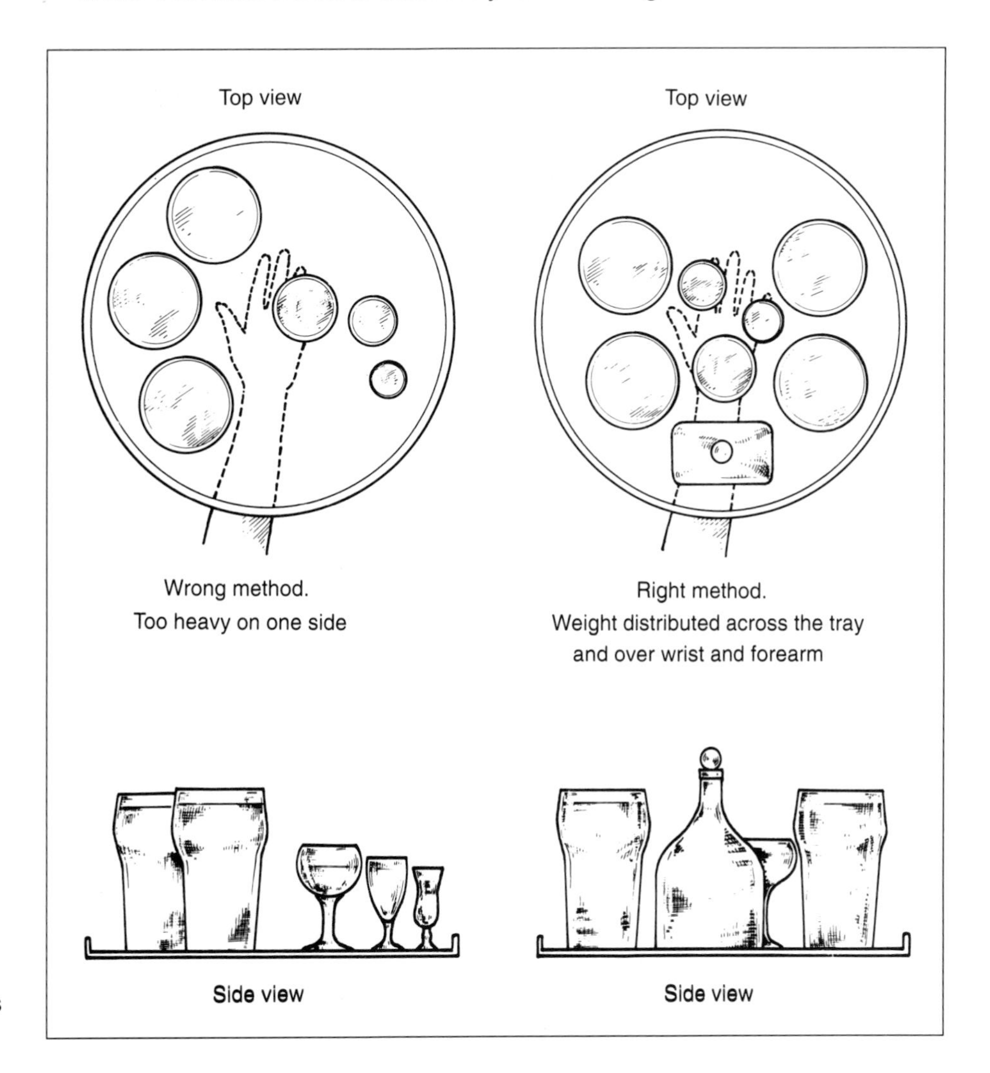

Right and wrong methods of loading a tray

Glassware

When placing or clearing glassware:

- handle stemmed glasses by the stem using the thumb and forefinger. Straight-sided glassware should be held by the base or low down
- do not place or clear glasses by putting your hand over the top of the glass or by putting your fingers inside a glass
- serve all drinks in a fresh glass even if it is a repeat order
- when clearing glasses, do not place glasses inside one another as this can lead to cracking and chipping
- remove glasses from tables as soon as they are empty
- serve or clear glasses to the right of the customer whenever possible.

Examples of the types of glasses used for different drinks and the right and wrong ways of placing and clearing them are shown on the next two pages.

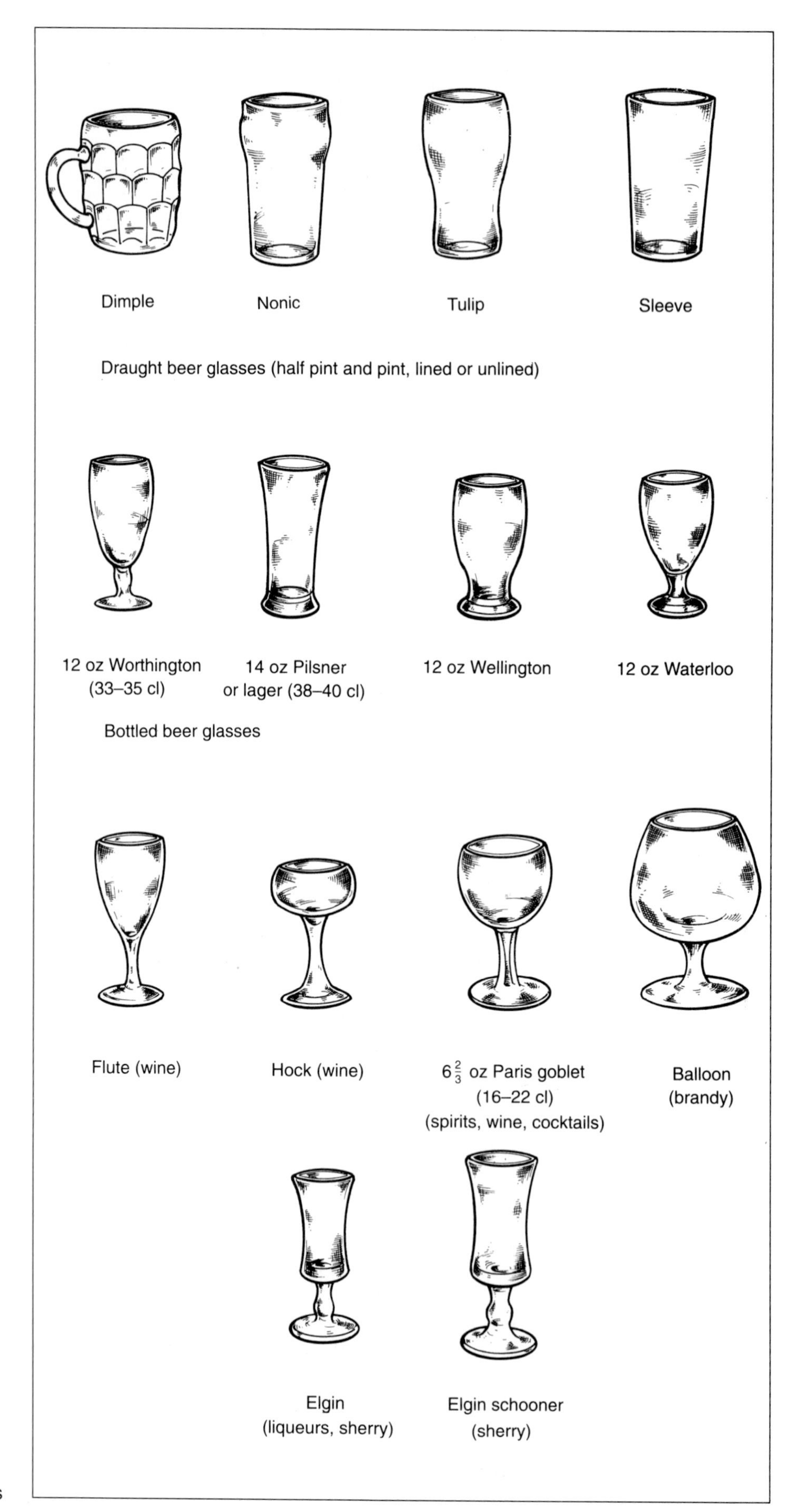

Popular shapes of glasses

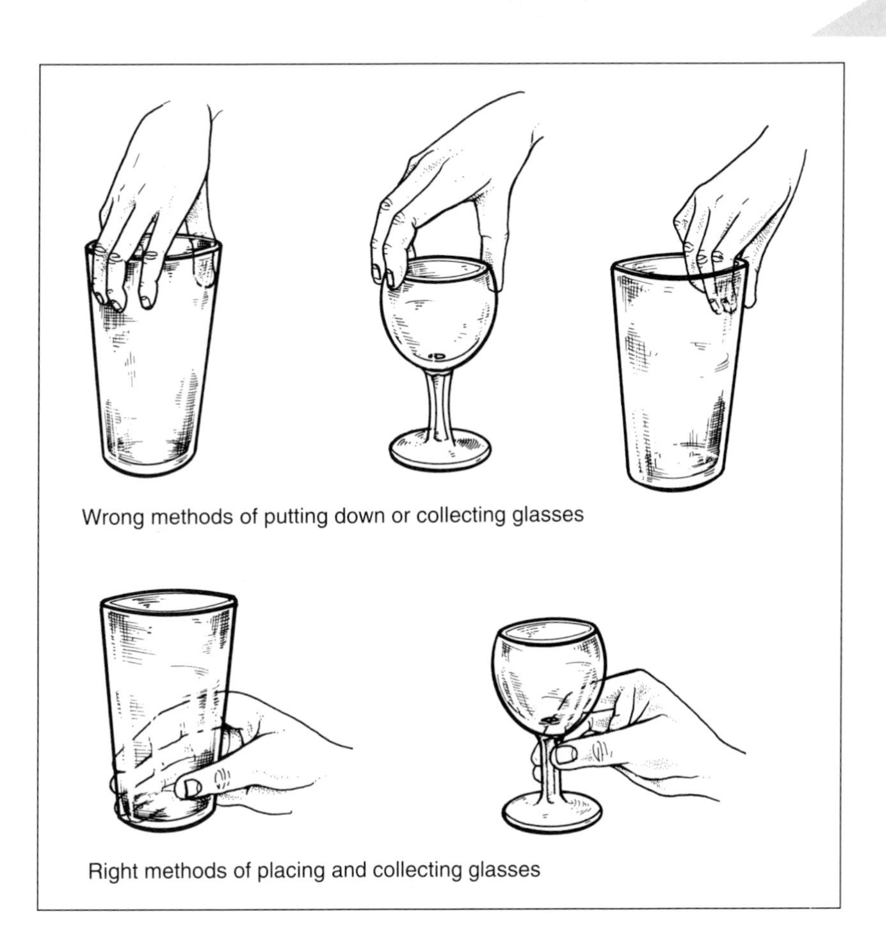
Wrong methods of putting down or collecting glasses

Right methods of placing and collecting glasses

Right and wrong methods of placing and collecting glasses

Serving draught and bottled beers

Draught and bottled beers are poured in the bar before being served at the table.

1. They are served in glasses or tankards which should either:
   - bear a government stamp and a quantity marking, and/or
   - have the required fill level marked by a line on the glass.
2. Ales such as bitter and mild should be be served at a temperature of 12–15.5 °C (54–60 °F).
3. Lagers are served chilled at 7–10 °C (45–50 °F)
4. Highly chilled beers such as Budweiser should be served at 4–6 °C (39–43 °F)

Cold and chilled beers should be served on a coaster as condensation forms on the outside of the glass and runs to the base of the glass.

When serving bottled beers, select a glass which will hold a larger amount than the bottle capacity to allow space for the head. For example, if you are pouring from a half-pint (10 fl oz) bottle, you will need a glass which holds about 12 fl oz. Lagers which are usually bottled in 330 ml bottles should be served in a 14 fl oz (38–40 cl) Pilsner glass.

Serving wine by the glass

The service of wine is dealt with in detail in Unit 2C6: *Preparing and serving bottled wines*. Wine is also sold by the glass and by the carafe in restaurants.

Wine is normally served in a tulip-shaped glass or a Paris goblet containing between 6 and 8 fl oz (18 and 22 cl). A glass marked with a line showing the correct fill height may be used.

White wine is usually served at cellar temperature (about 13 °C/55 °F) or lightly chilled at about 10 °C/50 °F. Red wine is served at room temperature.

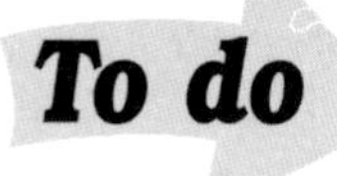

- Find out the procedure for obtaining drinks in your establishment.
  - What written documentation is used? By whom?
  - Do bar staff use a special key on the till for crediting drinks to the restaurant?
  - Who is responsible for taking a record of the order to the cash control point?
- Observe an experienced member of staff giving an order at the dispense point. Ask them if they use any particular sequence when giving the order to the barperson.
- Discuss with your supervisor if the establishment follows the Voluntary Code of Practice for the sale of wine by the glass. What measure is used by the establishment?

Serving spirits

The most popular spirit served in the restaurant is brandy, served after a meal, but other spirits may also be requested either as aperitifs or after the meal. They are often served with mixers or minerals, ice and other accompaniments. A Paris goblet or Slim Jim is normally used.

Obtain your order, then:

- carry the glasses and any bottles of mixers or syphon to the table. As baby bottles of minerals and mixers have a very narrow base, these are sometimes carried below the tray between the fingers of the left hand rather than on the tray. Follow the standard procedure for your establishment
- place the glasses on the table and ask the customer if he or she would like you to pour the mixer for them. If they agree, pour in the mixer steadily until they tell you to stop
- place the bottle on the table if there is any liquid left inside.

In some establishments, mixers are added at the bar. Follow your establishment's procedure.

Brandy

Some customers may prefer to take brandy in the same way as for other spirits (described above). In this case, it should be served in a Paris goblet.

However, if customers request a liqueur brandy after a meal, it should generally be served in a brandy balloon. Customers may request that the glass be warmed for them. If so:

- use hot water to heat the glass. Empty, wipe and polish the glass before pouring in the brandy. *Never* use direct heat (e.g. a flame from a candle or gas lamp) to heat a glass; if the glass becomes too warm, the aromas will disappear very quickly
- name the brandy to your customer when serving it. For example, 'Your Hennessy X.O., Madam.'

Serving liqueurs

Liqueurs may either be obtained from the bar or served directly from a tray or trolley. Various sizes and shapes of glass may be used, and some may have a line etched into the glass to indicate the appropriate fill height. In other cases, a 3 cl glass may be used which is not filled to the rim.

- One advantage of the line glass is that it eliminates the need to wash and clean a thimble measure when several different liqueurs are being served.
- If you are using a thimble measure (for example, when serving from a tray or trolley) have a bowl of warm water and a clean glass cloth ready to clean the measure before you serve a different liqueur.

- When using an unlined liqueur glass, fill it to just below the rim to avoid spillage or to allow flaming.
- Where a trolley is not used, the bottles and glasses can be brought to the table on a large salver. Present the appropriate bottle and pour the correct measure into the glass in front of the customer. Place it to the right of the coffee cup, but not too close to the edge of the table.

Serving cocktails

The two most important elements of the service of cocktails are that almost all are drunk cold and they should be served as fresh as possible.

- Carry them carefully to avoid spillages or dislodging any fruit decorations or garnishes.
- Name each cocktail to the customer as you serve it.
- As condensation will develop on the glasses, they should be placed on coasters or dripmats if possible.

Serving soft drinks

Not all customers will wish to take an alcoholic drink. The main types of soft drinks you may be required to serve are:

1. fruit squashes such as orange or lemon barley, crushes and pure fruit juices
2. natural mineral waters such as Vichy, Evian, Ballygowan or Perrier
3. manufactured minerals (often used as mixers) such as soda or tonic water, dry ginger ale, lemonade and bitter lemon.

Bottled squashes

- Bring a glass, the appropriate squash, ice, wrapped straws in a stand or glass and a stirrer to the table. A jug of water or a soda syphon should also be brought on the tray.
- Place the wrapped straws in their stand on the table and place the clean glass to the right of the customer.
- Pour a measure of the squash into the glass to the customer's requirement. Add ice. Fill up the glass with water or soda water.
- Stir the mixture lightly with the stirrer to disperse the squash.

To serve natural or manufactured mineral waters, pour some into the table glass and place the bottle to the right of it on the table.

Presentation of soft drinks

Soft drinks should be presented well.

- They should be served in an interesting shape of glass.
- Offer ice, lemon and straws with long drinks.
- Add orange slices to colas.
- Add wedges of orange or lemon to the rim of the glasses containing fruit drinks.

Besides fruit garnishes and ice, you should decorate soft drinks with swords, stirrers and miniature umbrellas to give them a cocktail appearance.

Serving hot drinks

Apart from tea and coffee, the hot drink most frequently offered after a meal is some type of speciality coffee. These drinks consist of a base spirit, white or Demerara sugar, hot black coffee and cream floated on the surface. They are often presented to the customer after being made up in the kitchen or bar, so ask if the customer prefers it sweetened or unsweetened when taking the order.

The sequence for making and serving a speciality coffee is as follows:

1. Write a check for whichever spirit or liqueur the customer has chosen and take this to the bar or liqueur trolley. Note that a separate check on the food pad may need to be written and taken to the stillroom in some establishments.
2. Pour hot water into the glass (usually a Paris goblet or a special glass with a handle). If the glass is not heatproof, place a tea or coffee spoon in the glass to prevent it cracking. When the glass is warmed, empty out the hot water back into the jug.
3. Place a spoonful of sugar (white or Demerara according to the customer's requirement) in the glass, leaving the spoon also in the glass. Add the liqueur or spirit.
4. Pour hot coffee into the glass until the liquid is 1–2 cm ($\frac{1}{2}$–$\frac{3}{4}$ in) from the rim. Stir until the sugar is dissolved.
5. When the coffee has stopped revolving, take the spoon and place it horizontally across the glass, until it is just touching the surface of the coffee, with the curved part of the bowl uppermost.
6. Gently pour unwhipped double cream over the back part of the spoon bowl so that the cream floats on the surface of the coffee. The collar of the cream should be 0.5–1 cm ($\frac{1}{4}$–$\frac{1}{2}$ in) thick.
7. Serve the coffee on a small sideplate covered with a doily. A tea or coffee spoon should also be placed on the sideplate.

If the customer is being served in a lounge, provide him or her with a paper napkin as the cream may stick to their upper lip.

Customer billing

Restaurant and residential service

The method for customer billing for beverages depends on the type of control system operated by the establishment. Some examples are given below.

1. In one system, when an order has been taken and delivered, the sommelier or waiter/waitress:
   - writes the price of each drink on the check and totals the bill (the total amount is normally circled)
   - takes the top copy to the dispense point and the duplicate copy to the cash control point (i.e. the cashier or receptionist) where the total bill for the meal and any beverages is made up.
2. If your establishment uses the café system, add the cost of drinks to the cost of the food and total them together at the end of service.
3. When guests staying in a hotel order drinks in the lounge or bar and request to have the cost added to their bill, take a copy of the check to the reception area or billing office and check that the person is really a resident if you do not know them.

   If a guest refuses to sign the bill, ask the head waiter or barperson to initial it to verify the drink has been served.

Lounge service

In normal lounge service, you should advise the customer of the total amount and place any cash on the tray or salver. After the drink has been paid for at the bar, return the change and any till receipt to the customer.

What have you learned?

1 Why does a skilled waiter or waitress need a thorough knowledge of the products he or she sells?

2 What difference to closing time will it make if your establishment holds
- a Supper Hour Certificate or
- a Special Hours Certificate?

3 State the types of persons you should *not* sell alcoholic drinks to in order to comply with the law.

4 Give two examples of offences against the Trade Descriptions Act.

5 What are the four main methods of making cocktails?

6 Give three reasons for providing customers with accurate information about the drinks you serve them.

7 What drinks could you suggest as an aperitif before a meal?

8 How would you clean the following:

- stainless steel trays?

____

- metal trays?

____

- silver salvers?

____

- wooden or plastic trays?

____

9 Why is it important that you take down customers' orders accurately?

____

____

10 How is the bill for drinks dealt with if an establishment uses the café system?

____

____

Extend your knowledge

1 Study the labels on packaged drinks in your establishment. Find out the alcoholic strength of the following:

- non-alcoholic and low alcohol beers
- cider and perry (Babycham)
- port and sherry
- spirits and liqueurs
- ales and stouts
- table wines
- vermouths

2 Obtain a book about spirits and liqueurs such as the *Penguin Book of Spirits and Liqueurs* by Pamela Vandyke Price. Find out the ingredients and flavour of the more popular spirits and liqueurs.

3 Obtain a copy of a guide to making cocktails such as the *International Guide to Drinks*, published by the United Kingdom Bartenders' Guild. Find out the ingredients of well-known cocktails and how they are made.

4 Find out the spirit or liqueur used as a base for the following speciality coffees:

- Balalaika
- Calypso
- Gaucho's
- Kentucky
- Witch's
- Cafe Napoleon
- Caribbean
- Highland
- Monk's
- Yorkshire
- Cafe Royale (French)
- Gaelic
- Irish
- Bonnie Prince Charlie's

UNIT 2C4

Providing a carvery or buffet service

ELEMENTS 1–3: **Preparing and maintaining a carvery or buffet display. Serving customers at the display and maintaining customer dining areas**

What do you have to do?

- Deal with customers in a polite and helpful manner.
- Keep the carvery or buffet table clean, free from damage and correctly positioned for food service.
- Arrange appropriate table linen, utensils and decorative display items, keeping them clean and free from damage.
- Present and display food items appropriately.
- Portion, serve and arrange food in accordance with laid down procedures and customer requirements, using the correct clean and undamaged equipment.
- Replenish food items at appropriate times.
- Keep the carvery or buffet and dining areas tidy and free from food debris.
- Clear customer tables as necessary of soiled and unrequired items and any left-over food or accompaniments.
- Remove soiled table linen and replace it with clean linen as required.
- Store and display food items in accordance with food hygiene legislation.
- Work in an organised and efficient manner to meet daily schedules, causing minimum disturbance to customers.

What do you need to know?

- How to identify customer requirements and provide them with accurate information, promoting establishment products and service.
- Why it is important to replenish and correctly display food items throughout service.
- Why dining and service areas must be kept clean and tidy.
- Why portions should be controlled when serving food to customers.
- Why information given to customers must be accurate.
- How to deal with spillages and breakages.
- Why waste must be handled and disposed of correctly.
- How to deal with unexpected situations.

Attractive presentation is essential when preparing a buffet

Introduction

Carveries and buffets are both types of service where the customers leave their tables to choose from a range of dishes and/or roast joints of meat on display. Customers may either be served by food service staff or chefs (who may stand behind the buffet or carvery) or they may help themselves.

Carvery and buffet types of service require less staff because customers serve themselves; this in turn helps to keep the cost of the meal down. However, as with other types of self-service, it is important that standards of presentation and hygiene remain high at all times.

When providing both buffet and carvery service you need to remain particularly aware of special customer needs: elderly and disabled customers should always be offered extra assistance.

ELEMENT 1: Preparing and maintaining a carvery or buffet display

Carvery service

Carvery service offers the guest the opportunity of choosing a starter and sweet from a table d'hôte type menu and a main course from the carvery display. Customers are greeted and seated by the head waiter or receptionist, the menu is presented and the first course is ordered. After the first course, the customer is invited to the carvery where they choose from a variety of roast meats or vegetarian alternatives. The chef carves the customer's choice of meat and the customers then help themselves to vegetables and accompaniments before returning to their table. After the main course has been cleared, customers order a sweet from the menu.

Positioning the carvery

When positioning the carvery, give careful consideration to the following:

- *access to the kitchen.* You need to be able to carry dishes to and from the kitchen and carvery easily and smoothly
- *space behind the carvery.* There needs to be enough space behind the carvery for staff to move around freely
- *customer access.* Customers should be able to reach the carvery easily, move along to make their selection and then return to their tables easily and safely
- *position of electric sockets.* Portable carvery units need to be situated close to suitable electric sockets.

Preparing the carvery

- Before setting up the carvery table, make sure that the plate warmer or hot cupboard is switched on in plenty of time for the plates to warm before the start of service.
- Check that all plates are clean and free from damage before setting up the carvery table.
- When setting up the carvery, check that there is an adequate supply of plates, carving utensils and equipment, and that these are in a clean and undamaged condition.
- When the main foods are brought to the carvery in readiness for service, check that the appropriate sauces and accompaniments are present.

Presenting and displaying food items and accompaniments

The carvery should be clean and large enough to hold all the food items without overcrowding. Display the food in an attractive manner, bringing it out for display at the last possible moment to ensure that food is in peak condition and to comply with food hygiene legislation. Joints of meat are often displayed under infra-red lamps to keep them hot during service and to improve the display.

Joints are usually positioned at the beginning of a carvery display and nearer to the carver than the customer (to prevent the carver having to lean across the display). Smaller items (such as Yorkshire puddings) are often displayed in front of the joints. The number of joints on display varies according to the establishment, price, occasion, etc.

When preparing the carvery, do not display cold food items such as salads too early as this can cause them to look 'tired'. Replenish food items (including accompaniments) as necessary. This ensures the smooth running of the operation and avoids causing customer delays and dissatisfaction.

Make sure that the carvery and the area around it is kept tidy and free from food debris at all times. This is important to prevent accidents or injury to yourself, your colleagues and customers and to prevent contamination risks.

The carvery menu

This includes a first and third course usually served to the customer at the table, and a middle (second) course where the customer approaches the carvery itself to select a dish. An example carvery menu is given overleaf.

Oven Hot Garlic Mushrooms
with Bread
Mousse of Smoked Salmon & Spinach
Melon Boat Gruyère
Chef's Country Pâté
with Oatcakes or Granary Rolls

* * * * *

Decorated Whole Fresh Salmon
Sugar Baked Decorated Danish Gammon
Roast & Rare Ribs of Beef
Seasoned Loin of Pork
Roast Prime Turkey with Cranberries
Salad Bowls to Include:
Nicoise, Broccoli & Yoghurt,
Tomato Vinaigrette with Dill, Coleslaw,
Waldorf with Carrot, Beetroot,
Curried Rice & Pimento, Egg Mayonnaise

Dressings:
Mayonnaise, French, Thousand Island, Blue Cheese

Breads:
Granary, Sesame Twist, French
Hot Buttered New Potatoes in Season

* * * * *

Apple Strudel
Orange & Lemon Soufflé
Strawberry Shortcake
Hazelnut Cheesecake

* * * * *

English Country Cheeses
with
Crisp Green Apples, Celery, Grapes

Coffee with Cream

Mints & Sweetmeats

An example carvery menu

Food hygiene: carveries

All hot food displayed on a carvery must be maintained and served at a temperature of 63 °C (145 °F) or above, because bacteria are unable to survive at these high temperatures. When working on a carvery, use separate implements for each dish, and ensure dishes remain covered for as long as possible to prevent cross-contamination. Remember the dishes must only be displayed for a maximum of four hours.

Essential knowledge

Food items should be replenished and displayed correctly throughout service in order to:

- maintain speed and efficiency of service
- avoid cross-contamination of foods
- ensure correct temperatures for hot and cold foods
- provide an attractive display.

Buffet service

This method of service is used successfully in a wide range of catering establishments. Customers visit the buffet table, select food items and then either sit down to eat or (at more informal occasions) remain standing.

There are three types of buffet: finger, forked and carved.

Finger buffets

Here customers help themselves to food from a buffet table or choose from food offered on dishes by staff circulating the restaurant. The type of food offered at a finger buffet must be capable of being eaten without a knife and fork; the choice is usually quite varied and can include: sandwiches, rolls, bouchées, canapés and open sandwiches. An informal finger buffet allows people to circulate and is ideal for cocktail parties, product launches and family occasions.

Danish Open Sandwich Selection
prepared on French Bread, Ryebread,
or Pumpernickel as preferred:
Danish Gammon
Smoked Salmon
Seafood
Salami
Beef Remoulade
Herrings
Blue Cheese
Pâté

* * * * *

Deep Fried Chicken Drumsticks
Seafood Barquettes/Seafood Quiche
Pinwheels of Smoked Salmon
Hovis & Asparagus Rolls
Cucumber & Cream Cheese Rings
Assorted Crudités with Spicy Dips

* * * * *

Fresh Cream Gâteau or Pavlova
Chocolate & Cognac Mousse
Dairy Cream
Cheeseboard
with Celery & Biscuits
Coffee with Cream

An example finger buffet menu

Seafood & Avocado Cocktail
OR
Melon with Cream Cheese & Peaches
OR
Hors D'Oeuvres 'CBC'
Granary Roll

* * * * *

Select two from:
Beef Stroganoff
Chicken Marengo
Scampi Provençale
Pheasant Casserole
Veal Fricassée with Cream
Venison & Game Pie with Cumberland Sauce
Coq au Vin
Braised Kidneys Turbigo
Whole Poussin Princesse
Fresh Salmon Pie with Asparagus
A Selection of three fresh Salads
Saffron Rice with Pimento
Baked Jacket or New Potatoes
A Medley of Seasonal Vegetables
Bread rolls – Butter

* * * * *

Sweet Table to include:

Fresh Orange & Grand Marnier Soufflé
Tipsy Trifle
Raspberry Pavlova
Belgian Apple & Cinnamon Flan

Cheeseboard with Celery

Coffee with Cream
Mints & Bon Bons

An example of a hot fork buffet menu

Fork buffets
In this instance, although some seating is provided at unlaid tables, the customers usually stand. They collect their food, a napkin and a fork from a buffet table. Presentation of food is similar to a finger buffet (above) but also includes items which can be eaten with a fork only, such as vol-au-vents, chicken pieces, veal and ham pie, goujons of fish and salad items.

Carved buffets
This style of buffet involves a more formal seating arrangement at tables which have been laid with cutlery appropriate to the menu. The guest visits the buffet table and selects the food he or she would like to eat for each course. When the guest has finished, each course is cleared away by food service staff.

The main course usually consists of decorated joints of meat, poultry and fish, carved at the buffet and served with a selection of salads and accompaniments. This type of service may be adapted according to establishment, customer and menu requirements. It is often used in hotels as a method of serving breakfasts and afternoon teas.

Preparing the buffet

Whichever type of buffet service is being used, there are certain basic principles to follow:

- the buffet should be set up in a *prominent position* in the room
- there should be *enough space on the buffet* to display and present all the food without overcrowding
- the buffet should be *within easy access of the kitchen* and wash-up so that food items may be replenished and dirty plates removed with the minimum disturbance to guests
- there should be *enough room for guests* to circulate freely
- there should be *sufficient occasional tables and chairs* for guests who may wish to sit down
- the *total presentation of the room* should be attractive and promote the correct atmosphere.

Arranging the table linen

Traditionally the buffet table is covered with suitable white tablecloths falling to within 1.25 cm ($\frac{1}{2}$ in) of the floor at the front and sides of the buffet. If more than one cloth is used, the creases should be lined up and the overlaps should run in the same direction: away from the entrance to the room or the main approach to the table (this makes them less noticeable). The ends of the buffet should be *boxed in* either by folding or by use of pins; this gives a more favourable overall presentation.

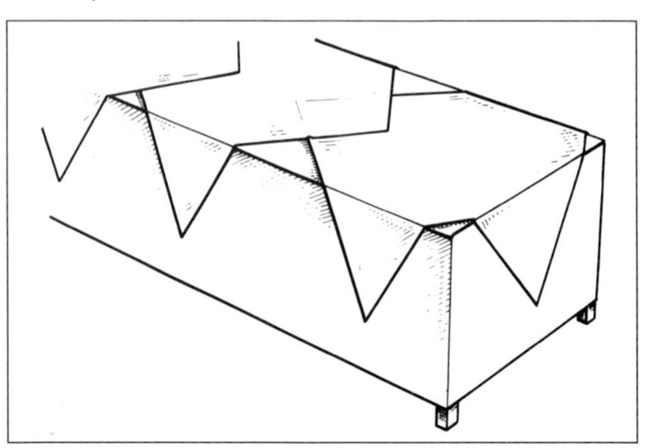

A 'boxed in' buffet cloth

Banquet rolls may also be used, where the required length is cut from the roll and then conveniently disposed of after the buffet has been cleared away. Slip cloths can be placed over the top of the buffet table to provide additional colour contrast to the table.

To do

- Find out what types of buffet are offered by your establishment.
- Find a sample menu of each of the types of buffet mentioned earlier.
- Ask your supervisor to show you how to *box in* a buffet cloth.
- Find out what types of display items are used on carveries and buffets in your establishment.

Arranging food on the buffet

By considering the following points and reaching appropriate decisions you can achieve the maximum effect from a buffet-style presentation.

- Food is displayed in this way to make it look more appetising, so avoid overcrowding the display with overly elaborate arrangements which distract attention from the food.
- Buffet tables usually have a main focal point with food items arranged and displayed around it. Items which are often used as a focal point are flower displays, fruit baskets, decorated hams or ice/butter carvings.

A buffet focal point

- Colour, height and shape can add interest to the buffet table. Try to use a variety of these dimensions to provide contrast without making the buffet look messy.
- Food which is difficult to serve should be positioned where customers can gain easy access to it.
- Hot foods should be positioned towards the end of the buffet so that they do not go cold on the plate while customers are still making further choices.
- In order to maintain the effectiveness of the display, empty dishes should either be removed or replenished as necessary.

Arranging utensils and accompaniments

- Appropriate accompaniments should be placed next to the food items, so that customers can match them to the correct food.

- A sufficient number of clean plates may be arranged either at one end of the table, at appropriate places along the table or on a smaller separate table.
- Depending on the style of buffet, tables will either be pre-laid with cutlery, napkins, condiments, etc. or these will be available at or near the buffet display, usually at the end.

Food hygiene: buffets

The maximum time food may be on display is four hours; after this time any bacteria present could multiply to significant numbers, increasing the risk of food poisoning. Ensure that food is kept at appropriate temperatures prior to service and remember to avoid airborne contamination by keeping foods covered until the last possible moment.

Essential knowledge

Dining and service areas must be kept tidy and free from rubbish and food debris in order to:

- prevent the transfer of bacteria to food
- prevent pest infestation in dining areas
- avoid the risk of fire
- maintain customer satisfaction
- comply with the law.

What have you learned?

1 Why should careful consideration be given to the positioning of a carvery?

____

____

2 At what temperature should hot food be maintained and served?

____

____

3 Why should food items be replenished and displayed correctly throughout service?

____

____

4 Briefly describe the three types of buffet.

____

____

5 Why must dining and service areas be kept tidy and free from rubbish and food debris?

6 Why is it important to consider access to the kitchen and wash-up when preparing a buffet?

ELEMENT 2: Serving customers at the carvery or buffet

Customer requirements

When serving food at a carvery or buffet you are representing your establishment, so it is important that you know how to deal effectively with customers and promote your restaurant's products and services correctly.

Always greet customers politely as they approach the buffet or carvery and be prepared to answer any questions they may have. Some customers may have special dietary requirements, so it is essential that you know what ingredients have been used in the dishes on offer and how they have been cooked. Customers will often want to know which dishes are suitable for vegetarians and which, if any, are low fat.

Essential knowledge

Information given to customers should be accurate in order to:
- ensure efficient customer service is maintained
- ensure that the establishment's products and services are correctly promoted.

Serving food

Before starting to serve food, check that you are familiar with the portion control methods you need to use (see *Portioning food* on the next page) and that you have all the necessary serving utensils to hand in a clean and undamaged condition.

When serving food, take care to arrange food items on customers' plates attractively. Try to place food items on the plate in such a way that the colours contrast in an appealing way. Remember to offer appropriate accompaniments.

Lift the lids from any hot dishes carefully, keeping your head away from the dish; steam rising from the opened dish can cause burns. Always replace the lids when you have finished serving each portion to ensure that the dishes keep hot.

Remember to use different carving knives and forks for each joint, and service spoons and forks for each other item to prevent cross-contamination. If you are unable to leave service utensils in the appropriate dish between serving customers (e.g. because of heat) keep a service plate available for holding them.

As dishes become empty, remove them and/or replenish as appropriate.

To do

- Find out what portion sizes are used in your establishment and the most common way of establishing these when serving.
- Watch your supervisor serving food at a buffet or carvery and notice how they arrange the food on the plate for maximum appeal.
- Find out what dishes are normally offered to vegetarians on buffet or carvery menus in your establishment.

Portioning food

Portion food correctly; this is important for several reasons:
- to maximise profits
- over-filled plates look unattractive and create wastage
- under-filled plates may create customer dissatisfaction
- it is important to ensure that all customers receive similar quantities of each dish.

Establishing portion size

There are several ways to identify the correct food portions:
- use of pre-portioned pies, flans and other food items
- use of measured quantity serving utensils
- use of garnishes or decorations to indicate portions (e.g. a rosette of cream may indicate each portion of a gâteau)
- plate size.

Essential knowledge

Portions should be controlled when serving food to customers in order to:
- control costs
- avoid wastage
- maintain customer expectations and satisfaction.

What have you learned?

1 Describe how you would greet a customer approaching the carvery.

2 Why should portions be controlled when serving food to customers?

3 What methods may be used to ensure portion control?

______

______

______

4 Why should information given to customers be accurate?

______

______

______

ELEMENT 3: Maintaining customer dining areas

Providing an efficient service

Buffet and carvery service usually involves customers leaving their tables, selecting food items from the buffet or carvery and returning to their tables with each course.

However, in certain situations, such as wedding buffets or hotel carveries, it may be necessary to prevent queues forming by 'inviting' individual tables to the buffet while assuring others that you will invite them in a 'moment'.

It is important for food service staff to be aware at all times, particularly at the end of each course, so that plates and cutlery can be cleared away promptly and efficiently along with other table items as appropriate; this should be carried out with the minimum disturbance to customers.

When all the customers have finished their meal, the buffet or carvery should be cleared of dishes, cutlery and crockery. Soiled table linen and breakages should be dealt with in the appropriate manner (see also *Unit 2C2: Providing a table service*, pages 133–54).

Dealing with spillages

If a spillage should occur on the buffet table during service it should be dealt with as quickly as possible to maintain the overall appearance of the display.

1 Remove a liquid spillage by mopping it up using a clean absorbent cloth. Remove a solid spillage (e.g. part of a food item) by scraping or lifting it onto a clean plate.
2 Remove the cloth or plate containing the spillage to the kitchen.
3 Cover the spillage stain on the linen with a clean slip cloth or napkin.
4 Place an old menu card or napkin underneath the slip cloth to help absorb excess liquid.
5 Remove any soiled linen to a service area and deal with it in accordance with establishment procedures.

See also p. 153 on dealing with larger spillages.

Essential knowledge

Waste must be handled and disposed of correctly in order to:
- prevent accidents
- prevent infection from waste
- avoid creating a fire hazard
- prevent pest infestation
- avoid pollution of the environment
- comply with the law.

Working safely

The restaurant must be kept tidy and clean at all times. Check the dining and service areas for potential hazards before service begins, and be aware of any developing problems during service. Waste, whether it is a small spillage, left-over food item, discarded tissue or something larger (such as an empty cardboard box), should be regarded as potentially hazardous. It can cause accidents, contamination, encourage pest infestation and pollute the dining environment. You are legally required to dispose of it safely and correctly.

Remember that you are responsible for your own, your colleagues' and your customers' health and safety. Work safely and efficiently, allocating your time appropriately to avoid any 'last minute rushes'.

Essential knowledge

Dining and service areas must be kept tidy and free from rubbish and food debris in order to:
- prevent the transfer of bacteria to food
- prevent pest infestations in dining areas
- avoid the risk of fire
- maintain customer satisfaction
- comply with the law.

Dealing with unexpected situations

During a carvery or buffet operation, unexpected situations may arise; it is important that you are able to take appropriate action as soon as possible. Make sure that you are familiar with the correct first aid treatment for cuts and burns, either of which might be sufferered by customers or staff. Always inform your supervisor of any accidents and ensure that the Accident Book is completed correctly.

What have you learned?

1 Describe how you would deal with a small spillage on a table.

____

____

2 Why must waste be disposed of correctly?

____

____

3 Why must dining and service areas be kept tidy and free from rubbish and debris at all times?

____

____

4 What should you do if a colleague accidentally cuts themselves?

____

____

Extend your knowledge

1 Investigate how breakfast and afternoon tea buffets may operate and what items would be included on the menu for these occasions.
2 Find out what specialised knives and other pieces of equipment might be used by the carver working behind a carvery.
3 Find examples of buffet menus that would be charged at varying ranges of prices. What kind of items and/or types of service increase costs?

Providing a silver service

ELEMENTS 1–2: Silver-serving food and clearing finished courses

What do you have to do?

- Prepare equipment and items for service.
- Clear courses to satisfy establishment and health and safety standards.
- Portion, serve and arrange a variety of food using the appropriate equipment.
- Check that all service equipment is clean and placed ready for service.
- Identify and meet customers' requirements while causing the minimum of disturbance.
- Clear courses from the table at the appropriate time with assistance from other staff.
- Deal with surplus food and used service equipment in accordance with laid down procedures.
- Carry out work in an orderly and efficient manner taking into account priorities and laid down procedures.

What do you need to know?

- How to deal with customers correctly.
- Why care has to be taken to serve and arrange food correctly.
- What sequence to follow when clearing.
- Why food has to be carefully portioned during service.
- The procedures of service.
- What action to take when dealing with unexpected situations.

Introduction

Silver service, sometimes known as *English service* is a form of table service where the food is served from a flat or dish onto the customer's plate at the table. The food is usually transferred using a spoon and fork, although occasionally the food is served using two forks, two fish knives or some other type of specialist service equipment. Some restaurants have moved away from this style of service, but within the hotel industry as a whole the skill is still required for many occasions. It is almost always used, for example, for a banquet, and for meals in many top class hotels, restaurants and cruise liners.

Silver service has both advantages and disadvantages. The main ones are listed below and overleaf.

Advantages

- Many portions of food can be carried and served by one person.
- Portions can be controlled by the food server.

- The service is flexible, and can be used with a combination of other types and styles of service.
- Customers feel they are getting special service.
- It is a quick form of service when organised, trained staff are used.
- It presents an opportunity to demonstrate quality food, presentation and service.

Disadvantages

- It is more expensive to provide, requiring well-trained staff.
- There may be a high initial cost for specialist equipment (if needed).
- More space is needed between tables, which reduces the number of covers to be served.
- When groups of people are served, the presentation of food to the final guests served can be adversely affected.

Skills

When training to be a silver service waiter you need to develop certain skills in addition to the technical ones required, such as:

- local knowledge (customers may ask you about local facilities, attractions, etc.)
- menu knowledge (customers may need dishes translating or explaining, or may require information concerning special dietary requirements)
- a polite, and courteous manner
- a sense of urgency
- communication skills.

You will generally spend a considerable amount of time in contact with customers, so attention to personal hygiene and customer care is imperative. Remember also that you are the direct representative of the establishment and the person best placed to meet the customers' requirements and needs.

When clearing courses, always act in a professional manner, as this also reflects the standard of the establishment.

Planning your time

A well-planned and efficient service will keep your customers satisfied. When thinking about how to carry out your tasks effectively, take into account both national and establishment procedures, and consider health, safety and hygiene points as well as the task in hand. The following principles will help you to maintain a time-efficient service:

- ensure you are fully prepared for service
- make journeys worthwhile; for example, you could return dirties on a journey back from the restaurant to kitchen/wash-up
- while customers are eating one course, prepare for the next; make sure any necessary cutlery, crockery, glassware is clean and ready
- keep sideboards fully stocked
- coordinate service if serving several tables; for example, serve one table and then clear the next
- before leaving the kitchen make sure you know the portioning of the dishes to be served; this will avoid waste and control costs
- anticipate your customers' needs and time your service accordingly (e.g. serve cold food before hot).

ELEMENT 1: Silver serving food

Preparing for silver service

- Check any dishes or flats to be used for the service *before* service to make sure they are clean and undamaged. If they are to be used for the service of hot food, they must be hot themselves; likewise cold if for cold food.
- When using dishes, prepare underliners of the appropriate size.
- The portioning of food is very important. As the food server, you must be able to identify the number of portions on the flat. Portions can easily be identified if, for example, two slices of meat are garnished on the flat slightly further away from the next two slices. If the portions are not identifiable, you may serve two portions instead of one by mistake and have to return to the kitchen for more. If in doubt, ask.
- Ensure that your sideboard is fully prepared with all necessary equipment and has space for you to place down loaded trays.
- Check that food which has been heated on flats has not stuck to the flats, making service difficult and possibly spoiling presentation.
- The speed of service is very important. An experienced food server could be expected to serve between 10 and 15 customers from one flat for functions and banquets; this means that the food would have to be very hot when coming from the kitchen and the food server would need to serve quickly enough for even the last customer served to have hot food.

Carrying clean plates

Your service cloth

A service cloth is a very important part of your service equipment as well as a part of the food server's uniform. It must be kept clean and ironed at all times and only used as a service cloth for such things as:

- carrying hot plates
- final polishing of plates and cutlery
- wiping small spills
- brushing crumbs onto a service plate
- wiping the underside of plates before placing them on the table
- protection against hot service dishes.

Adjusting cutlery

The adjusting of cutlery is done as soon as the customer's order has been taken or before each course is served. This is to ensure that the cutlery on the table is correct for the dishes chosen. For a table d'hôte cover you would need to remove any unnecessary items from the cover and re-lay any extra items after taking the customer's order. For an à la carte cover, however, you would lay the cutlery required for each course just before serving that course.

Carrying cutlery

There are several points to note.

- You will need a service plate or salver covered with a napkin. Cutlery is placed on the service plate or salver when it is being moved, because this is safer, easier for distinguishing the different pieces of cutlery and more hygienic than carrying it in the hand or pocket. Always tuck the top of knives under any forks for safety reasons.
- You need to work around the table, removing and placing cutlery from the left of one customer, then turning and removing and placing cutlery on the right of the next customer.
- You must not go between two customers who are having a conversation.

Placing plates on the table

Full silver service will require you to place hot and/or cold plates onto the table before serving food items. The method for carrying this out correctly is given below.

- Cover the palm of your hand with one end of your service cloth.
- Place the plates in that covered palm and wrap the rest of the cloth round the plates.
- On reaching the table, wipe the top plate, then pick it up using your thumb and fingers on the rim. Place the plate carefully in front of the customer, bending your knees slightly and leaning gently forward.
- Continue around the table repeating the sequence for each plate. Serve female guests first, working anti-clockwise around the table, then serve the male guests and lastly, the host.
- Place the plates onto the table following any establishment procedures. For instance, if the plates are decorated with a company crest or logo, the plate would normally be placed so that the crest is at the top of the cover.

Technical silver service skills

Silver service is a skill which can be learned quickly, but needs practice to acquire competence. Occasionally you will need to use some specialist service equipment, but your principal items of service are the service spoon and fork.

Using a serving spoon and fork

- With the curve of the fork in the bowl of the service spoon, hold both handles in the palm of the hand.
- Push your first finger between the handles so pinching the fork between your finger and thumb.
- By making a slight adjustment to the holding position, you will be able to keep the spoon supported while being able to lever the fork open and closed.

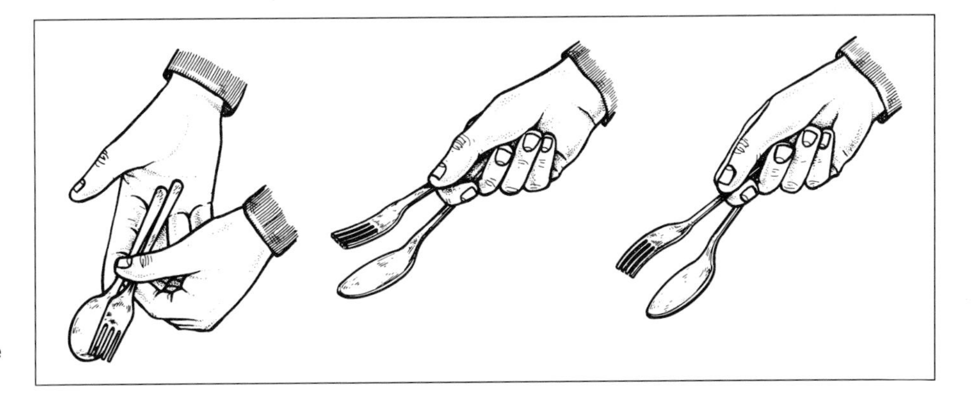

Holding a spoon and fork for silver service. Far right: the fork is inverted to serve round objects

Useful tips

If the fork is inverted (i.e. with the prongs facing down) it is easier to serve round objects such as potato; while peas, for example, need only the spoon. For delicate flat items, such as fish fillets or omelettes, two splayed-out service forks or fish knifes are sometimes easier to use. Some dishes involve special service equipment such as tongs, sauce ladles, etc.

To do

- In order to become a competent silver food server you will need to practise and master the skills of using the service spoon and fork. Select different sized items of various types to simulate food items and practise picking them up and placing them down, adjusting the spoon and fork as necessary.
- Use an old customer order to practise adjusting cutlery at an empty table.

Performing silver service

1. Hold the service flat or dish on the palm of your left hand cushioned by your service cloth. (If you are left-handed, hold the dish in your right hand.)
2. Present the dish to the customer/s before actually serving, generally while standing to their left (see *Service side* below). By doing this you allow customers to admire the dish fully arranged and decorated, and to confirm it is the one ordered. If lids or cloches are used take care when lifting them off as condensation can drip onto a customer or the tablecloth.
3. Bring the flat or dish to the level of the customer's plate and hold it just over the rim.
4. Carefully lift the food with the spoon, using the fork to hold the item and then place it on the customer's plate. Transfer any garnishes in the same way.
5. If a sauce or gravy is on the flat, this can be served by tilting the flat and using just the spoon to serve the sauce or gravy.
6. On completion, thank the customer and move on to the next.

Service side

There is no hard and fast rule on which side of the customer you should serve from, although each establishment has its particular procedures and rules. There are however, two methods that may be adopted in part or full:

- *English service*: all food is served from the left and cleared from the right. All beverages are served and cleared from the right
- *Continental service*: plates and glasses are placed from the right; coffee and food from the left; drinks are served from the right; and all items are cleared from the right.

There are occasions when a food server should be allowed to judge this for themselves; for example, if a customer is sitting next to a wall, it would be wrong to ask another customer to move so that the server had room to reach. However, it is important to be consistent to avoid confusing the customer.

Service priorities

The following points need to be considered when determining priorities of service:

- serve female guests first and the host last
- serve hot food on hot plates, cold food on cold plates
- warn customers of hot plates
- serve cold food before hot food
- do not touch food on the plates
- serve accompaniments (e.g. sauces) as soon as all other food items have been served
- serve from the left unless establishment procedures or seating positions require you to act otherwise
- if a customer asks for a larger portion than allowed, serve the normal portion to that customer and place a supplementary order. Do not serve another guest's portion, leaving them to wait
- use clean cutlery for each food item.

Talk to your customers and take note of their likes and dislikes. If you do your job well they are more likely to return to the restaurant on another occasion. As a food server your work includes public relations, sales and marketing through efficient service.

Serving particular dishes

Serving soup

Before serving soup you will need to lay the correct cover: soup spoon for soups, dessert spoon for consommés.

For one portion of soup an individual soup tureen is often used.

1 Approach the customer from the left, holding the soup tureen on a service salver or underliner and the soup bowl and its liner on your forearm.
2 Place the soup bowl (with liner) in front of the customer, then position the service salver so that it just covers the rim of the soup plate.
3 Keeping the service salver level, pick up the individual tureen, move to the edge of the service salver and pour slowly into the soup bowl away from the customer. The tureen is placed on an underplate/flat to act as a drip plate so preventing any spillage going on the table or customer.
4 Return the tureen to the sideboard and offer the customer the appropriate accompaniments.

For multiple portions of soup a large soup tureen would be used. The soup would then be served, using a service ladle, at the sideboard or from a service table (guéridon) at the table, and the soup bowls then carefully placed in front of the customer.

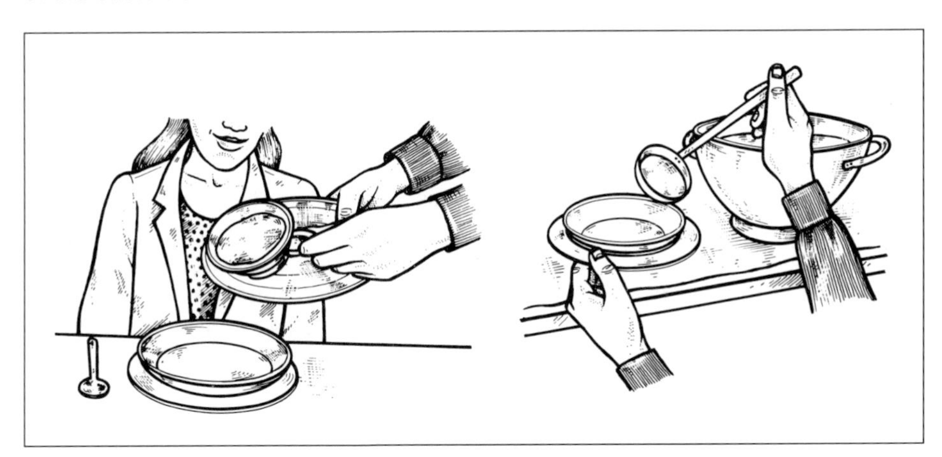

Left: serving soup from an individual tureen. Right: serving multiple portions of soup from from a large soup tureen

Serving fish and large or delicate items

Before serving fish, check that the correct cutlery has been laid; i.e. a fish knife and fork. When serving, you will sometimes find that fish fillets or large thin slices of meat are difficult to serve with a spoon and fork and it may be necessary to adopt one of the following options:

1 use two forks or two splayed fish knives
2 cut across the middle with your service spoon, serve and reassemble on the customer's plate remembering arrange it attractively.

Serving meat or poultry

Before you start, check that the correct cutlery has been laid; i.e. a joint knife and fork with a hot joint plate for hot food, and a cold plate for cold food.

1 If some cold dishes have been ordered take them to the sideboard or serve them first.
2 Approach each customer from the left and present the dish. The customer can then see the presentation work of the chef as well as seeing the completed dish from the kitchen.
3 Lower the service dish or flat so as to slightly cover the rim of the joint plate.

4. Using your service spoon and fork, place the meat portion onto the customer's plate at the 'six o'clock' position along with any garnish. If there is a sauce or gravy on the flat, tip the flat slightly forward and use your spoon to serve the sauce.
5. If more than one portion of meat is being served from the same flat, rotate it so that the portion to be served is nearest the plate each time. If the meat portion is correctly positioned there should be plenty of room for any potatoes and vegetables.

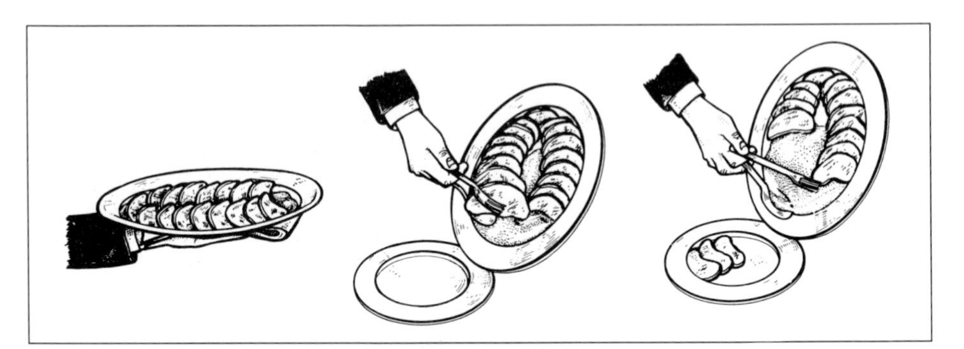

Serving meat

Serving potatoes and vegetables

The general rule is to serve potatoes before vegetables, although each establishment will have its own procedures.

1. Place the serving dish on a salver or service plate.
2. Have a separate service spoon and fork for each different type of dish to be served.
3. Present the dish, then lower the service dish so as to slightly cover the rim of the customer's plate.
4. Using your service spoon and fork, serve each potato dish starting from the far side of the customer's plate and working your way back. Remember to rotate the dish as you serve each item with its own service equipment.
5. Once the potatoes have been served, use the same procedure to serve the vegetables.

Once you are practised and competent, service time can be speeded up by placing the potatoes and vegetables onto a large service salver or underflat. In this case, you would serve from the front of the salver or flat and then rotate it, to bring the next type of vegetable to the front of the flat before serving it.

Serving potatoes and vegetables

Essential knowledge

Care has to be taken to serve and arrange food correctly in order to maintain:
- cost controls
- the attractive appearance of dishes
- customer satisfaction.

Accompaniment sauces

The sauce should be served from a sauce boat placed on an underplate with a ladle.

1 Position the sauce boat so that it is over the rim of the customer's plate and pointing towards it.
2 Take a ladle full of sauce, then run the under-edge of the ladle on the side of the sauce boat to remove any drips which may otherwise fall on the cloth or customer.
3 Pour the sauce gently over the portion of meat. (Note that for certain dishes the sauce should be poured to the side of the plate.)

Ladling gravy onto food

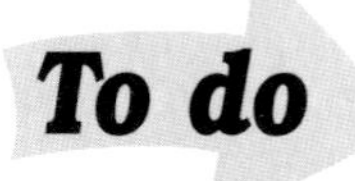

- Watch experienced food servers serving soup in your restaurant, noticing equipment and techniques used.
- Ask your supervisor what implements are used in your establishment for serving fish and large or delicate items.
- Practise serving, using different items which are similar in size, shape and weight to the food items you might serve.
- Practise ladling liquid from a sauce boat to a dish.

Serving cheese

Before serving cheese, check that the correct cover is laid and that the correct accompaniments are placed on the table: i.e. a side plate and side knife, a dish of butter, celery and cruets. Other accompaniments may be offered according to establishment procedures. Check that you have a clean knife for the service of each cheese.

1 Present the cheese board from the customer's left-hand side.
2 When the customer has made their choice, rest half the board on the table edge while holding the other half in your hand; this will give a firm base for cutting as well as freeing a hand to cut with.
3 Cut a portion of the chosen cheese and place it onto the customer's plate using the double prongs on the cheese.
4 Offer a selection of cheese biscuits or place a selection on the table either in a basket or on an underplate.

When cutting cheeses, care should be taken to achieve the correct portioning so as to satisfy the customer while controlling costs. For each type of cheese there is a special method of cutting; see the illustration on page 145.

Serving cheese

Essential knowledge

Food must be carefully portioned during service in order to:

- control costs
- avoid wastage
- maintain customer expectations and satisfaction.

Plating food from a side table or trolley

This type of service is a little easier as both hands are free, allowing you to hold a piece of service equipment in each hand. This is helpful when serving or arranging delicate items such as hors d'oeuvres, pies, puddings, flans and gâteaux.

- Collect all the equipment required for service before starting to serve.
- Wheel the service table or trolley to the customers' table, positioning it so that they can see the tasks have been carried out. Besides serving and arranging food, these tasks could include carving and jointing of meats, filleting of fish, the making of salad dressings or the portioning of desserts.
- Present the dish/es to the customers.
- Working quickly, serve each customer by transferring the portion from the dish to the customer's plate together with any accompanying garnish.
- Pick up the plate by the rim and place it carefully in front of the customer.

Plated service (from side trolley to table)

Service and timing

In order to maintain customer satisfaction and ensure a speedy and efficient service, the timing of service is critical. The following points will help to maintain a smooth, time-efficient service:

- place any cold accompaniments required onto the table before serving
- as soon as possible after taking the order, serve the first course
- inform the customer if there are going to be any delays
- as soon as everyone has finished eating, clear that course
- take the dessert order promptly
- suggest coffee and liqueurs after the dessert course has been cleared.

Unexpected situations

The type of unexpected situations that might occur during silver service are covered in Unit 2C2: *Providing a table service*, pp. 152–4.

What have you learned?

1 Why is the adjusting of cutlery carried out?

2 What points need to be considered when deciding on priorities of service?

3 Why must food be carefully portioned during service?

4 Why should you take care to serve and arrange food correctly?

5 Why are dishes presented before they are served?

6 How can the service spoon and fork be held to make it easier to serve round items?

7 How can the service of fish fillets be made easier?

8 What point on the plate is meat placed?

9 How can a cheese board be supported for the service of cheese?

ELEMENT 2: Clearing finished courses

When to clear

Each course should be cleared once all of the customers have finished eating. If the host of a party is known, clear their plate last. Clearing should be systematically carried out round the table.

At a function, where a large number of people are eating together, the supervisor will give a signal for clearing to start.

Clearing main courses

1. Approach each customer from the appropriate side; this is usually the right.
2. Lean forward slightly and take hold of the plate by the rim; remove the plate from in front of the customer, leaning back and away as you do so.
3. Turn slightly away and back from the customer (so that you are out of his or her vision). Put the plate into your other hand with your thumb on top, two fingers underneath, and the other fingers held back and pointing upwards (see the illustrations on p. 149).
4. Scrape any left-over food items to the front of the plate and arrange the knife and fork at right angles to each other with the knife blade tucked under the bridge of the fork. This prevents the cutlery from sliding around or falling to the floor.

Carrying dishes and underplates

5 Remove the second plate as before, but this time place it on the platform made by your held-back third and fourth fingers, thumb base and inside wrist, checking its balance as you do so.
6 Place the second knife under the fork on the first (lower) plate.
7 Scrape any food items forward onto the first plate.
8 Place the second fork with the first on the lower plate.
9 If more plates have to be cleared, continue as above, collecting only as many plates as you can safely carry. While scraping and stacking always turn away from the customers.
10 Once you have collected all the plates and stacked them neatly onto your forearm, move the first plate with all the debris, knives and forks onto the other (top) pile.
11 Hold the whole pile with both hands and remove it to your sideboard or wash-up area.

Clearing plates or dishes with liners

This procedure is much the same as above, except that there is another plate or dish to stack in each case.

Once the second plate is in position on the forearm (Step 5 above), the cutlery from the first dish is moved up and into the second dish, then the second dish (holding the cutlery) is placed onto the lower dish leaving a liner plate on the forearm.

Clearing dishes with liners

The sequence is repeated until all dishes are cleared. The lower stack can then be placed on to the forearm, collected into both hands and removed to the sideboard or wash-up area.

Clearing by salver

On some occasions it may be appropriate to use a salver to help with clearing. The salver is held in one hand and the cleared plates stacked onto it.

Key points

- Clearing should be done as quietly as possible; noise can unsettle customers.
- If there is a lot of debris, clear a few plates at a time; large piles of waste can become unsightly.

- Carry out clearing as quickly as possible, making as few visits to the table as you can. Working with assistants as a team will help give speed and efficiency of service.
- If you do drop something when clearing, do not bend over to pick it up while you have plates stacked; remove them to the sideboard or wash-up then return to pick up the item.
- Each time you clear a course, look at the table to check that the cutlery and crockery is in order for the next course. If it is not, correct it before serving the next course.

- Practise clearing two or three plates without food, until you feel confident that you can do it without dropping cutlery or plates or spilling waste.
- Notice how often cutlery is cleared or changed during a meal in your restaurant.

Crumbing down

Crumbing down is a task that is normally carried out after the main course has been cleared although it should be done whenever the table needs it, whichever course has been cleared. The purpose is to remove crumbs and debris from the table. The items of equipment needed are a service plate and a service cloth. After the course has been cleared:

- approach the customer from the left-hand side
- position a service plate just under the table lip
- working from the centre of the cover position, use a folded service cloth or small brush to brush any crumbs onto the service plate
- If a à la carte menu has been served, there will not be any cutlery left on the table. However, if a table d'hôte cover has been used the dessert spoon and fork will be at the top of the cover: move the fork down to the left-hand side of the cover
- move round to the right-hand side of the customer and repeat the same crumbing down procedure. On completion move the dessert spoon down to the right-hand side of the place setting for a table d'hôte cover.

When the service cloth is not in use, hold it with your fingers under the service plate. During the whole crumbing down procedure do not reach across a customer: if this is unavoidable, excuse yourself first.

Clearing other table items

Ashtrays

If during the meal an ashtray is dirty yet not being used it must be changed or removed. To do this you will need a service plate or salver with a napkin on top and a clean ashtray.

To change or remove an ashtray:

- approach from the nearest point to the ashtray
- stand side on to the table holding the salver in the hand furthest away from the table
- hold the clean ashtray upside down in the other hand and place it on top of the dirty ashtray
- pick up both together (this will prevent cigarette or cigar ash from being blown onto the table) then place them onto the salver
- return the clean ashtray to the table, turning it up the right way
- before moving across the room, cover the dirty ashtray with the napkin.

Glasses

As courses are cleared, and depending on the wine served, it may be necessary to clear glasses. If you need to do this, approach the table from the right-hand side of each customer and pick up the glasses by their stems or bases. Place them on a salver before removing them to the sideboard, wash-up or bar area.

Condiments, accompaniments and table decorations

Condiments and accompaniments for each dish should be removed when that course is cleared. Cruets are normally left until the main course is cleared. Table decorations, in most cases, are left throughout the meal although some establishments remove them before coffee is served.

Maintaining sideboards

It is important to keep the sideboard clear throughout service and at no time to allow debris, dirty crockery and cutlery to be on the sideboard at the same time as dishes to be served. This would increase the risk of contamination and food poisoning.

What have you learned?

1 What action should you take if you drop an item during the clearing of a course?

2 When is crumbing down carried out?

3 Why should you cover a dirty ashtray with a clean one when removing the dirty ashtray from the table?

4 When should you begin to clear a table?

Extend your knowledge

Although silver service is regarded as the higher standard of service, flambé work is the most impressive to watch and requires a skilful and informed performer. By working through the list below you can begin to build up your knowledge of this skill.

1 Find out what the term *flambé* means.
2 Look through a catering equipment supplier's brochure. Find the pieces of equipment required for a basic flambé operation and cost them out.
3 Find out what principle characteristics must be present in food items to enable them to be cooked at the table.
4 What precautions need to be considered before flambé work can be carried out?
5 Apart from flambé, what other work is carried out in front of the customer at a gueridon?
6 What is *Canard à la presse* and how is it done?

UNIT 2C6

Preparing and serving bottled wines

ELEMENT 1: Preparing and serving bottled wines

What do you have to do?

- Deal with customers in a polite and helpful manner, attending to them without unnecessary delay.
- Promote wines to customers, giving them accurate information as required.
- Present and serve wines, meeting customer requirements.
- Serve wines at the correct temperature using the appropriate equipment.
- Carry out all work in an organised and efficient manner taking account of priorities and laid down procedures.

What do you need to know?

- What type of customers may not be served alcoholic drinks.
- How to identify customer requirements correctly.
- How to deal with unexpected situations.
- All relevant legislation and establishment procedures.

Introduction

Most restaurants now offer wines with meals, whether their list consists of a small number of wines given under the dishes on the menu, or an extensive number of wines on a separate wine list. Only the more expensive restaurants, however, employ one or more wine waiters (or *sommeliers*). This means that as a food server, you need to know not only how to serve these wines, but also how to promote them, by acquiring a good working knowledge of the wines served in your establishment. This unit will introduce you to the basic categories and characteristics of wine, together with the techniques you will need to prepare and serve wine in a restaurant.

Legal requirements

When serving wines you will need to be familiar with the relevant legal requirements, i.e. certain details from the following legislation:

- licensing legislation
- weights and measures legislation
- trade description legislation
- health and safety legislation
- food hygiene legislation.

Details of these are given in *Unit 2C3: Providing a table drinks service* pp. 155–78. You will also need to be familiar with all relevant company procedures that operate alongside these requirements.

Essential knowledge

In order to comply with the law, the following types of customers may not be served alcoholic drinks:

- any person on licensed premises that you suspect is under 18 years of age or any person attempting to buy a drink for them
- any person in a restaurant or area put aside for table meals whom you suspect is under 16 years of age
- any customer requiring service outside licensing hours
- any customer acting in a drunken, violent or disorderly manner or under an exclusion order.

Dealing with customers

When dealing with customers, remember that you are the most direct link they have with your establishment, and you are therefore a representative for the company. At all times be polite and helpful, offering assistance without delay when appropriate.

As the person responsible for the sale and service of wines, you play an important part in promoting the wines on offer. Customers may appreciate some help or advice in selecting wines to drink with their meal, and you will need to be able to give them accurate information on types available, their

Always be ready to give advice or assistance

flavours, prices, origins and the wines that best complement the dishes they have chosen. However, remember at all times that the customer should be allowed to make their own choice of wine, even if the choice seems inappropriate to you (see *Food complements* on p. 216).

In order to provide this information you will need to familiarise yourself with your establishment's wine list, learn how to interpret wine labels and, over time, build up a general knowledge of wine and the food it complements. A *sommelier*, or wine waiter, would be expected to have a thorough knowledge of wines available; if your establishment employs some one in this capacity, try to learn more about wines from him or her by watching them work. If a customer asks for advice which you are unable to give, refer to your sommelier or supervisor for assistance.

The wine list

The wines available in your establishment will have been chosen both to cater for a variety of customer needs and tastes, and to complement the menu on offer in both style and price. Many establishments today feature one or two low-alcohol or non-alcoholic wines, in response to changes in drink-driving legislation and concern over health issues. Many also feature a 'wine of the month', which promotes a particular wine or wine region for a limited length of time (e.g. Beaujolais Nouveau when it becomes available on the third Thursday in November).

THE HOUSE WINES

WHITE WINES	*glass*	*bottle*
Paul Bocuse	2.25	7.95
Sauvignon Blanc, Portal del Alto 1991, Chile	2.45	9.75
Semillon Chardonnay, Crazies Hill 1992, Australia	2.45	10.95
RED WINES	*glass*	*bottle*
Paul Bocuse	2.25	7.95
Cabernet Sauvignon, Santa Helena 1990, Chile	2.45	9.75
Cabernet Sauvignon, Hamilton Estate 1991, Coonawarra, Australia	2.45	10.95

THE MAIN LIST

Chardonnay, Hamilton Estate 1991, McLaren Vale, Australia	11.95
Villa Antinori 1991, Tuscany, Italy	12.55
Chardonnay Tiefenbrunner 1992, Alto Adige, Italy	13.95
Sauvignon, Château Thieuley, 1992, Bordeaux	13.95
Sauvignon Blanc Pask 1992, Hawkes Bay, New Zealand	14.50
Chardonnay, Hawk Crest 1991, Napa Valley, California	16.45
Sancerre Paul Prieur 1991, The Loire Valley	18.75
Chablis Domaine des Manants JM Brocard 1991, Burgundy	18.75
Chardonnay Cloudy Bay 1991, Marlborough, New Zealand	22.50
Rioja, Marquės de Cáceres 1989	12.95
Shiraz Cabernet, Crazies Hill 1990, Barossa Valley, Australia	13.95
Merlot, Carrascal 1985, Bodega Weinart, Argentina	15.45
Julienas Claude Joubert 1991, Beaujolais Cru	15.75
Shiraz Leconfield 1991, Coonawara, Australia	15.80
Cabernet Sauvignon, Hawk Crest 1989, Napa Valley, California	16.45
Chianti Classico Reserva Villa Antinori 1989, Tuscany, Italy	16.85
Chateauneuf du Pape Domaine de la Roquette, Brunier Frères 1989, The Rhone Valley	19.95
Connetable de Talbot 1988, 2nd wine Ch. Talbot St. Julien	24.75

HALF BOTTLES

David Marie NV Brut Champagne 14.50

Sauvignon Blanc Ashbrook 1991, Barossa Valley, Australia	8.25
Sancerre Paul Prieur 1991, The Loire Valley	9.95
Chablis Domaine des Manants JM Brocard 1990, Burgundy	9.95
Cabernet/Merlot St. Hallett 1989, Barossa Valley, Australia	8.45
Chateau Malescasse 1989, Cru Bourgeois Haut Medoc	8.75
Chianti Classico Reserva Villa Antinori 1989, Tuscany, Italy	9.45

PINK WINES

Cotes de Ventoux, la Vieille Ferme 1992, The Rhone Valley	11.25
Sancerre Paul Prieur 1990, The Loire Valley	18.75

DESSERT WINES

	glass	*bottle*
Muscat Beaumes de Venise, The Rhone Valley	2.95	14.95
	glass	*bottle*
Vino Santo, Villa Antinori, Tuscany, Italy	2.95	14.95

MINERALS

	small	*large*
Hildon House Still	1.45	2.45
	small	*large*
Hildon House Sparkling	1.45	2.45

An example wine list

The wines available may either be listed on a separate section of the menu, on a blackboard alongside dishes of the day, or in a separate wine list. The wine list, in whatever form, is effectively a piece of sales literature, and it is through this that the restaurant promotes the sale of its wines. Most wine lists contain the following information:

- the name of the wine
- a brief description of the country and region of origin
- the wine's main characteristics (i.e. whether it is white, red, rosé, sparkling, sweet, dry)
- the price per bottle, per ½ bottle, per carafe or per glass
- the reference number, called the *bin number*, which is given for ease of ordering.

The wine list may be divided by countries and their wines or by wine colour or type (e.g. house wines, white, red or rosé wines, sparkling wines and champagne, fortified wines). We discuss the various categories and types of wine in the next section.

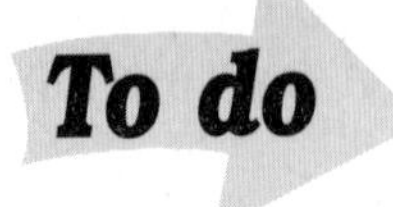

- Re-read Unit 2C3: *Providing a table drinks service*, with special reference to the legal conditions under which you may or may not serve wine.
- Go through your establishment's wine list with your sommelier or supervisor, asking them to point out which wines are sold most frequently and why.
- Find out if your establishment has any special wine promotions planned. If so, ask your supervisor how to help promote this particular wine or wines.

Types of wine

Wines are distinguished by colour (red, white, rosé), by their sparkling or still quality, by their year (vintage or non-vintage), and by how dry or sweet they taste. They are also said to be *light*, *medium* or *full-bodied*. Finally, there is a group of wines known as *fortified wines*. All of these types and distinctions are discussed below.

Colour

Remember that whatever the colour of wine, it should always be a clear, bright liquid. If it is cloudy it should not be served, as this indicates either that the wine contains sediment which has been shaken up into the wine or that there is something more fundamentally wrong with the wine.

- **Red:** Red wine is made from black grapes, and the grape skins are left in the fermentation (i.e. during production) as the wine is being made to achieve the rich colour. Young red wines are usually a purple shade of red, while older wines tend towards a redder brown. As a general rule, most red wines are dry, although there are a few exceptions.
  Examples include: Bordeaux wines (e.g. clarets such as Médoc or Graves, St Emilion) and Burgundies (e.g. Nuits St George, Beaujolais) from France; Chianti and Valpolicella from Italy; Rioja from Spain; Dão from Portugal; Shiraz from Australia; Zinfandel and Cabernet from the USA. (Note that the wines of North America often take their names from the main grape variety used for the wine.)
- **White**: White wines can be made from any colour of grape (or even a mix), but when black grapes are used the skins are removed as soon as pressing is complete, to ensure that the wine remains white. The actual colour range

of white wine includes a colourless liquid to a honey or even light brown colour, with some of the younger wines having a green tinge.
Examples include: Bordeaux wines (e.g. Entre-deux-Mers), Burgundies (e.g. Chablis, Pouilly-Fuissé) and Loire wines (e.g. Muscadet and Sancerre) from France; Frascati and Soave from Italy; Riesling and Liebfraumilch from Germany.

- **Rosé**: Rosé wines are usually made from black grapes, where the grape skins are only left in the fermentation for a short time to achieve the pink colour. Occasionally rosé wine is made by blending a small amount of red wine with a large amount of white wine.
Examples include: Anjou Rosé and Lirac Rosé from France.

A selection of wines; from left: Hawk Crest Chardonnay (USA); Villa Antinori (Italy); Marqués de Cáceres Rioja (Spain); Leconfield Shiraz (Australia); Paul Prieur Sancerre (France); Bollinger Champagne (France)

New world wines

Note that many North American, Australian and New Zealand wines are named after the European areas that produce the same type of wines. You will therefore find wines from these countries labelled chablis, graves, burgundy, hock and claret.

Sparkling wines and champagne

Champagne, famous as a celebration drink, is only produced in the Rheims district of France. The name is jealously guarded and cannot legally be applied to any other type of wine. Almost all champagne is a a crystal clear, sparkling white wine, although a small amount of pink (rosé) champagne is also produced.

Sparkling wines produced following the champagne method but made in other regions of France or in other countries are said to be made by *méthode traditionelle*; this is then indicated on the label. Other methods for making sparkling wines include *cuve close*, the *transfer method* and *carbonation*.

Examples of sparkling wines include: Sekt (from Germany), Cava (from Spain), Asti Spumante (from Italy), St Peray (from France).

The sparkle of these wines and champagne is achieved by trapping the gas produced during fermentation; in champagne this is trapped in the bottle, while in sparkling wines it is usually trapped in the large sealed tanks in which the wine is fermented. This gas is also produced during the making of still wines but is allowed to escape.

Vintage wines

Wines which have been made from a single year (and therefore a single harvest) are known as *vintage wines*. The harvest in these cases was an exceptionally good one, and the year is always included on the label.

Non-vintage wines, on the other hand, are wines made from poor harvests blended with surplus wine from better years. In this case the label does not display the year of production.

Fortified wines

These wines are given added strength either by the addition of grape spirit (e.g. sherry, port, Madeira, Marsala) or by the addition of grape spirit, sweetened with sugar and flavoured with herbs and spices (e.g. Martini, Cinzano). The latter type of fortified wines are also known as *vermouths* and occasionally as *aromatised* wines.

Fortified wines are often requested as *aperitifs* (drunk before the meal) or *dessert wines* (drunk after the meal). Their alcoholic content is approximately 20 per cent. They are also often used as a cooking ingredient because of their strong flavour.

A selection of fortified wines

Wine characteristics

Dryness or sweetness

During the fermentation of dry wines, all the sugar is consumed by the yeast, leaving a dry taste. In sweet wines, however, some sugar may remain in the wine after the yeast has died, leaving a distinctively sweet taste (e.g. Sauternes).

Body

Wines are referred to as being *light, medium* or *full-bodied.* This relates to the alcoholic content and flavour or fruitiness. A full-bodied wine would have a high alcoholic content (upwards of 12 per cent vol) which causes the wine to 'sit heavily' on the palate, and a full, strong flavour. A light-bodied wine has a lower alcohol content (below 12 per cent vol) and a lighter, less pronounced flavour. A medium-bodied wine is one that is felt to lie midway along this range.

Bouquet

This refers to the smell of the wine. It is also known as the *nose* or *aroma.* After the label, the bouquet provides the taster with the most information about a wine. An experienced wine taster can determine the origin, grape content, age and character of a wine by testing its bouquet.

The table below lists the principal grape varieties used for wine-making and their associated bouquet.

Grape varieties and their associated bouquet

Grape	Associated bouquet	Wine example
Pinot Noir	Strawberries, cherries, plums	Red Burgundy, Champagne
Cabernet Sauvignon	Blackcurrants	Red Bordeaux (claret)
Gamay	Strawberries	Beaujolais
Chardonnay	Ripe melon, fresh pineapple	White Burgundy, Champagne
Sauvignon Blanc	Gooseberries	White Bordeaux, Sancerre
Riesling	Apricots, peaches	Hocks, Mosels

When serving wine, notice if any unexpected smell comes from the opened bottle. A smell of vinegar or mustiness would indicate a problem and the wine should not be served.

Flavour

The flavour, or taste, of the wine should confirm the promise of the bouquet. When judging flavour, an expert will consider dryness or sweetness (see above), fruitiness, acidity or bitterness, the body (see above) and possibly the tannin content. Wines high in tannin have been produced to improve with ageing, while those low in tannin should be drunk while young (e.g. Beaujolais Nouveau).

- Find two examples each of red, white, rosé and sparkling wines from your wine list.
- Compare the prices of vintage and non-vintage wines on your wine list.
- Find out which fortified wines are regularly drunk as aperitifs in your establishment. Are they served alone or with mixers?
- Go to a wine tasting (these are often held by wine merchants). Ask for help in tasting the difference between light, medium and full-bodied wines, and in distinguishing bouquets/grape types.

Bottle and label information

Much of the information you will need can be gained from learning how to recognise bottle shapes and how to interpret the label. Note that the standard size for a wine bottle is 75 cl, while a half bottle normally holds 37.5 cl. Champagne is also available in a range of larger bottles, from a magnum (the equivalent of 2 bottles) to a Nebuchadnezzar (the equivalent of 20 bottles).

Bottle recognition

The shapes of bottles often relate to the types of wine they hold. For instance, Bordeaux wines (both red and white) are square shouldered, while Burgundy wines (both red and white) have a more gently sloping shape. Other distinctive shapes include wines from Alsace, Provence, the German Hock and Moselle

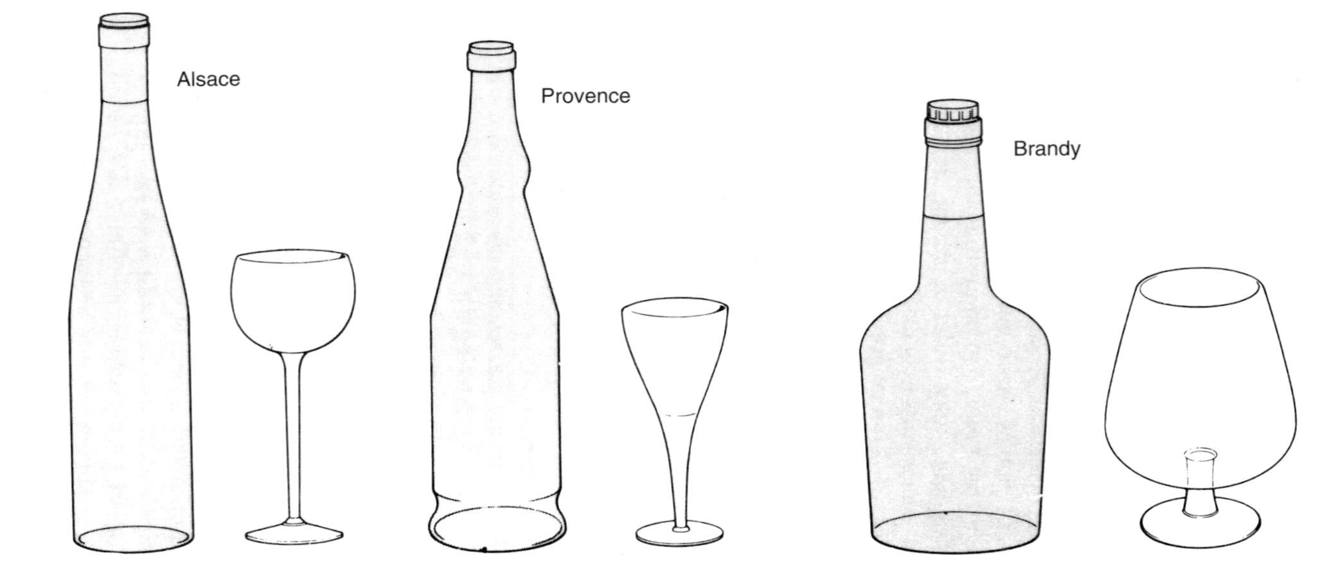

Example wine bottles and glasses

regions and Chianti (see the illustration on p. 214). Wine that is said to have similar characteristics to these wines is bottled in a similar way; for instance a Spanish wine believed to have Burgundy-type characteristics would be bottled in the distinctively sloping-shouldered shape.

Information from the label

The label will provide you with the following information:

- the name of the wine
- the country and region of origin (on non-blended wines)
- on a vintage wine only: the year the wine was made (a non-vintage [NV] wine will not display a date)
- the alcoholic strength (in percentage by volume: % vol)
- the quantity of wine contained in the bottle (normally 75 cl)
- the trademark or name and address of supplier/bottler.

Common label terms

English	French	German	Italian	Spanish	Portugese
Dry	Sec	Trocken	Secco	Seco	Seco
Medium	Moelleux	Lieblich	Amabile	Semi-dulce	–
Sweet	Doux	Suss	Dolce	Dulce	Doce adamado
Sparkling	Mousseux	Schaumwein	Spumante	Espumoso	Espumante
Lightly sparkling	Pétillant	Spritzig	Frizzante	Petillant	–
White wine	Vin blanc	Weisswein	Vino bianco	Vino blanco	Vinho branco
Red wine	Vin rouge	Rotwein	Vino rosso	Vino tinto	Vinho tinto
Rosé wine	Vin rosé	Schillerwein	Vino rosato	Vino rosado	Vinho tosado
Vintage	Vendange	Hauptlese	Vendemmia	Vendimia	Colheita

You will also need to be familiar with certain other definitions that might appear on the label:

- **vin de table** (table wine); a wine of low to moderate quality that may be made up of a blend of wines from more than one country of the EC (European Community), with an alcoholic content of at least 8.5%
- **vin de pays**; French country wines typical of their region with an alcoholic content not less than that specified by the region. Slightly better quality than vin de table

An example label

- **AOC** (*Appellation Origine Contrôlée*); quality wines from a defined area of France (which might be as large as a region or as small as an individual château)
- **VDQS** (*Vins Délimité de Qualité Supérieure*); very good second-quality wines (i.e. just below AOC status) from minor districts of France
- **QmP** (*Qualitätswein bestimmte Anbaugebiete*); the highest quality German wines
- **DOCG** (*Denominazione di Origine Controllata e Garantita*); the highest quality Italian wines.

Food complements

It is generally accepted that certain types of wine complement certain types of food, for instance most people would choose a red wine to drink when eating red meat. However, these are not hard and fast rules; many 'experts' disagree with them in certain instances, preferring occasionally to drink sweet white wine with lamb, for instance. When reading through the suggested complementing food and wines below, remember that the customer may prefer a different combination to those suggested, and they should never be made to think that their choice is 'wrong' in any way. Always accept the customer's choice, but be ready to give help and advice when requested.

Dishes and their complementary wines

Type of dish	Type of wine	Example wines
Fish		
(fried)	Dry, full-bodied white wines	Alsace Riesling, White Burgundy, White Jura
(in sauce)	Full-bodied, sweet white wines	Barsac, a kabinett Hock
(shellfish)	Dry white wines	Chablis, Pouilly-Fuissé, Muscadet, Frascati
Lamb and beef	Red wines	Burgundy, claret, Chianti, Chinon, Zinfandel, St Emilion, Côtes du Rhône red
Pork and veal	Medium white wines	Liebraumilch, Graves
Chicken and turkey		
(roast)	Light red wines/medium rosé wines	Beaujolais, Chinon rosé, Corbières rosé
(cold)	Light white wines /dry rosé	Alsace Riesling, Côtes de Provence white, Côtes de Rhône white, Moselle
Game (duck, hare)	Full-bodied red wines	Burgundies, claret, Chianti, Rioja
Cheeses*	Dry red wines	St Emilion, Pomerol, Hermitage Red, Médoc, Mâcon red, Bordeaux red
Desserts	Sweet white wines or sparkling wines	Sauternes, Trochenbeerenauslese/ champagne (demi-sec), Asti Spumante

*Traditionally, port is served to accompany Stilton cheese

Fortified wines

Some fortified wines are best drunk as aperitifs; i.e. they are consumed before the meal to stimulate the appetite. Sherry and vermouth are typical examples.

Brandy and liqueurs may be served at the end of the meal, sometimes accompanying coffee. Port is often served with cheese (see the note to the table above).

Wine temperature

Wine needs to be served at the correct temperature to bring out the full flavour and bouquet. The following temperatures are those generally accepted as correct:

- *dry white wines and rosé wines*: 7–12 °C (43–54 °F)
- *semi-sweet white wines, champagne and sparkling wines*: 7–10 °C (43–50 °F). Note that sparkling red wines are usually served chilled
- *red wines:* room temperature, i.e. approximately 18 °C (65 °F). Some customers prefer light red wines (e.g. Beaujolais Nouveau) to be served slightly colder, at approximately 10–12 °C (50–54 °F).

Restaurants often keep a stock of white wines in a refrigerator set to 8–10 °C (47–50 °F). Note that temperature changes should always be achieved slowly; never place white or rosé wines in a freezer, nor red wines in a hot cupboard or on a hotplate. If you do need to raise the temperature of wine quickly (if, for instance, a customer requires a red wine to be served above the normal service temperature), warm a decanter and slowly pour in the wine, allowing the heat to transfer slightly from the decanter to the wine.

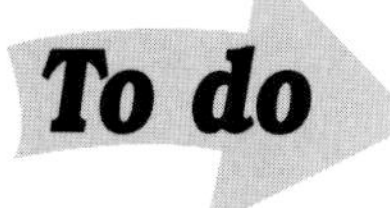

- With permission from your supervisor, inspect your establishment's wine stock, noting the different shapes of bottle according to wine type.
- Compare the labels on at least four different types of wine. What information have you gained?
- Ask your supervisor to go through your establishment's menu with you, recommending wine to accompany the various dishes. Make a note of these for future reference.
- Find out how wine is chilled in your establishment.

Equipment for preparing and serving wines

You will need to use several pieces of specialised equipment for presenting and serving wine, although the actual types used will depend on your establishment. Make sure you are familiar with all the necessary equipment and know how and when to use it.

An ice bucket

Ice buckets or wine coolers

These are used for keeping white or rosé wines cool once the glasses have been filled for the first time. However, they might also be used when a customer prefers the wine to be at a lower temperature than for normal service, in which case the ice bucket can be used to chill the wine further, rather than just maintaining the temperature. In this case, remember that a mix of water and ice will lower the temperature more quickly than ice alone.

The bucket or cooler needs to be deep enough for the ice or ice and water to reach the shoulder of the bottle. When serving wines at the table, either place the ice bucket in a stand beside the table, or place it on top of a napkin-covered plate on the table (to the right of the host's cover), depending on establishment procedures.

Carafes and decanters

Old, red wines collect (throw) a sediment at the bottom of the bottle which should not be disturbed before the wine is drunk. In order to avoid this, the wine may be *decanted* or *cradled* (see below).

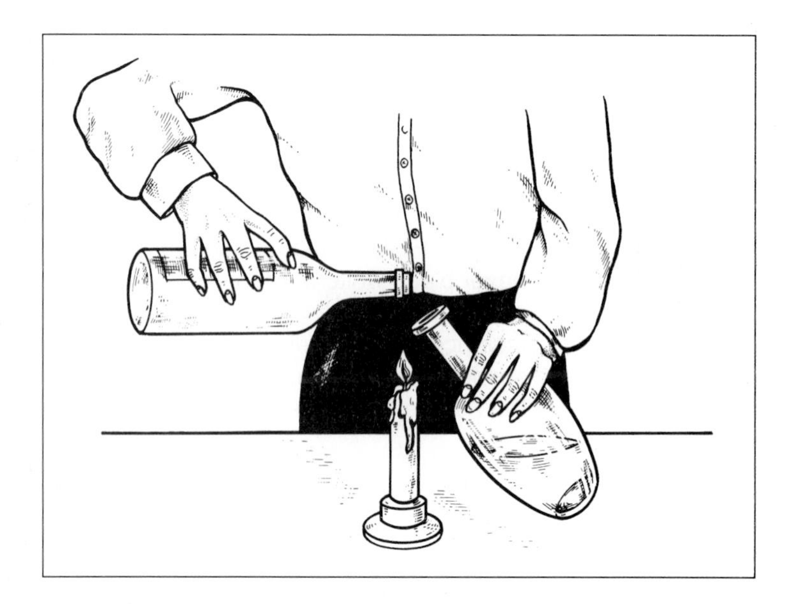

Decanting wine over a light so that the sediment is visible as it approaches the neck of the bottle

To decant wine:

1 Prepare a clean decanter at room temperature.
2 Uncork the bottle of wine without shaking it or disturbing the sediment, then wipe around the top of the bottle with a clean cloth.
3 Lift the bottle carefully, bringing the top of the bottle level with the top of the decanter and resting it there.
4 Raise the bottle slowly until the wine begins to pour slowly into the decanter. Watch the liquid running through the neck of the bottle: as soon as this becomes at all cloudy, stop pouring.

A wine cradle

Wine cradles

Some customers prefer their wines to be served in the bottle, so that they are sure it is the wine they selected. For this reason, wines that would be expected to have a sediment may be *cradled*, i.e. moved from the cellar to the table without any real change of position. This is done by placing the wine in a napkin-lined basket (or cradle) in the same (almost horizontal) position that the wine held in the cellar.

Care must be taken when serving to prevent the sediment from being disturbed and spoiling the wine.

Corkscrews

The three main types of corkscrew used are the waiter's friend (or lever corkscrew), the winged corkscrew and the screwpull corkscrew (see the illustration overleaf). The waiter's friend is most commonly used, because it fits neatly into a pocket, and it contains a small knife for cutting through the foil on the wine bottle. This foil, or capsule, must be cut away before the cork can be removed. To do this, cut around the foil just below the glass lip of the bottle

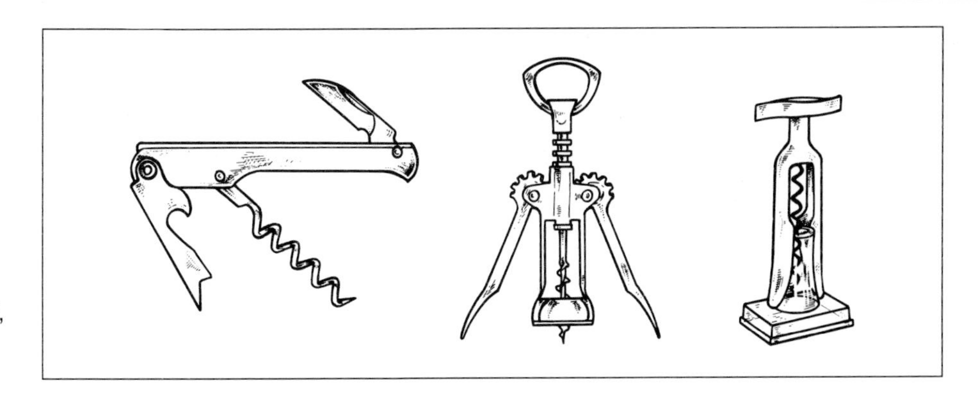

From left: a waiter's friend, a winged corkscrew, a screwpull corkscrew

(see illustration below) with a small sharp knife (such as that found on the waiter's friend) and then wipe around the lip of the bottle with a clean dry cloth before beginning to withdraw the cork.

Key points

When using corkscrews, note the following points:

- turn the screw clockwise through the cork, working gently and smoothly to prevent disturbing the wine or damaging the bottle
- do not allow the corkscrew to go right through the cork; always stop short of the bottom of the cork to prevent pieces of cork from falling into the wine
- when using a waiter's friend, use the lever against the bottle lip to help retract the cork

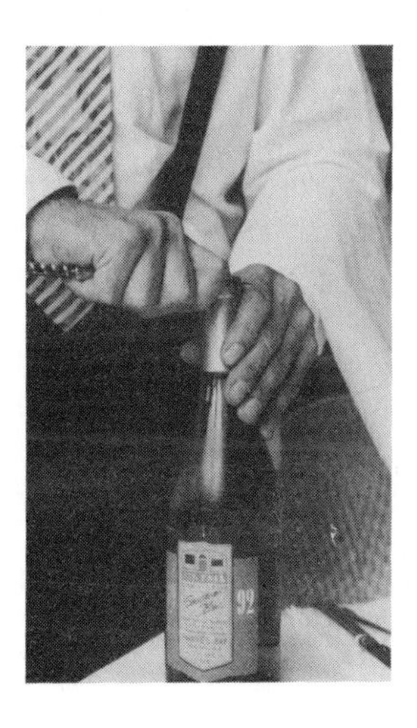

Left: cut through the foil. Middle: use leverage to pull out the cork. Right: wipe the mouth of the opened bottle.

- gently pull the cork out of the bottle until approximately 10 mm ($\frac{1}{2}$ in) is left in the bottle, then twist your thumb and fingers to release the cork completely. This prevents any jerking movement which might disturb the wine
- once the cork has been removed, wipe around the top of the bottle with a clean, dry cloth to remove any traces of cork. Check that there is no unpleasant smell coming from the cork
- never hold the wine bottle between your legs or under your arm when extracting the cork.

Glassware

- Wine glasses should generally be clear in colour, except when a German white wine is being served (in this case brown or green stemmed glasses may be used).
- The shape of the glass chosen for drinking wines should enhance the wine's colour, bouquet and taste.
- The top of the bowl of a wine glass should be tapered, curving inwards to 'trap' the bouquet.
- The bowl of the glass should be larger for wines that need to be swirled in order to encourage the release of the bouquet (e.g. red Burgundies).
- The glass should be stemmed, so it can be held without warmth from the hand transferring to the wine, so raising the temperature. White wine is therefore traditionally served in glasses with longer stems.
- Champagne and sparkling wines should be served in glasses with narrow bowls to prevent the bubbles from dissipating.
- Brandy is traditionally served in balloon glasses. The large bowl allows the guest to wrap their hands around the glass, warming the brandy and releasing the bouquet.

See also Unit 2C1: *Preparing and clearing areas for table service* on the handling of glasses, and Unit 2C3: *Providing a table drink service* for further information on glassware.

Serving cloths

There are many points at which you will need to use clean serving cloths during the preparation and service of wine:

- *when presenting wine*: hold a clean serving cloth under the wine as you present it in your hand to the customer, making sure that the label is clearly visible at all times. If using a cradle, make sure it is lined with a clean service cloth before placing the wine inside and presenting it to the customer
- *when uncorking wine* (see p. 219)
- *when lifting a bottle of wine from an ice bucket*: dry the bottle with a clean serving cloth before pouring. This cloth should be kept at the side of the wine cooler for use each time the bottle is lifted out
- *when serving wine*: hold a clean, folded cloth in your empty hand. As you finish pouring each glass you should gently twist the bottle neck to avoid drips, but should any form on the bottle neck these can be wiped away with the cloth
- *while waiting as the host tastes the wine*: hold the cloth directly under the bottle as you stand to one side of the host
- *when serving red wines*: after pouring, place the folded cloth on a clean sideplate and position the wine bottle on top. Place the plate near the host's right-hand side, with the label facing towards him or her.

To do

- Find out if decanters are used in your establishment. If so, watch your sommelier or supervisor decanting a bottle of wine; notice the equipment and techniques used.
- Find out what type of corkscrews are used in your establishment. Make sure you know how to use them correctly.
- Ask your supervisor to show you which wine glasses should be used for the wines on your wine list. Make a note of these.

Taking the wine order

- Offer the opened wine list to the host for an order to be taken (note that the host may invite one of their guests to make the selection). If the wine is to be served as an accompaniment to food, present the wine list from the right-hand side after the food order has been taken.
- Allow customers time to make their choice, while not appearing to abandon them. They may need to ask for assistance in making their choice. If you do have to leave them, reassure them that you will return shortly and apologise for the delay when you come back to take their order.
- Be ready to offer information about any wines your establishment is trying to promote, and answer any queries the customers may have. If you are unable to provide the information they need, refer to your sommelier or supervisor.
- Be patient when customers are indecisive or change their minds.
- Take the order, recording the information accurately onto the check. Remember to record the bin number and the amount ordered (one bottle, one glass, etc.).
- If the wine is to be served with a meal, ask the host/guests when they would like the wine to be served. If it is to be served alone, prepare it for service immediately.

Taking the wine order

Presenting wine

Before presenting wine, make sure that you have everything you need:
- the correct glasses on the table
- the appropriate equipment for holding the wine (e.g. cooler, cradle, decanter)
- a corkscrew
- a clean serving cloth

and that the wine is at the correct temperature.

Presenting wine in the bottle

Wine in the bottle is usually presented against the white background of a serving cloth (as shown in the illustration below) with the label facing uppermost. Present the wine to the host so that the label can easily be read. Confirm that this is the wine ordered by mentioning it by name. For example, you might say to the host, 'Your Beaujolais Nouveau, madam'. Always present an *unopened bottle*, in case you have accidentally brought the wrong wine to the table, and handle the wine carefully to prevent any sediment from being disturbed.

Once approved, the wine can be removed to the sideboard and opened. Note that white and rosé wines may be opened while in the cooler or ice bucket.

Presenting wine

Presenting wine in a cradle or decanter

Before serving decanted wine, present the empty wine bottle and cork to the host when you bring the decanter full of wine to the table. This acts to reassure the customer that the wine in the decanter is the wine from the bottle, and therefore the wine he or she ordered. As you actually serve the wine, you should tell each guest the name of the wine being served.

When presenting wine in a cradle it is particularly important not to shake the bottle in any way. Present the unopened bottle in the cloth-lined basket, with the label uppermost, to the host by standing to their right-hand side. Once the wine has been approved, either place it on the guest's table or remove the bottle to the sideboard and then open it carefully, retaining the angle that the bottle has been held at since being removed from the cellar.

Opening wine bottles

Refer to *Corkscrews* on p. 218 for details on opening still wine using a corkscrew.

Champagne and other sparkling wines require a different method of opening, as given below.

1. Lift the wine from the ice bucket, dry it with a clean serving cloth and present it (label uppermost) to the host.
2. Place the bottle on a flat surface. Cut the foil just under the wire and remove it.
3. Put the thumb of your left hand on top of the cork and wire, and gently untwist the 'tie' of the wire. Loosen the wire around the bottle neck.
4. Lift off the wire muzzle with one hand, keeping the thumb of your other hand pressed down against the cork.
5. Lift the bottle, holding it at an angle of 45°, with the top pointing away from the table and not towards any one in the room.
6. Firmly grasping the base of the bottle with one hand and keeping your other hand fully around the cork, slowly twist the bottle until the cork begins to ease out. Let the cork out slowly, keeping the bottle at a 45° angle until it gently pops out.

Make sure that you are standing with quick and easy access to the host's glass in case the wine should fizz over. As with still wines, make sure there is no unpleasant smell from the cork.

Serving wine

Once the bottle has been opened, begin service by pouring a small amount of the wine into the host's glass for approval. Stand to the right-hand side of the host, and, keeping the bottle label uppermost and clearly visible, pour a sample amount in the glass. This 'taster' allows the host to check that the wine is in good condition and at the correct temperature, and to test bouquet, flavour, etc.

When the host has given approval you may serve the remaining guests. Female guests are usually served first, and you would normally work anti-clockwise around the table, by moving to the host's right. Serve the woman to the host's right and then the other female guests, working anti-clockwise around the table, and then serve the men, still working anti-clockwise around the table. Lastly, return to the host and fill their glass to the correct level. It is customary to fill wine glasses between a half to two-thirds full, to allow the bouquet room to gather at the top of the glass.

Key points for pouring wine

- Stand to the right of the person whose glass you are filling.
- Hold the bottle with the label uppermost, making sure you are not obscuring it with your hand.
- Place the lip of the bottle just over the edge of each glass, without touching the glass and tilt the bottle neck downwards to achieve a steady flow.
- As you finish pouring, ease the bottle back up, giving it a little twist to the right as you do so, to prevent any drips. If the bottle does begin to drip, wipe the lip of the bottle with your serving cloth before going on to serve the next guest.
- Never lift a glass to the bottle; always bring the bottle to the glass.

After service

When the host has been served, you need to leave the wine on or near the table, depending on what type of wine and presentation has been selected.

- *Chilled wine*: return this to the ice bucket or cooler which should be positioned to the right of the host. Place a clean, folded cloth over the bottle neck.
- *Red wine, carafes or decanters*: place the wine on a cloth-covered sideplate on the table to the host's right (near their wine glass), with the label facing towards him or her. The cork is also often left on this sideplate.

Refilling glasses

While serving in the restaurant generally, you will need to remain aware of guests' wine requirements. When you notice that most of the guests at a table have nearly-empty glasses, return to the table and refill as necessary. When the bottle is empty, ask the host politely whether another bottle is required. Note that empty white and rosé bottles are generally replaced upside down into the ice bucket when empty.

Planning your time

Always work in an organised and efficient manner, taking account of priorities and laid down procedures. Make sure that you have everything you need before beginning to present or serve wine so that you will not suddenly have to leave the table. Check your establishment procedures for chilling or warming wine, and make sure the wine you need is at the correct temperature for service.

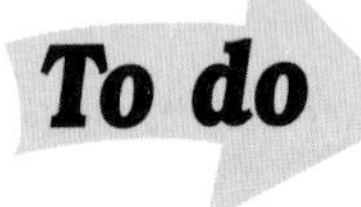

- Watch an experienced wine waiter or food server taking a wine order. Notice what kind of questions they are asked and how they respond to the guests.
- Ask your supervisor to demonstrate the way in which wine should be presented in your establishment.
- Watch an experienced wine waiter or food server serving wine. Notice how they work around the table and the techniques they use for pouring the wine cleanly and effectively.

Unexpected situations

Unexpected situations will sometimes occur and you will need to be aware of your own areas of responsibility and the appropriate action to take. When serving wine, there is always a possibility of wine being spilled onto the table, either by yourself or a customer. If this occurs, firstly apologise to the guest if it is your fault. If wine has fallen onto a customer's clothing, offer them a clean, damp cloth to remove the spillage. If they need to retire to the cloakroom, return their meal to the hotplate to keep warm until they return.

If the spillage is on the tablecloth, move any items that are in danger of becoming dirtied, then place a menu card or folded white paper under the tablecloth below the stain. Place another menu card on top of the stain and unroll a clean napkin over the card. Return any items you moved to their original position.

Make sure that you know what to do in the event of an emergency, particularly fire, sudden illness or accident. Details of appropriate responses to these are given in Unit G1: *Maintaining and safe and secure working environment.*

What have you learned?

1. What types of customer must not be served drinks?

2. What are *vintage* wines?

3. When might you describe a wine as *full-bodied*?

4. What information could you expect to gain from a wine label?

5. What kind of wine would you recommend to complement roast beef?

6. List the order in which you would serve wine to guests around a table.

7. How would you open sparkling wine?

Extend your knowledge

1. Find out what the following French terms mean: cru, grand cru, premier cru, cuvée réserve.
2. Find out what terms may appear on labels in addition to those given in this unit. What do they mean?
3. If possible, visit a vineyard and go on a tour of their cellar. You will probably also be invited to a tasting, which can be very informative.
4. Find out how wine is made and the ideal storage conditions for the different types of wine.
5. Investigate the different types of glassware available for serving wine. Why do certain types of wine require a particular type of glass?

Index

Page references in italics indicate illustrations